Voices from the *fuente viva*

The Bucknell Series in Latin American Literature and Theory
Series Editor: Aníbal González, Pennsylvania State University

The literature of Latin America, with its intensely critical, self-questioning, and experimental impulses, is currently one of the most influential in the world. In its earlier phases, this literary tradition produced major writers, such as Bartolomé de las Casas, Bernal Díaz del Castillo, the Inca Garcilaso, Sor Juana Inés de la Cruz, Andrés Bello, Gertrudis Gómez de Avellaneda, Domingo F. Sarmiento, José Martí, and Rubén Darío. More recently, writers from the United States to China, from Britain to Africa and India, and of course from the Iberian Peninsula, have felt the impact of the fiction and the poetry of such contemporary Latin American writers as Borges, Cortázar, Garcia Márquez, Guimarães Rosa, Lezama Lima, Neruda, Vargas Llosa, Paz, Poniatowska, and Lispector, among many others. Dealing with far-reaching questions of history and modernity, language and selfhood, and power and ethics, Latin American literature sheds light on the many-faceted nature of Latin American life, as well as on the human condition as a whole.

The aim of this series of books is to provide a forum for the best criticism on Latin American literature in a wide range of critical approaches, with an emphasis on works that productively combine scholarship with theory. Acknowledging the historical links and cultural affinities between Latin American and Iberian literatures, the series welcomes consideration of Spanish and Portuguese texts and topics, while also providing a space of convergence for scholars working in Romance studies, comparative literature, cultural studies, and literary theory.

Titles in Series

Mario Santana, *Foreigners in the Homeland: The Latin American New Novel in Spain, 1962–1974.*

Ronald J. Friis, *José Emilio Pacheco and the Poets of the Shadows*

Robert T. Conn, *The Politics of Philology: Alfonso Reyes and the Invention of the Latin American Literary Tradition*

Andrew Bush, *The Routes of Modernity: Spanish American Poetry from the Early Eighteenth to the Mid-Nineteenth Century*

Santa Arias and Mariselle Meléndez, *Mapping Colonial Spanish America: Places and Commonplaces of Identity, Culture, and Experience*

Alice A. Nelson, *Political Bodies: Gender, History, and the Struggle for Narrative Power in Recent Chilean Literature*

Julia Kushigian, *Reconstructing Childhood: Strategies of Reading for Culture and Gender in the Spanish American Bildungsroman*

Silvia N. Rosman, *Being in Common: Nation, Subject, and Community in Latin American Literature and Culture*

Patrick Dove, *The Catastrophe of Modernity: Tragedy and the Nation in Latin American Literature*

James J. Pancrazio, *The Logic of Fetishism: Alejo Carpentier and the Cuban Tradition*

Frederick Luciani, *Literary Self-Fashioning in Sor Juana Inés de la Cruz*

Sergio Waisman, *Borges and Translation: The Irreverence of the Periphery*

Stuart Day, *Staging Politics in Mexico: The Road to Neoliberalism*

Amy Nauss Millay, *Voices from the* fuente viva: *The Effect of Orality in Twentieth-Century Spanish American Narrative*

Voices from the *fuente viva*

The Effect of Orality in Twentieth-Century Spanish American Narrative

Amy Nauss Millay

Lewisburg
Bucknell University Press

Associated University Presses
2010 Eastpark Boulevard
Cranbury, NJ 08512

The paper used in this publication meets the requirements of the American National Standard for Permanence of Paper for Printed Library Materials Z39.48-1984.

Library of Congress Cataloging-in-Publication Data

Millay, Amy Nauss, 1970–
    Voices from the fuente viva : the effect of orality in twentieth-century Spanish American narrative / Amy Nauss Millay.
        p. cm. — (Bucknell studies in Latin American literature and theory)
    Includes bibliographical references and index.
    ISBN 0-8387-5594-1 (alk. paper)
1. Spanish American fiction—20th century—History and criticism. 2. Literature and folklore—Latin America. 3. Tradition—Latin America. 4. Cabrera, Lydia—Criticism and interpretation. 5. Arguedas, José Maria. Rios profundos. 6. Bernet, Miguel, 1940—Criticism and interpretation. 7. Burgos-Debray, Elisabeth—Criticism and interpretation. 8. Roa Bastos, Augusto Antonio—Criticism and interpretation. I. Title. II. Series.

PQ7082.N7M535 2005
863'.60998—dc22

                                2004009361

PRINTED IN THE UNITED STATES OF AMERICA

Contents

Contents

Acknowledgments

This book was conceived in a New Haven classroom, when María Rosa Menocal brought to life the songs and stories of the fourteenth-century *Libro de buen amor*. Without her inspiration and fine teaching, I might never have embarked on this journey to discover a strikingly similar oral tradition in the books of twentieth-century Spanish American writers. I feel fortunate to have María Rosa as a friend and mentor.

I am equally indebted to Roberto González Echevarría for his meticulous reading of this manuscript at every stage of the process. He generously opened his library to me, and taught me to recognize and appreciate the marvelous relationships between Spanish American narrative and non-literary forms of discourse. Both he and Rolena Adorno encouraged me to "take the final quarter turn" and turn my doctoral dissertation into a book.

I am grateful to Tufts University, and especially to Mark Hernández and Claudia Kaiser-Lenoir, for the support and encouragement I received while preparing this book. I would also like to express my gratitude to Andy Klatt, whose superb skill as a translator has helped me capture the poetic language of all of these writers. Finally, the insightful comments of Aníbal González, editor of the Bucknell Series in Latin American Literature and Theory, have been invaluable.

I owe the most fundamental recognition to the many individuals who have encouraged me to pursue my interest in Spanish since the beginning. In particular, I have profited tremendously from the dedication and magnificent teaching of Martha Forbes in high school and Raúl Bueno of Dartmouth College. Very special thanks to my parents and to my entire family, whose unwavering generosity has given me the freedom to research and write.

This book is dedicated to my husband, Todd Millay, who began this journey with me in New Haven and has never faltered as a source of inspiration and wisdom.

Voices from the *fuente viva*

1
Anthropologist-Writers as Singers of Tales

Sɪɴᴄᴇ ᴄᴏʟᴏɴɪᴀʟ ᴛɪᴍᴇs, sᴘᴀɴɪsʜ ᴀᴍᴇʀɪᴄᴀɴ ᴡʀɪᴛᴇʀs ʜᴀᴠᴇ sᴏᴜɢʜᴛ ᴛᴏ ᴄᴀᴘᴛᴜʀᴇ the voices of their countries' native inhabitants in writing. When El Inca Garcilaso conceived his *Comentarios reales* (*The Royal Commentaries of the Inca*), he undertook to translate and transcribe "lo que mamé en la leche y vi y oí a mis mayores"[1] [what I imbibed with my mother's milk, and saw and heard from my elders] into written form, according to the modes of a culture steeped in humanist thinking. Likewise, Felipe Guaman Poma de Ayala produced a hybrid text, reflecting the complexity of the colonial subject; it was composed of dissonant voices, and formed by layers of stories, songs, and performances, and yet simultaneously influenced by the literate colonizing class. Since Columbus's arrival, Spanish American writers have sought to mediate between two cultures, one oral and autochthonous, and the other deemed superior in part because of its writing system.

The orality/literacy duality is present throughout the history of Spanish American writing. Singers, musicians, and storytellers are human archives of collective lore; they store information and perpetuate tradition. Some of the most memorable voices of Spanish American narrative tradition are singers of tales: Macario, the archetypal storyteller of *Hijo de hombre* (*Son of Man*), the bards of *La guerra del fin del mundo* (*The War of the End of the World*), and Martín Fierro, the roving gaucho, whose verses founded gauchesque literature. These speaking subjects illustrate that oral tradition is manifold not monolithic. Their voices occupy the space of the oral, but only one who has access to writing can inscribe their songs and stories. Writers like Augusto Roa Bastos, José María Arguedas, Mario Vargas Llosa, and José Hernández have reproduced the voice of the Other in their fiction, in part out of a desire to preserve orality from contamination by contact with written culture.

11

This process of mediating between writing and speech is manifest in both literary and anthropological discourse. Riobaldo's stream of consciousness narration in João Guimarães Rosa's *Grande sertão: Veredas* (*The Devil to Pay in the Backlands*) juxtaposes the intervening editorial notes of the absent investigator. In Mario Vargas Llosa's novel *El hablador* (*The Storyteller*), the narrator-protagonist frantically seeks to identify the mysterious storyteller of the Machiguenga, who represents the heart of their civilization and is entrusted with the people's dreams, myths, and fictions. Similarly, Esteban Montejo's verbal retelling of Cuba's historical epochs in *Biografía de un cimarrón* (*Autobiography of a Runaway Slave*) is deemed by its editor, the anthropologist-writer Miguel Barnet, superior to official historiographical accounts. Anthropology is a principal mediating element that has enabled Spanish American writers to translate and inscribe cultural traditions.[2] It is also a self-reflexive discipline through which Western thinkers articulate their own identities vis-à-vis other cultures.

The writers considered here fashioned themselves as mediators between distinct cultures and languages. They turned to native speech out of a sense of social responsibility and nostalgia. Their texts masquerade as firsthand accounts, ethnographies, autobiographies, and faithful transcriptions. For these anthropologist-writers, fictionalization of oral discourse provided the most authentic manifestation of the written voice. Writers who attempt to "give voice" to other cultures are essentially ventriloquists. They try to erase all traces of their authorial presence from the text by creating a simulacrum of authentic speech. In their efforts to recuperate the past by creating a textual effect of orality, stories, songs, and oral performances are transformed into a fiction of the present. As a result, their texts often tell us more about first-world intellectuals' needs and interests than about third-world oral traditions.[3]

Writers who inscribe oral discourse are faced with a rhetorical predicament: How can one safeguard orality from the violence imposed by writing when the process of inscription affirms the power of writing over an oral aesthetics? In my view, this dilemma is resolved by strategically projecting, in writing, an illusion of oral discourse. Therefore, any written text that claims to recuperate orality and celebrate the essence of oral culture is perpetually dismantling itself and enacting its own difference.[4] An important part of this discursive strategy is the underlying notion that orality and literacy represent two essences in opposition. I shall argue that the identification of conflicting realities has served as a means for validating cultural production.

In this context, I contend that presupposed notions of differences between oral and written culture are best perceived as rhetorical strategies in the elaboration of literature, specifically modern fiction in Spanish America. Writers' attempts to fashion themselves as mediators between distinct linguistic and cultural systems reflect their underlying desire to redefine their respective national literatures. Oral discourse enters their writing as artifice and illusion. Texts that purport to inscribe oral discourse enact a crucial paradox that underlies Spanish American literature: writers who address the theme of the great divide between oral and written cultures inevitably perpetuate this artificial dichotomy because its existence enables them to play the role of mediator between two worlds. The whole enterprise of inscribing the oral presupposes a questionable conception of orality and literacy that pits the two practices against one another.

For the anthropologist-writers Lydia Cabrera, José María Arguedas, and Miguel Barnet, oral tradition was a rich resource for their attempts to rewrite their respective cultures by salvaging traditions threatened by literate culture. They invoked native voices because of their discontentment with the ways written discourse portrayed oral cultures. All three sought to expand notions of national culture to include marginalized groups whose predominantly oral traditions were deemed at odds with a central writing system. Cabrera, Arguedas, and Barnet turned to orality out of a longing for a past that preceded the processes of modernization symbolized by writing. They attempted to redefine national identity by incorporating oral culture in all of its variants.

How, then, does one inscribe the Other's speech within Western literate culture, a culture seemingly at odds with the dynamics of oral expression? The contradictory insider/outsider position of the anthropologist-writer lies at the heart of the complex problem of writing the oral. Although motivated by the shared desire to preserve oral cultures, Cabrera, Arguedas, and Barnet composed from within the context of literate culture. Their texts attempt to forge an "alliance" between the oral and the written, and by extension, between two distinct cultures.[5]

Arguedas, in particular, experienced at first hand the dilemma of mediating between cultures. His quest to engage oral cultures stemmed from his personal position with regard to both the Quechua-speaking and Hispanic peoples of Peru. Arguedas ultimately straddled two worlds, but belonged wholly to neither. His ambiguous position is emblematic of the other anthropologist-writers considered here. Can one revive the Other's oral memories without doing violence to the very traditions one seeks to vindicate? In order to resolve this dilemma, Arguedas, Cabrera, and Barnet fashioned themselves as cross-cultural mediators, and imbued their texts with an artistic effect of orality.

For these writers the project of inscribing oral discourse was manifestly political. Josefina Ludmer has examined the representation of voice in writing in the context of issues of national identity. She defines the genre of gauchesque literature as the "use" of the voice of the gaucho by literate culture. In this context, a centralized legal system, symbolized by writing, confronts and differentiates primarily oral communities. The author who transcribes the voice of the gaucho ultimately fulfills his own political desire by constructing the oral to include in its interiority the written and political word, *his word,* that appears quoted and reproduced by the voice of the gaucho.[6] Anthropologist-writers are similarly motivated by the desire to reproduce the voices of the disenfranchised peoples of their respective nationalities. Their texts, both anthropological and narrative, enact the union of linguistic and cultural systems that the writers perceive to be distinct.

Since the Conquest, Spanish American intellectuals have defined their culture as a literate one. According to Angel Rama, the establishment of the "ciudad letrada" [learned city] culminated in the formation of national literatures at the end of the nineteenth century. With these changes emerged the figure of the "letrado," whose access to writing awarded him prestige and power. Aníbal González explains the outcome of this preoccupation with writing:

> [Spanish American culture's] profoundly literate character, as Angel Rama's *La ciudad letrada* demonstrates, has paradoxically little to do with literacy rates and more with the fact that this is a society founded on a pervasive utilization of writing and a deep respect for it. In spite of this foundation, or perhaps even because of it, writing was from the very beginning regarded in Spanish America with a mixture of mistrust and awe.[7]

In Rama's opinion, modernization resulted in the silencing and death of splendid songs and stories. Implicit in this argument is a condemnation of writing as a violent form of language and a source of political oppression. Rama links Fernando Ortiz's notion of "transculturación" [transculturation] to Spanish American authors who demonstrate an interest in the popular cultures of their native regions in an attempt to revive and preserve traditions and languages of a vanishing Other.[8] Rama groups writers like Augusto Roa Bastos, José María Arguedas, Juan Rulfo, João Guimarães Rosa, and Gabriel García Márquez as "narrators of transculturation," narrators whose texts mediate between social realms, geographic regions, and opposing cultural worlds.[9]

Martin Lienhard views these narrative texts as battlegrounds for the opposing forces of oral culture and print culture. Cross-cultural narrative can never achieve a fusion of pen and voice; it can only create an illusion of oralized writing. He proposes the idea of an alternative kind of literature that is inscribed when hegemonic and marginalized sectors of society meet.[10] Similarly, Antonio Cornejo Polar maintains that Spanish American books in which two cultural worlds coincide (colonial texts, gauchesque literature) occupy an ambiguous and conflictive space, and can be read as the meeting grounds for heterogeneous discourses. Orality enters the written work, particularly Andean literature, as artifice—as gestures, performance, and lyric. The outcome is the destabilization of literary discourse and the emergence of a literature that functions as a point of intersection for multiple cultural systems.[11]

Carlos Pacheco elaborates on Rama's analysis of "narrators of transculturation" by arguing that writers like Roa Bastos, Guimarães Rosa, Arguedas, García Márquez, and Rulfo are primarily concerned with invoking the oral cultures of the interior regions, or "comarcas," of their respective nations. The inscription of oral communication, gestures and intonations confers on the written text an oral "flavor" that achieves each writer's ideological objectives.[12] According to Pacheco, the fictionalization of oral discourse by appropriation of certain discursive strategies associated with orality creates an aesthetic effect of orality. These texts do not only fictionalize, but actually embody the conflictive interaction between counterposed universes that are geographically, socially, and culturally diverse.[13]

These observations regarding the incorporation of oral discourse in Spanish American writing are predicated on the assumption of a great divide between speech and writing. Rama and others share with "narrators of transculturation" the desire to create pure totalities of knowledge. In essence, they have taken for truth the fictional dichotomy that makes books like *Hijo de hombre* and *Los ríos profundos* (*Deep Rivers*) so appealing. Strict binary distinctions between writing and speech, dominant culture and marginalized culture, and Spanish and native language uphold the we-they comparisons that serve the writers' respective ideological agendas. They are best understood as rhetorical devices in the elaboration of fiction. Spanish American writers' attempts to inscribe oral discourse in their narratives reveal crucial ways in which orality is influenced by the power of the written word.

In his study of oral poetry, Paul Zumthor defines "oral" as "any poetic communication where transmission and reception at least are carried by voice and hearing," whereby "every oral communication posits an act of authority, a unique act, one never identically reiterable." It is this authority of voice that the Spanish American writer seeks to inscribe in a written text. Since orality is best perceived as a kind of performance, writing the oral implies recreating the circumstances and context of the original speech act.[14] It is not productive to think of oral culture as existing independent from literate culture. Rather, orality coexists and interacts with writing.

It is commonplace in studies of orality to associate oral discourse with a specific consciousness or mentality that favors communal knowledge and the accumulation of information. Carlos Pacheco formulates a coherent definition of orality that is echoed in the written texts of Cabrera, Arguedas, and Barnet. He asserts that orality is best understood as a particular cultural economy, capable of substantially affecting not only the acquisition, preservation, and diffusion of knowledge, but also the development of worldviews, value systems, and particular cultural products, both historical and current. Orality is about processes, conceptions, and products that differ significantly from those found in cultures that have established and diffused writing, printing, and communication technologies.[15]

Modern-day studies of orality tend to associate spoken language with self-presence and value. This gesture is mimicked by Spanish American writers who create an illusion of orality in their texts to fulfill a shared desire to inscribe an origin of autochthonous cultural expression. Ironically, writing, a vital part of inscribing speech, is condemned for threatening the superiority of orality.

Aníbal González asserts that Spanish American literary tradition, from its very beginnings, has expressed suspicion of the written word. The corollary to this ethical argument is that orality, in contrast to writing, constitutes a positive and value-laden form of human discourse:

> Alongside the paeans to literacy in Western culture, there have always been the paeans to orality, viewed as a "superior" form of language because of its associations with thought and self-presence, which are in turn linked to metaphysical notions such as truth, beauty, and good. Within this hierarchical system, speech is the father, the source of truth and goodness, the lord and master of writing, and the written word is always under suspicion as a potentially subversive, malevolent, and rebellious form of language. From the outset, then, graphophobia is implicit in Western culture.[16]

Texts that allegedly "oralize" writing attempt to escape the oppression and violence associated with literate culture. They create an illusion of presentness, authenticity, and communal experience by incorporating the voices of the disenfranchised and the powerless.

Theories on orality and literacy have tended to dichotomize oral and literate cultures by conceptualizing them as pure cognitive systems. In his

Preface to Plato (1963), Eric A. Havelock describes the efficacy of oral poetry in Homeric Greek culture. For the Homeric poet, who aimed to preserve the collective memory of a society, the ability to recollect oral discourse served as a source of power. The Homeric poet memorized verses in discrete units. Thus, according to Havelock, the oral style is characterized by variation and repetition, and lacks integration. These judgments, however, are based on criteria established by a literate culture and reflect biases implicit in Havelock's analysis. *Preface to Plato* argues that advances in literacy that accompanied the birth of Greek philosophy resulted in a restructuring of cognitive processes, causing a great divide between cultures.

Jack Goody's *Domestication of the Savage Mind* (1968) has focused on the effects of the advent of literacy in modern nonliterate societies. He perceives the shift from orality to literacy in evolutionary terms, and sees the onset of literate practices as enabling individual thought.[17] Goody suggests that literacy bestows on members of communities objective thought that enables them to distinguish between myth and history. Brian Street's arguments to the contrary are compelling: "Not only does modern literacy foster uncritical belief in specific, 'modern' renderings of the world, it also contributes to a weakening of the kinds of sensibility and skepticism that may have been fostered in oral tradition."[18] Goody's tendency to regard the acquisition of writing as a positive cognitive advance implies that power relations are embedded in the dialectic. Rather than contrasting speech with writing, whereby orality is defined as lacking social function, I would argue that interactions between the two cultural systems are crucial sources of heterogeneous cultural expression.

The literate/nonliterate dichotomy that underlies the works of Havelock and Goody is presented by Walter J. Ong in his renowned book *Orality and Literacy: The Technologizing of the Word* (1982) as a sweeping claim for a great divide between orality and literacy. Ong, one of the founders of orality theory, studies examples of "primary orality" in groups not exposed to writing. He focuses on the differences in "mentality" between oral and writing cultures, arguing that oral thought is tied closely to memory and open-ended communication, whereas print fosters a sense of closure and fixation. For Ong, sound is linked to interiority and presentness. Oral communication is participatory, formulaic, thematically organized, and repetitive. He writes that oral cultures do not conceptualize linear history in the modern sense; rather, one witnesses a confluence of present and past, an entanglement of myth and history.[19]

There is a striking tendency for hegemonic discourses to idealize oral culture. But literary work that seeks to understand an oral mentality contains a fundamental contradiction. As Jacques Derrida points out, Plato is trapped in a literate frame of mind when he denounces the effects of writing in favor of authentic spoken language. Derrida offers a reformed concept of the classical debate surrounding the relationship between speech and writing by alleging that speech already shares many writerly features with writing, and that all language is, in a sense, a writing.[20]

There are compelling reasons to be suspicious of dichotomizing concepts like those that inform most orality theory. Cultures are not pure and static objects, but rather complex processes of negotiation. Brian Street's ideas surrounding the orality/literacy debate run contrary to most orality theory and shed light on the assumptions and ideological practices that structure widely accepted notions of the opposition between oral culture and written culture. Street contends that an ethnocentric bias underlies the concept of a great divide between speech and writing. He likewise criticizes Ong for embellishing the ideality and evanescent nature of oral communication, and condemns Goody for exaggerating the link between literacy and rational, objective thinking. As Street points out, Ong attributes to literacy a unique tendency to fix the fleeting sounds of oral experience, when oral language already possesses this quality of fixing and separating concepts. Street asserts that orality and literacy should not be explained apart from their social contexts. Instead, he advocates an "'ideological' model of literacy," which emphasizes specific social practices involved with reading and writing.[21] I argue for a fluid approach that does not consider orality and literacy in purely oppositional terms. Like Street, I believe that it is far more fruitful to look at interactions between speech and writing, and to treat supposed differences between literacy and orality as means of sustaining belief in a great divide between languages and cultures.

Jorge Marcone has perceptively reformulated the debate by analyzing the ideologies of writing culture that uphold the opposition between orality and writing as a discursive tool in cultural production. His influential book *La oralidad escrita* (1997) (Written Orality) develops a general theory of orality as a category that functions within writing. Inscription of oral discourse cannot occur apart from the institutions and ideologies of writing. Marcone introduces the concept of "modern and post-modern discovery of orality," which entails a search for an alternative writing in which oral discourse functions as the key to a conceptualization of language and writing itself becomes more "natural" due to this association.[22] Thus, it is problematic to interpret orality as an authentic form of representation. According to Marcone, the whole notion of orality is invoked as a strategic measure to undermine the ideologies of literate culture. It signifies an object of desire or a discursive utopia to satisfy the writer's personal agenda. As Marcone points out, the gesture of inscribing oral discourse paradoxically affirms the power of writing.

Therefore, how can an intellectual claim and inscribe orality without causing the demise of the very tradition one seeks to represent and preserve? I would suggest that this predicament is internalized and displayed in texts that profess to represent an oral aesthetic. The identification of a strict division between orality and writing, an impasse between two cultures, has served as a rhetorical device in the production of literature in Spanish America. Thus, the outcome of inscribing the oral in written texts is the innovation of a discursive form that aims to subvert ideologies upheld by writing culture, and not a faithful expression of the *essence* of oral culture.

The first three chapters of this book trace the evolution of these ideas in the writings of Cabrera, Arguedas, and Barnet. The final chapter discusses ways in which Augusto Roa Bastos has understood better than any other Spanish American author the relationship between orality and literacy in the context of national identity. He is a good example of a Spanish American writer who has upheld the theory of a great divide between oral and literate cultures to legitimize his role as a cross-cultural mediator. His theories of orality are echoed in the texts of Cabrera, Arguedas, and Barnet. Roa Bastos's ideas surrounding oral cultures have been dominated by the notion that speech is distorted by written discourse. He has articulated a coherent thesis regarding the relationship between speech and writing, maintaining that the opposition between the "told" in indigenous song and the "written" in Paraguayan colonial literature signals a significant distinction: that which moves from the living and collective oral tradition to the "dead zone" of literary writing, the product of a sole individual.[23] Roa Bastos conceptualizes a system of binary oppositions—Guaraní/Spanish, speech/writing—to describe Paraguay's cultural dualism and to account for the country's turbulent history. His narrative works exemplify his struggle to redeem his nation's marginalized culture by infusing the written with features of Guaraní oral tradition.

Michel de Certeau maintains that discourses on the Other, what he terms "heterologies," enable us to gain knowledge by establishing a relationship with other cultures:[24]

These different "heterologies" (sciences of the different) have the common characteristic of attempting to *write the voice*. The voice reaching us from a great distance must find a place in the text. Thus primitive orality has to be written in the ethnological discourse: the "genius" of "mythologies" and religious "fables" (as the *Encyclopédie* puts it) has to be written in a scholarly discipline, or the "voice of the people" has to be written in Michelet's historiography. What is audible, but far away, will thus be transformed into texts in conformity with the Western desire to read its products.[25]

Ethnographers seek to translate the Other's experience by collecting and decoding oral discourse. They cast speech as a source of original expression and native culture. To what extent does this practice of collection and translation satisfy a Western longing for coherent tradition and communal existence? Does oral expression actually presuppose presentness, interiority, and intimacy? And does its fleeting nature accord it value and originality? Or, is the notion of a great divide between writing and speech merely a Western ideological construction?

Although profoundly enmeshed in writing, ethnography remains very close to orality. Recently, anthropologists have considered the literary qualities of anthropological writing.[26] These recent trends highlight the writerly nature of ethnography, and suggest that we should read the anthropological writings of Cabrera, Arguedas, and Barnet in conjunction with their narrative texts. Both ethnography and literature are embedded with multiple discourses and a plurality of voices. These writers' ethnographies are literary insofar as they are the proving ground for an inventive "ethnographic poetics."[27] For all three, poetry provided a perfect medium for creating an artistic effect of orality.

Ethnographic practices, which developed in the first half of the twentieth century, are based on present, experiential, oral interactions. Expectations of authenticity and wholeness are built into the desire to create coherent representations of other cultures. Ethnographers like Cabrera, Arguedas, and Barnet base their observations on the intimacy of fieldwork experience: they, unlike their readers, can claim to having truly "'been there.'"[28] This claim enables them to speak from the informant's point of view. In their writings, both anthropological and narrative, they reproduce the voices of their "fuentes vivas" [living sources] in textual form. The Western outlook of the transcriber complicates this process of inscribing native voices. As a consequence of these cultural constraints, ethnographers typically fashion themselves as sources of truth and authenticity.

Jorge Luis Borges's story "El etnógrafo" (The Ethnographer) stands as a classic fable of the anthropologist's quest to translate and inscribe oral tradition in the postcolonial world. In the story, Fred Murdock journeys into the hinterlands, hoping to write a thesis that will reveal the sacred rituals and traditions of an indigenous tribe to the Western world. At the beginning of his stay, he follows the rigorous ethnographic methodology he has learned as a student of anthropology and indigenous languages. But, after living in teepees on the open prairie for some time, he destroys his copious notes, forgets his friends and native city, dreams in a new language, and even begins to think in a way that his accustomed logic rejects. Murdock eventually recounts his dreams to a wise shaman, who in turn discloses the tribe's sacred secret.

Upon returning to his university, the young ethnographer informs his professor that he will not reveal the shaman's secret. The professor asks if perhaps he is bound to silence or if the English language is inadequate as a means of translation. For Murdock, the secret is so precious that science, by comparison, seems frivolous.

"El etnógrafo" chronicles the unraveling of the ethnographer's quest for spoken truths, pure knowledge, and original sources. Murdock's journey is essentially that of anthropologists and fiction writers alike. The desire to retain orality by inscribing and transforming other voices is part of the history of Spanish American literature. Borges's story tells us that one must become the Other in order to attain the promised land of pure tradition. Murdock's experience implies that the processes of mediation linked to Western hegemonic discourses do not lead to understanding the "essence" of native culture.

The political and cultural system of the colonial period created the permanent "otherness" of the New World vis-à-vis Europe. The economic relationship of the colonies with Spain and Portugal established a social structure of center and periphery that continued long after emancipation in the early nineteenth century. Within this hierarchy, intellectuals perceived indigenous voices as backward and antimodern with respect to written culture. Thus, as Carlos Alonso has argued convincingly, for Spanish American individuals modernity has always been elsewhere, a model that is simultaneously desired and rejected:

> The discourse of modernity constitutes both the core of the Spanish American work and the center from which it has to flee in a centrifugal flight for the preservation of its own rhetorical authority. The uniqueness and particularity of the Spanish American postcolonial/neocolonial cultural situation is founded on this radically ambivalent movement toward and away from modernity.[29]

Since the late nineteenth century, Spanish American intellectuals have expressed their desire for cultural autonomy by recuperating indigenous voices and by broadening their respective country's concepts of nationalism to include them.

The whole enterprise of inscribing oral culture can be regarded as an attempt to create literature that reflects autochthonous reality. The desire to achieve expression of autochthonous culture has been a chief concern of Spanish American writing. Alonso has raised important issues linking anthropological interpretation with autochthonous literature:

> Through its preoccupation with autochthony the subject necessarily enters into a relationship of mediation with respect to its own culture, a circumstance that opens the way to counterfeit, exoticism or ideological expediency: "a falsifier, a tourist, or an Arab nationalist." In any event, the outcome of this inevitably centrifugal displacement is the formulation of a partial vision of cultural essence that willfully isolates certain elements— camels, for instance—and advances them as representative of the totality of cultural experience.[30]

For our purposes, a camel might be a Lucumí legend or an Andean song. The inscription of native voices purports to represent a collectivity, and therefore is in perpetual danger of essentializing this culture. This gesture harks back to the first colonial writers who implored indigenous peoples of the New World to reveal their secrets; and it is mimicked by writers of testimonial novels who reconfigure the stories of their informants.

For Spanish American anthropologist-writers, authority stems from proximity to the subject. Nevertheless, this privileged relationship places the writer in a unique circumstance, one that sets in motion essentialism and exoticism. Since voice is boundless, and seemingly at odds with the confines of writing, any inscription of oral discourse is by necessity incomplete. Underlying the process of inscribing oral culture is the problematic assumption that a partial vision of a culture can faithfully represent it. Alonso makes the crucial observation that one must conceive of a culture as static and closed before describing it as being in danger of losing an element that binds and connects it. As a result, the written text that seeks to celebrate the essence and presentness of an oral culture seems condemned to never be able to participate in this culture.[31] Spanish American texts that inscribe oral discourse display this permanent state of conflict.

It could be argued that inscription of oral discourse and an obsession with the contamination of oral tradition by written culture are fundamental elements of Spanish American cultural production. Nevertheless, they are incompatible with Spanish American intellectuals' shared desire to be modern. Alonso writes, "The crisis produced by Spanish America's insertion in the modern world historical order—which I have proposed to characterize as a rhetorical predicament—is 'resolved' creatively by Spanish

American writers in the continual affirmation of a cultural specificity that is perceived to be, consciously or not, discontinuous with modernity."[32] The anthropologist-writers Cabrera, Arguedas, and Barnet display this rhetorical dilemma in their ethnographies and narratives. Oral tradition is textualized as an exotic feature of New World cultures. In his analysis of intellectuals' ambiguous relationship with the discourse of modernity, Alonso insists, "For Spanish American writers authority resides in the prestige of the discursive models that they invoke and that are appropriated precisely to lend status to their writing."[33] For Cabrera, Arguedas, and Barnet, anthropological knowledge provided an ideal discursive tool for appropriating the Other's voice. Their writing is marked by tension, by a fundamental need to uphold writing culture as the discourse that constitutes the bedrock of each text's articulation, and also an implicit desire to reject all that this cultural discourse implies.

Spanish American authors have continually founded their work upon the myths and songs of an ephemeral origin. No book tells this story better than Alejo Carpentier's *Los pasos perdidos* (*The Lost Steps*). The narrator-protagonist is a figure belonging to two cultural worlds. His quest for authentic artistic expression mimics that of Cabrera, Arguedas, and Barnet. The narrator-protagonist's interest in native cultures is sparked when he visits a museum exhibit of musical instruments that predate the colonization of the Americas. He embarks on a journey away from the decadence of the city, in search of a cosmic origin where he can find the source of pure artistic creation. In a place steeped in authenticity and essence, he decides to compose an epic musical poem. After several days of frenzied composition, the narrator-protagonist realizes that his supply of paper and ink is insufficient to capture the songs and sounds that surround him. He decides to leave the jungle and sets out on a painful return to civilization. Upon returning to Santa Mónica, he finds that the carved inscription that once marked the route to the sacred source of music is submerged beneath the waters of the swelling river. In the end, he fails to complete his poem.

The narrator-protagonist's arduous journey confirms his belief that he straddles two cultures, and belongs wholly to neither. His failure to return highlights the futility of any quest for an origin of artistic expression. His search is for a passage from the oral to the written. Ironically, the desire for pure and authentic expression presupposes that songs, myths, and poetry inhabit the *origin* of literature and culture, and that oral culture is inevitably compromised by writing. If we assume that writing is at odds with speech, then retrieving an origin by inscribing the spoken word endangers the very conceit of originality. Writers endeavoring to salvage cultural authenticity uphold the notion that spoken utterances are somehow bound to their origin in a unique way that distinguishes them from writing. Given the fluidity of an oral tradition as context, any quest for an origin or a source is not only quixotic, it is illogical.[34]

The quest described in *Los pasos perdidos* is the same search undertaken by Cabrera in her efforts to convey the magical realm of the *monte* in writing. For Arguedas, the quest was strikingly personal; through language, he sought to reconcile the contradictions inherent in his bicultural identity. The very fragmentation of his final novel reflects the irreconcilable conflicting voices that plagued him. Cabrera, Arguedas, and Barnet confronted the dilemma of uniting seemingly incompatible cultural and linguistic worlds. By inventing an ethnographic poetics, each writer bypassed this predicament by creating an illusion of authenticity, a fictionalized orality.

Culturalist allegories stand behind the fictions of difference that make up ethnographic accounts.[35] For example, *El monte* and *Biografía de un cimarrón* play out the archetypal Spanish American trope of a recovered origin, reinvented in the present. Similarly, *Los ríos profundos* and *Hijo de hombre* are the stories of a symbolic return to an oral poetics. These books value the uniqueness and authenticity of the spoken word. Their yearning for origins is not limited to anthropology or literature; it marks the history of writing.[36]

The aesthetic goal of these writers was realistic cultural representation. Their texts are authenticated by the portrayal of actual encounters with other voices. In both their narratives and ethnographies, oral language is organized into coherent accounts, and orality takes on an aesthetic function. It evokes a culture that favors repetition, that is communal rather than individual, and that is highly poetic and rhythmic. Otherness, thematized as a return to the oral, is conveyed in these writers' texts through the fictionalization of oral discourse. Oral language is replete with poetic rhythms, onomatopoeia, repetitions, nonlinear sequencing, interpolated songs, and colloquial sayings. Cabrera, Arguedas, Barnet, and Roa Bastos adhere to Barthes's notion of the "reality effect"—the aesthetic of verisimilitude—by contriving a kind of orality effect for the written text.[37] Their texts are similarly committed to the master trope of recuperation and reinvention. Cabrera, Arguedas, and Barnet responded to the ethnologic quest of cultural invention that took hold in the twentieth century. Only Roa Bastos was aware of the irony of representation. His involvement in poststructuralist debates surrounding speech and writing compelled him to rewrite his widely acclaimed novel *Hijo de hombre* and compose *Yo el Supremo* (*I the Supreme*), where the whole debate is parodied; it stands as a monument to a writerly orality.

By stressing the differences between speech and writing, these anthropologist-writers establish themselves as mediators who can bridge a great cultural divide. Ironically, they simultaneously uphold notions of opposing cultures—oral vs. written, dominated vs. dominant—in their very attempts to dismantle these hierarchies. Their efforts to recover oral expression reflect a desire to foster cultural diversity in an age of modernization.

Illuminating the false dichotomy of the "great divide" between orality and literacy helps to resolve the ambiguous role of orality in defining authentic culture. The inscription of oral discourse is not simply logocentric, nor is it a false construct that is pleasing to Western expectations. Instead, I argue that orality is a single crucial thread among the multitude that make up the complex tapestry of Spanish American national identities and literary tradition.

This book traces the efforts of anthropologist-writers to portray orality in narratives and ethnographies. I focus on selected key figures in Spanish American literary history whose writings best exemplify the issues described above. Lydia Cabrera was one of the first Spanish American intellectuals to draw both from the disciplines of anthropology and literature in her explorations of Afro-Cuban cultural practices. The first chapter of this book describes her interest in ethnographic surrealism, which culminated in her masterwork, *El monte*, perhaps the best example of Spanish American narrative that is not a novel. The utopian desire of inscribing native voices and preserving a lost origin is most poignant in Cabrera's writings in exile, where the dynamics of memory and oral history influence the process of textual production.

Arguedas was similarly committed to the project of inscribing other voices to raise awareness about the social realities of Andean peoples. Throughout his career as a writer, he struggled with the theoretical challenge of expressing in written Spanish the stories and thoughts of Quechuan speakers. By exploring the literariness of his ethnographies and the role of anthropological mediation in his narrative, we can better understand Arguedas's commitment to resolving this ideological predicament. In *Los ríos profundos*, his most poetic novel, Quechuan orality is conveyed as a superior and ideal form of cultural expression. Arguedas's writings explore his personal quest to represent in writing the complexities of his bicultural upbringing and, by extension, the encounter between modern literate culture and oral tradition.

The incorporation of orality as a rhetorical device is most apparent in testimonial narrative, a Spanish American literary invention that took hold in the 1960s. *Testimonios* are composed primarily by literate intellectuals who share with ethnographers a commitment to represent faithfully the life story of a non-Western subject. They echo the earliest colonial texts that record New World encounters between literate Spaniards and nonliterate indigenous peoples. The third chapter of this book argues that some *testimonios*, like Barnet's *Biografía de un cimarrón*, masquerade as scientific documents; this demonstrates that the genre represents a point of intersection for multiple disciplines. In complicity with their subjects, testimonial writers invoke native speech as a means of inscribing otherness. Recently, the whole genre has undergone serious debate in light of the controversy surrounding the veracity of Rigoberta Menchú's life story, written by Elisabeth Burgos in *Me llamo Rigoberta Menchú y así me nació la conciencia* (*I, Rigoberta Menchú: An Indian Woman in Guatemala*).

Can the oralization of writing grant one access to a collective and vanishing world? Or, does the process of inscription preclude any complete understanding of Spanish American oral culture? The intermingling of anthropology and narrative in texts by these writers reaches to the core of issues of representation opened by El Inca Garcilaso and Guaman Poma. Since the colonial period, Spanish American authors have sought to express, in writing, the relationships between their countries' heterogeneous populations. This practice of recuperation and redemption is based on the premise that oral traditions convey values and knowledge that Western literate culture lacks. In the twentieth century, anthropologist-writers like Cabrera, Arguedas, and Barnet invoked ethnography as the chief mediating element to translate the timeless stories and songs of other cultures into writing. Ultimately, however, each was bound to writing, a practice associated with the irretrievable loss of oral tradition.

2

Oral Poetics in
Lydia Cabrera's *El monte*

LYDIA CABRERA (1900–1991), A PIONEER IN AFRO-CUBAN CULTURAL STUDIES, EXCELLED in the fields of literature and anthropology, and creatively melded the two in her writings. During her lifetime, she published many ethnographic investigations and collections of short stories in Paris, Cuba, Spain, and the United States, yet her oeuvre, like that of so many Cuban writers who fled their homeland over the course of the twentieth century, has been largely overlooked. Until now, her literary works and her anthropological studies have been predominantly regarded as separate enterprises. Her fiction has been the subject of a handful of dissertations, and ethnographies like *El monte* have had a lasting impact on the understanding of Afro-Cuban culture.

Lydia Cabrera, the eighth daughter of Raimundo Cabrera y Bosch and Elisa Marcaida y Casanova, was born in Havana at the turn of the century. Her father, a lawyer by training, was active in political and cultural life in Cuba during the first two decades of the 1900s and participated in the Liberal Revolution of 1917. In 1897, he founded *Cuba y América,* a magazine that celebrated the separatist cause of Cubans and was in circulation until 1915. Lydia's first writings appeared in her father's magazine. In 1913, at the age of fourteen, she began to publish her anonymous column *Nena en Sociedad* (Young Woman in Society). Her mission, as articulated in the column, was to chronicle social happenings in Havana.

Lydia enjoyed some early success as a painter, displaying her paintings in the Salon des Beaux Arts in 1922. In collaboration with Alicia Longoria de González, she established a commercial enterprise called Casa Alyds that was dedicated to the importation and sale of European decorative goods. As a young artist, Cabrera demonstrated a passion for foreign artworks—antique furnishings, decorative curiosities, and handicrafts. Her inquisitiveness later drew her to explore non-Western art forms, in particular

African contributions to Cuban culture. Although initially intrigued by cultural artifacts that could be exhibited, Lydia eventually turned to stories and verbal accounts as items to be displayed.

In 1922, Cabrera took part in the founding of the Association of Retrospective Art, which proposed to commemorate Cuba's artistic tradition by holding an annual exposition. She articulated the association's agenda in an article published in *Diario de la Marina*: "Es el amor al pasado y la comprensión del pasado lo que nos prepara y nos hace capaces de amar y comprender el presente."[1] [It is the love of the past and the understanding of the past that prepares us and enables us to love and understand the present.] The exposition called "Old Havana" was well received by the Cuban public. It was not until several years later, on the banks of the Seine, that Cabrera would expand her vision of Cuba's cultural tradition to include Afro-Cuban practices as its primary component.

The death of Raimundo Cabrera in 1923 affected Lydia deeply, and she virtually disappeared from the public eye. Over the next few years, she resolved to achieve financial independence and to save enough money to spend some years pursuing her interests abroad. In the same year as her father's death, Cabrera attended the inaugural session of the Society of Cuban Folklore, presided over by Fernando Ortiz. Although Lydia claims that her brother-in-law was not the driving force behind her interest in Afro-Cuban studies, her initiation into the field prior to her travels to Paris was certainly definitive.

DISCOVERING CUBA ON THE BANKS OF THE SEINE:
CABRERA'S INTRODUCTION TO ETHNOGRAPHIC SURREALISM

Lydia Cabrera's original intention upon arriving in Paris in 1927 was to study painting in L'Ecole du Louvre, from which she obtained a degree in 1930. Soon thereafter, she resolved to burn her paintings and to pursue her intellectual interests by attending lectures. Her professors included Grousset, Dayés, and Conteneau, and Cabrera recalls discussions with Miguel Angel Asturias, who was studying ethnology under Georges Raynaud at the time. Her encounter with Asturias was significant, for the two most likely responded to the intellectual climate of Paris in similar ways. Both writers were inspired by their studies in Paris to explore the alluring autochthonous voices of their homelands in their attempts to understand other beliefs and other modes of thought. These explorations resulted in the simultaneous publication of collections of stories by Cabrera and Asturias by the Parisian publishing house Gallimard in 1936.

Over the course of her years in Paris (1927–38), Lydia became enchanted with Buddhism, Indian culture, and Chinese folklore. Her studies of Asian mythology sparked memories of African stories recounted innumerable times by her childhood *tatas* (nannies). Her belief in a transcendental harmony of all cultures led her back to Cuba:

> Pongamos por caso las leyendas, todas las religiones en el fondo se parecen. De niña había oído muchos cuentos de los negros de casa, el de "espíritu del árbol," por ejemplo. Todo esto lo redescubría en el folklore japonés ¡cuántas leyendas parecidas!, algunas casi iguales a los cuentos que escuché en mi infancia. Comenzó entonces mi interés por lo negro-cubano.[2]

> [Let's suppose that with regard to legends, all religions are essentially similar. As a young girl, I heard many stories from the black people of the house, the one about the "spirit of the tree," for example. I would rediscover all of this in Japanese folklore. So many similar legends, and some almost identical to the stories I heard in my childhood. Thus began my interest in the Afro-Cuban.]

Lydia's separation from her native culture and language inspired her to reflect on her own past and Cuba's present from an objective perspective. She regarded oral memories as a rich source of artistic inspiration.

Lydia returned to Cuba several times over the course of her stay in Paris. In 1928, upon returning to Havana, she recalls that she already felt a great restlessness about approaching "black culture."[3] Her first contacts began through Omí Tomí, in the neighborhood of Pogolotti. Cabrera's preliminary ethnographic field notes are dated 1930, but Alejo Carpentier attests that he crossed paths with the anthropologist-writer in the field as early as 1927, when Lydia was observing a Ñáñigo oath ceremony being celebrated in the middle of the swamp, in the outskirts of Marianao.[4]

During these early years, Cabrera established important contacts with informants who would prove to be vital sources in her future studies: Calixta Morales (Oddedeí), José de Calazán (Bangoché), and Teresa Muñoz (Omí Tomí), among others. Calixta is the protagonist of these notes. In a significant entry, the ethnographer records "[c]osas oídas a Calixta y notas sobre su biografía" [things heard from Calixta and notes about her biography], a compilation of Calixta's biography as well as a list of colloquial sayings. It was a preliminary version of what later became Cabrera's collection of *Refranes de negros viejos* (1955) (Proverbs of Old Negroes).

Lydia Cabrera's observations could at times be mistaken for entries in her own diary. In a typed report, she recounted her evolving friendship with and trust in her informant. These early encounters planted the seed for both her literary as well as her ethnographic projects. Cabrera's 1930 field notes reflect an interest in individuals as protagonists of a narrative, rather than in the formal, more scientific, aspects of their religious practices.[5] From the outset, the ethnographic account and the narrative tale were inextricably linked in Lydia's thinking processes. Informants in her ethnographies and narrators of her stories were virtually interchangeable. She was primarily interested in transcribing a multitude of Afro-Cuban voices. Her early field notes represent the first step involved in creating an oral context for her writings.

The artist-turned-writer took these transcriptions back to Paris at the beginning of the thirties. Although *El monte*, her masterwork of ethnology, did not appear until 1954, it seems that it was in its beginning stages in Europe in the 1930s. Paris proved to have an intellectual climate that was more receptive to studies of Africa than that of Havana. In the wake of World War I, it was the site of a fervent passion for a new aesthetic, one that prized exotic artifacts and sought to explore the otherness of nonhegemonic cultures. Theories of the German philosopher-historian Oswald Spengler echoed throughout Europe and the Caribbean. In his *Decline of the West* (1917), which appeared in Spanish translation in 1923, he dismissed all notions of Europe's superiority and placed European civilization on par with other world cultures. Spengler's theories reached the Spanish-speaking world via Ortega y Gasset's *Revista de Occidente* (Journal of the West), which Carpentier referred to as "our guiding light."[6] Roberto González Echevarría writes about the crucial impact that Spengler's ideas had on the ideas of Carpentier: "In the case of Carpentier and Afro-Cubanism, Spengler furnishes some of the basic tenets for the postulation of a radical new beginning. . . ."[7] The notion of Europe as a fallen civilization was in vogue at the time that Cabrera educated herself in Paris, and had direct repercussions on the thinking of writers, ethnographers, and artists who sought to incorporate new subject matter into mainstream intellectual pursuits. She shared with her contemporaries a longing for acceptance of the world's diverse cultures.

Lydia Cabrera joined many European intellectuals and artists who turned to Africa or, in her case, Afro-Cuban cultural practices in her own nation. Translations of German anthropologist Leo Frobenius's *Histoire de la civilisation africaine* circulated in Paris and contributed to a trend that debunked previously unquestioned notions of colonialism.[8] In the early 1900s, Black Africa was coming to the foreground in ethnographic studies. The 1920s saw the formation of a new generation of Africanist ethnographers at the Institut d'Ethnologie, led by Paul Rivet, Lucien Lévy-Bruhl, and

Marcel Mauss. This organization endeavored to train ethnographers and to serve as a forum for their publications. Although Cabrera did not undergo any formal training in anthropology, she was a close acquaintance of Roger Bastide, who would go on to teach Severo Sarduy, Pierre Verger, and Alfred Métraux, a student of Mauss at the Institut. Cabrera would later collaborate with Verger and Métraux in a 1956 excursion to Matanzas that resulted in a poetically written ethnographic study entitled *La laguna sagrada de San Joaquín* (The Sacred Lagoon of San Joaquín).

By 1931, "Africanism," having acquired its own nomenclature to distinguish it from "Orientalism," was accepted as an independent field of investigation. Christopher Miller perceptively observes that the very notion of a discrete "Africanist" discipline implies a "gesture of reaching out to the most unknown part of the world and bringing it back as language—the process . . . ultimately brings Europe face to face with nothing but itself, with the problems its own discourse imposes." Miller highlights the irony that epitomizes Africanist discourse as it developed in Paris in the 1930s. Just as Said's "Orient" is portrayed as a negative entity of Europe, Africa similarly embodied what the West was not, "producing a single, symmetrical Other."⁹ Europe once again affirmed its colonial dominance by relegating Africa, an invention of the West, to a permanent position of otherness. Black francophone writers who rallied behind ideals of Negritude, of whom Cabrera was a fervent admirer, criticized these tendencies to fetishize black culture.

During the interwar period in Europe, when Lydia was residing in Paris, the development of ethnography and surrealism coincided. In 1925, the same year that the Institut d'Ethnologie was established, the surrealists published their first manifesto. Cabrera was in Paris at a time when the surrealist movement was shaping the ethnographic studies of African culture. As part of their opposition to the principles of Western civilization, surrealists cultivated affinities for non-Western societies, and rejected colonialist attitudes of cultural dominance. Cabrera was not an active member of the surrealist group, but she respected its quest, which sympathized with peoples of color. Surrealism extended far beyond any particular school or group of thinkers, and embraced an entire aesthetic that arose from an affinity for issues of displacement, exile, and otherness. The theories of Sigmund Freud appealed to surrealists, because his emphasis on the subconscious and repressed primordial instincts enabled them to delve into the "primitive" that Africa purportedly signified.

James Clifford notes a parallel between ethnography and surrealism and sheds significant light on the processes intertwined: "[Both share] an abandonment of the distinction between high and low culture. . . . Ethnography cut with surrealism emerges as the theory and practice of juxtaposition. It studies, and is part of, the invention and interruption of meaningful wholes in works of cultural import-export."[10] This melding of scientific investigation and poetic invention became a central part of Cabrera's literary and ethnographic writings. Long after her departure from Paris, Lydia Cabrera's writings were marked by surrealist elements described by Clifford. She was a collector of linguistic curiosities, incorporating fragments of discourse and juxtaposing cultural variants. By adopting surrealist techniques, she enhanced the "oral" nature of her prose. All of her writings exhibit a dynamic interplay of voices, songs, and stories.

Cabrera acknowledged that her fascination with non-European cultures and religions coincided with the preoccupations of the surrealist group in Paris. She, like many of her contemporaries, sought to redefine the aesthetics of portraying other cultures. In doing so, these writers tapped a reservoir of oral traditions they feared would vanish. Literature of color was hardly foreign to Spanish America; it dated back to the nineteenth century, when romantic and realist texts idealized "primitive" cultures, treating Indians and blacks as analogous civilizations. Cabrera, well-read in world literature, was certainly familiar with Chateaubriand's accounts of Indians, which were echoed in novels by Spanish American writers like Jorge Isaacs and Gertrudis Gómez de Avellaneda. However, she diverged from these romanticized tales in her efforts to faithfully represent African voices.

The European fascination with African cultures coincided with modernism, as the French tired of the conventional, staid art forms produced in the last decades of the 1800s. Gauguin's paintings at the turn of the century, incorporating black Haitian subjects, represented a call for a new aesthetic. In the wake of World War I, new democratic ideals gave rise to an avant-garde that looked beyond Europe. This call for artistic innovation was not limited to the visual arts; jazz arrived in Paris in 1918, when a black orchestra played at the Casino de Paris. During the first decades of the 1900s, Paris celebrated its "Banquet Years," a period that inaugurated, as Roger Shattuck observes, a new kind of thinking: "Man is, by nature, an unnatural animal, and it requires a suitably primitive art not to distort this nature, but to reveal it."[11] Although the postwar decades showed a decline in the festive tone of the "Banquet Years," avant-garde artists continued to explore the realities of primitive societies. A popular vogue for *l'art négre* and black music, imported from the United States, coincided with the rising importance of African societies as subjects of ethnographic studies. Paris in the 1920s and 1930s was fertile intellectual ground for writers like Cabrera, Carpentier, and Asturias, who were captivated by the tantalizing otherness of the African and indigenous cultures of their respective homelands.

THE NEGRITUDE WRITERS: A POETICS OF DISPLACEMENT

Between 1932 and 1946, francophone Caribbean writers in Paris came into contact with French surrealists. Developments in the arts and ethnographic studies provided the impetus for a new group of writers who espoused ideas of racial equality and a fervent self-awareness that came to be known as Negritude. Lydia Cabrera's publications indicate that she was on the fringes of this movement, which was led by natives of the Caribbean who sought to expand notions of African culture. Much later in her career she wrote an important article entitled "Notas sobre Africa, la Negritud y la actual poesía yoruba" (Notes concerning Africa, Negritude, and Present-day Yoruba Poetry), which consisted of brief biographies of Léon Damas, Aimé Césaire, and Léopold Sédar Senghor, the founders of the Negritude Movement. It was complemented by a mini-anthology of Yoruban poems.[12] The title of her article indicates that Cabrera's own project coincided with the goals of the Negritude poets. The works of these poets were instrumental in the creation of her unique ethnographic poetics, because they made her aware of poetry's affinity for the oral. From Damas, Césaire, and Senghor, Lydia learned that poetry provided a perfect medium for creating an artistic effect of orality.

On June 1, 1932, a red pamphlet entitled *Légitime défense* was issued in Paris by a group of black students.[13] Among the many readers of this manifesto-like booklet were Damas, born in French Guiana and educated in Martinique; Senghor, a native of Senegal; and Césaire, from Martinique. In 1934, these three intellectuals went on to establish their own journal, which claimed the title *L'Etudiant Noir*. This new publication transcended national boundaries and called for an end to the tribalization that divided blacks into their national groups. The founders of *L'Etudiant Noir* championed the self-awareness proclaimed by *Légitime défense*, but their writings assumed a less politicized tone. The group that formed around *L'Etudiant Noir* was skeptical of contemporary Western ideologies. They were also reserved in their acceptance of surrealism, supporting the aesthetic only insofar as it could be used as a means for vindicating the African voice.

Years later, Damas, Césaire, and Senghor came to call their group's passionate self-awareness and nostalgia for a native past "Negritude," a term that denoted a literary movement as well as the group's ideology. The intellectuals advocated an appreciation of black cultural values and an end to an aesthetic that regarded blacks as exotic subjects. In a speech delivered in 1959, Senghor reflected on the inception of Negritude: "To be really ourselves, we had to embody Negro African culture in twentieth-century realities. To enable our Negritude to be, instead of a museum piece, the efficient instrument of liberation, it was necessary to cleanse it of its dross and include it in the united movement of the contemporary world."[14] These ideals, which played a significant role in Lydia Cabrera's thinking, were reflected in the poetry of the three intellectuals. Paris was essentially the birthplace of black francophone literature, and a parallel process of displaced discovery informed the works of other writers like Cabrera and Carpentier, who saw the significance of African elements in Cuban society oceans away from their native country.

The first of the *L'Etudiant Noir* group to publish his works was Léon Damas. He, like Cabrera, had abandoned his studies (of law, in his case) to pursue an interest in oriental languages. His studies of Asia led him back to his original roots, and he trained as an ethnologist. Like Cabrera, he straddled the fields of literature and anthropology and knew well the hardships of exile. His book of poems entitled *Pigments* was published in Paris in 1937. Lydia was an avid reader of Damas's poetry. In an article paying homage to the Guianese poet, Lydia wrote she had read his early works and sympathized with his honesty, his violence, his pride in being black, and his thirst for justice.[15] In the brief article written in exile in Miami, Cabrera expressed her gratitude for his attention to issues that engaged her in her personal struggle to incorporate black culture into the Cuban intellectual community. Damas, like Cabrera, was deeply troubled by the social discrimination and disenfranchisement of the African peoples of his homeland. It was this concern that inflected both writers' treatment of African oral culture in their writings.

In 1938, Damas was commissioned by the Musée d'Ethnographie de Paris to lead a mission to French Guiana to investigate the social effects of colonization and the impact of the penal colony imposed by the corrupt colonial regime. He collected testimonies of convicts to support his denunciation of French programs of assimilation. The resulting report, entitled *Retour de Guyane*, appeared in 1938 and was regarded by French authorities as a political publication. During this return to his homeland from exile in Paris, Damas became fascinated with Guianese oral folklore. Years later, he translated some of these legends and tales, and published them with the title *Veillées noires*. Cabrera learned from Damas that the ideals of Negritude could be used to serve her own political agenda and evoke the poetics of a suppressed culture. Like Damas, she turned to Afro-Cuban oral culture as a means of liberating unheard voices.

Lydia Cabrera's contact with Negritude writers was not limited to Damas. She also admired the works of Martiniquan Aimé Césaire. As a young student in Paris, Césaire devoured books by Frobenius and Delafosse that extolled the virtues of a rich African heritage. Marx, Engels, and Freud also played a decisive role in his intellectual formation. Césaire's first pub-lication, and masterwork, appeared in an almost complete version in 1939 in the French journal *Volontés*. This early rendition of *Cahier d'un retour au pays natal* (*Notebook of a Return to the Native Land*), a long poem, followed in the footsteps of Damas's *Pigments*, but did not enjoy the same early success. It was not until shortly after Lydia Cabrera's translation of Césaire's poem was published in Cuba in 1943 under the title *Retorno al país natal* that the piece became popular in Paris. The 1947 Bordas edition of *Retour* published the poem in toto and was prefaced by an article written by Breton that regarded the poem as a lyric triumph. As a translator, Lydia learned that poetry could express the aesthetics of oral language.

Césaire's *Retour*, like Damas's *Pigments*, coupled political aggressive-ness and rebelliousness with a lyrical voice and telluric images. Critics praised the work for its insightful penetration of the African soul. *Retour* is a poem of extremes; it juxtaposes violence with tenderness. Césaire, like his Guyanese colleague, derided assimilation as the destiny of coloniza-tion. These excerpts from Lydia Cabrera's fine translation exemplify Césaire's combative tone:

> Escuchad al mundo blanco
> horriblemente cansado de su esfuerzo inmenso
> sus articulaciones rebeldes crujir bajo las estrellas duras
> su rigidez de acero azul traspasando la carne mística
> escuchad sus victorias proditorias pregonar sus derrotas. [...]
> Acepto... acepto... enteramente sin reserva...
> mi raza que ninguna ablución de hisopo y de lirios mezclados
> podría purificar. [...][16]

> [Hear the white world
> horribly weary from its immense efforts
> its stiff joints crack under the hard stars
> its blue steel rigidities pierce the mystic flesh
> hear its deceptive victories tour its defeats
> hear the grandiose alibis of its pitiful stumbling. . . .
> I accept . . . I accept . . . totally, without reservation . . .
> my race that no ablution of hyssop mixed with lilies
> could purify. . . .][17]

Césaire writes passionately about the hypothetical return that he would indeed undertake a few months after the outbreak of war. Ironically, the poem had a more decisive impact on the community he abandoned than on the one to which he returned.

Like the Negritude poets, Cabrera was first inspired to explore her homeland's black culture while in Paris. She drew from their writings an interest in oral folklore, and began to identify orality with cultural identity. Cabrera shared with Damas and Césaire a disdain for colonial forces that impinged on the expression of black heritage. By celebrating Afro-Cuban orality she subtly criticized Cuban literate culture. Combining anthropology with poetry, these writers sought to introduce the marginal cultures of their respective regions to a Western audience.

CUENTOS NEGROS DE CUBA: CABRERA THE COLLECTOR VS. CABRERA THE CREATOR

Lydia Cabrera's first literary endeavor echoed the cultural vindication that the black Negritude poets advocated. At the time when she first conceptualized the *Cuentos negros de Cuba* (Tales Told by Black Cubans), Paris was primed for this kind of autochthonous literature. *Cuentos* unflinchingly focuses on the black cultural phenomena that comprise, in Cabrera's eyes, a fundamental component of Cuban national identity. This theme developed from her contacts with Omí Tomí, Oddedeí, and Calazán Herrera when she visited Cuba in 1930. Teresa de la Parra accompanied her on several of these excursions to the Pogolotti neighborhood of Havana, where the two explored an occult world that was still essentially closed to whites. When Teresa became ill in Paris, Lydia entertained her with stories told to her by black servants in her childhood home in Havana. Eventually, with the aid of the ethnographic notes recorded in 1930, Cabrera wrote down these oral memories in the form of short stories to send to De la Parra, who was bedridden in a sanatorium in Switzerland.

Lydia shared a copy of this collection with her friend Francis de Miomandre, who was so impressed that he brought it to Paul Morand, the director of Gallimard, a prominent editorial house in Paris. Miomandre's translation of Cabrera's *Contes nègres de Cuba*, dedicated to Teresa de la Parra, appeared in 1936, the same year that Gallimard published Asturias's *Lègendes du Guatemala* (Legends of Guatemala). Lydia's collection represented an innovative literary adaptation of Afro-Cuban folklore. It was one of the first versions of *patakíes* (Lucumí legends) and *kutuguangos* (legends proceeding from the Reglas Congas) recorded in a Western language. Although the intended public of Cabrera's stories was initially her ailing friend, the *Contes* were ultimately published for a European readership charmed by non-Western cultures.

Alejo Carpentier immediately acclaimed the book in a revealing re-

view, written in Paris in 1936 and published in the Cuban magazine *Carteles*;
Carpentier had been an editor of the magazine in the twenties and was now
its correspondent in Europe. During the 1930s, Carpentier sent numerous
articles to the Havana weekly, informing Cubans of the latest trends in
Europe. Carpentier heralded the arrival of a new kind of Cuban national
literature, "a unique work in our literature," and a new writer as well. For
him, the collection of black tales constituted a new genre in the domain of
an essentially creole poetics. Carpentier praised the stories for locating
Antillean mythology within the context of universal values. Arguably, he
wrote, Lydia's collection should be shelved beside the works of Kipling
and Lord Dunsany. The review is a curious gesture, since Cabrera's book
was not made available to a Spanish-speaking public until four years later,
thereby affirming the collection's presumably elite, European readership.

   Carpentier's reading incorporated the work into the Western canon. He
maintained that the collection could not have been composed by a man,
and that it represented a milestone because it deviated completely from the
usual concerns of Cuban woman writers. Carpentier thus welcomed
Cabrera's collection into Cuba's national letters. Even more striking are
his meditations on the probable process of composition:

> Pero sería un error creer que la escritora se ha contentado con transcribir
> ese folklore en sus narraciones. Con notas acumuladas en cuadernillos de
> colegiala—notas referentes principalmente a los cuentos negros y lucumíes,
> "cuentos con música," cuya tradición está casi perdida en Cuba—ha
> construido relatos personalísimos, enriquecidos por suntuosas visiones de
> paisajes y costumbres criollos.[18]

> [But it would be an error to believe that the writer has merely transcribed
> that folklore in her narrations. With notes collected in a schoolgirl's note-
> book—notes relating primarily to black and Lucumí stories, "stories set to
> music," a tradition that is practically lost in Cuba—she has constructed
> highly personal tales, enriched by sumptuous views of landscapes and Creole
> customs.]

This assessment captures the remarkably ambiguous nuances tied up in the
combination of anthropology and inventive poetics in Cabrera's writing.
Carpentier most likely knew these methods well, as his own fieldwork was
instrumental in recording stories and songs that appeared in his 1946 study
of Cuban music, a scholarly book titled *La música en Cuba*. As in the case
of Cabrera, Carpentier's transcriptions spill over into literary works, such
as his 1933 novel *¡Ecue-Yamba-O!*

   Conspicuous in Cabrera's *Cuentos negros* is the absence of a preface written by the author describing her methods of transcription and creative processes. Such an introduction became an enlightening part of all of her later publications. This void was filled by Fernando Ortiz in the 1940 Spanish version of the *Cuentos negros de Cuba*, printed by Cuba's publishing company La Verónica. His prologue is actually an abbreviated version of an article published in a 1938 issue of *Estudios Afrocubanos*, a Havana quarterly of which he was the president.[19] While Carpentier hailed the collection as a literary triumph, Ortiz read Cabrera's *Cuentos* as a faithful transcription of African mythology. Ortiz's assessment diverged significantly from Carpentier's review of Lydia Cabrera's masterwork of Cuban literature. The two Cuban critics reacted in very different ways to the contradictions inherent in the relationship between literature and anthropology displayed in the collection.

Ortiz's review appeared in the section of *Estudios Afrocubanos* devoted to recent publications and, like Carpentier's *Carteles* article, introduced the collection of stories to Cuba's reading public. In the opening sentences, Ortiz recalled Lydia's induction into the group of Afro-Cubanists. Her curiosity led her into the "forest" of black legends. Later, for pure pleasure, she began transcribing and collecting them. For Ortiz, Cabrera was essentially an ethnographer: a collector, a translator, and a transcriber of black folktales.

The first portion of Ortiz's review summarizes the critical reception of *Contes nègres* in Paris. Ortiz cites at length Jean Cassou's favorable review of Cabrera's book. Cassou admits that Europeans are shockingly unfamiliar with American culture, and that Cabrera's stories serve as an important remedy for this ignorance. Ortiz denounces the prejudicial notions that tinge Cassou's assessment of the black tales as devoid of morality and didactic intention. He then proposes an alternative approach to definitions of black morality, stating that it would be preferable, from an ethnographic standpoint, to observe, not a lack of morality, but rather diverse moral and social values.[20]

But Ortiz's views are also fraught with contradictions. While, on one hand, he defends the productive elements of black and white coexistence, his reading is highly contingent on a modern Western view of literature that excludes African elements. Ortiz is preoccupied with the "authenticity" of the Yoruban tales, yet places them in the category of Aesop's fables. In stark contrast to Carpentier, Ortiz undermines the artistic and inventive role of the author. He describes the collection as a second translation of black legends.

Although *Cuentos* represented the first effort to present Afro-Cuban folklore to a European public, the collection was not the first of its kind to be published in Spanish. Two years before Cabrera's stories were published in Havana, Rómulo Lachatañeré published a compilation of twenty-one *patakíes*, or Yoruban legends, in Matanzas. This author, a mulatto of Franco-Haitian descent, cultivated relationships with his informants in much the same way as Cabrera. In the preface of the 1938 edition, he describes his close friendships with members of the Yoruban cult.[21] Comparing Ortiz's prologues of Cabrera's *Cuentos* and Lachatañeré's collection, one is struck by the latter's emphasis on the genre as a whole and the ideological implications of the transcriptions. Ortiz heralds Cabrera's and Lachatañeré's works as the inauguration of a new kind of writing, one that "brings to light" a hidden, yet vital, black literature.

For Ortiz, Cabrera and Lachatañeré were essentially collectors, and their texts were analogous to an archive, or a museum full of works of art that evoked the essence of Afro-Cuban culture. A similar "culture collector" inhabits Carpentier's *Los pasos perdidos* (*The Lost Steps*), the paradigmatic story of the plight of an anthropologist-writer who seeks to recuperate a lost origin by inscribing a linguistic beginning in the form of an oral poem. Ortiz's assessment of the Cuban writers' journeys into an obscure literary "jungle" parallels the narrator-protagonist's symbolic return in Carpentier's novel. For both Ortiz and the narrator-protagonist, songs and stories are valuable artifacts.

James Clifford explains, "The notion [that] this gathering involves the accumulation of possessions, the idea that identity is a kind of wealth (of objects, knowledge, memories, experience), is surely not universal. In the West, however, collecting has long been a strategy for the deployment of a possessive self, culture and authenticity."[22] Within such a context, recorded stories are strategically selected to form a coherent representation of an alien tradition. Remnants of a vanishing oral tradition are regarded as authentic and pure. Ortiz suggests that prior to the arrival of *¡¡Oh, mío Yemayá!!* and *Cuentos*, the field of black popular literature was regarded as taboo and unworthy of consideration. His articulations reflect ideas of cultural authenticity for both Cuban blacks and their oral literature that proceed from Western assumptions about order, wholeness, and essence.

Ortiz's articles also reveal certain misguided assumptions about oral tradition that have influenced ways in which readers approach collections like *Cuentos*. In his opinion, the collector of stories is faced with the difficult task of transposing oral texts into intelligible, written Castilian. He asserts that this process involves the impossible translation from musical languages that are distant both spatially and temporally. One of the distant languages to which Ortiz refers is Yoruba, or Lucumí, as it is called in Cuba. A rich body of *patakíes,* or legends, has passed from generation to generation, primarily via oral recitation. For the devotees of the Regla de Ocha, or Cult of Ocha, these myths are not regarded as fiction; rather, they constitute the sacred memory of the group. Given this distinction, Ortiz is particularly concerned with the chasm separating oral and literate practices, and how these opposing conventions impinge on the task of the translator. In his prologue to Lachatañeré's collection, Ortiz claims that orality, in part archaic, esoteric and senseless, in part communal and lacking professional style, is expressed by Lachatañeré in African languages that are slowly vanishing, becoming ignored even by a great majority of African descendants.[23] Ortiz's appraisal of the value of orally transmitted texts is fraught with ideological assumptions that associate literacy with progress. His assessment implicitly links the development of literacy with notions of civilization and permanence. Orality, by default, is defined as a lack, and oral literature therefore lacks modernity, sense, and an aesthetic style.

Brian Street would group Ortiz with theorists like Walter J. Ong and Jack Goody, who have overstated the superiority of literacy practices to oral traditions. Street points to the fundamental contradiction inherent in any piece of written analysis that seeks to understand an oral mentality. In a broad sense, it is more productive to think about all language as possessing qualities that fix or classify experience: "Fixing, separating, abstraction all happen without literacy."[24] Rather than conceiving orality and literacy as mutually exclusive concepts, it is far more fruitful to see the interactions between speech and writing.

Ortiz, like Ong and Goody, is trapped in a literate frame of mind when he evaluates the difficulty, and even the impossibility, of faithfully transposing oral literature into written form. For Ortiz, transposition, a process that implies difference, can only result in a loss, because written Spanish cannot adequately express the rhythmic and melodic nuances of African languages. Ortiz argues that orality is fundamentally distinct from literacy insofar as it is tied up in experience with music and fleeting intonations. The collector/translator's task is to "fix" these pure oral texts, risking the betrayal of what Ortiz refers to as "the fidelity of primary thought."[25]

Ortiz analyzes the process of transposition and translation with regard to Lachatañeré's and Cabrera's collections of fiction, anticipating issues that will be central to the appraisal of Cabrera's ethnographic and literary works. For Ortiz, Cabrera's *Cuentos* represent a meaningful contribution to the field of Afro-American ethnography. He does not, however, appreciate the literary elements shared by fiction and ethnography. Cabrera faced the same issue. She offered no introductory remarks in her first literary publication; but her later collections of stories indicate that she, too, regarded her own eclectic oeuvre somewhat ambiguously. Although Cabrera claimed merely to transcribe the anecdotes her informants provided, it is clear that her texts illustrate that the gestures involved in an ethnographic transcription do not exclude those effected in a literary retelling.

By upholding the notion of a "great divide" between oral and literate cultures, Lydia embellished her own role as the preserver of an oral tradition that was losing out to the processes of modernization. Her *Cuentos* exemplify her desire to salvage a threatened tradition by inscribing oral memories. Assuming that speech and writing are mutually exclusive, she adhered to an ideological premise that allowed for fictionalization of the oral. This assumption, albeit unsound, is necessary for the construction of fiction. Her project was ethnographic in its conception, yet she found that the most effective way to "write" orality was a mimesis of African storytelling. Lydia Cabrera imbued her texts, both literary and anthropological, with an aesthetic of the oral to convey her belief in the authenticity and integrity of Afro-Cuban culture.

Lino Novás-Calvo, Lydia Cabrera's friend and compatriot in exile, was one of the first critics to explore the mediations that distinguish various moments in Cabrera's texts. In 1969, he wrote the prologue to a complete edition of her short stories, including those contained in *Cuentos negros de Cuba* and *Por qué... Cuentos negros de Cuba* (1948) (Why . . . Black Stories of Cuba). In an article published in *Exilio* in 1969, Novás-Calvo draws distinctions between the methods employed by Lydia Cabrera the short-story writer and those employed by Lydia Cabrera the ethnographer:

> Sabia trajinera, como sus bibijaguas, fue acumulando datos, llenando ficheros, que guardaba en una especie de cuarto de los misterios. Los más explosivos, una vez confirmados, fueron a dar finalmente a ese tesoro de magia, santería y brujería que es *El monte*. Ahí está la ciencia. Los otros, los menos controlables, los más comunicables, pasaron a los cuentos. Ahí está el arte.[26]

> [As an astute communicator, she diligently went about gathering data, filling index cards that she kept in her treasure chest of mysteries. The most explosive elements, once confirmed, eventually made their way into that treasure chest of magic, *Santería* and witchcraft that is *El monte*. Therein lay the science. Others, less easily described but more readily imparted, ended up in the stories. Therein lay the art.]

Taking Novás-Calvo's observations one step further, the complexity and richness of Lydia Cabrera's works can be attributed to the fact that science and poetry intermingle in all of her writing. Novás-Calvo asserts that the classification of *El monte* as a purely academic treatise is arbitrary and misleading, since the book "está cundido de historias que son también obras de creación y de arte; y en todos los cuentos de Lydia Cabrera está la mano y el cerebro de una investigadora. [...] *El monte* se lee como una biblia, un milyunanoches, un decamerón negro; y los cuentos se leen como páginas escapadas del *monte*"[27] [is filled with stories that are also works of creation and art; and in all of Lydia Cabrera's stories one finds the hand and mind of a researcher. . . . *El monte* reads like a Bible, a *One Thousand and One Nights*, a black *Decameron*; and the stories read like pages that have escaped from *El monte*].

The stylistic gestures in Cabrera's literary experiments diverge significantly from Fernando Ortiz's description of sterile and methodical steps of transposition and translation. Lydia, the short-story writer, found a new aesthetic and formulated an ethnographic poetics of cultural invention that derived from black oral tradition. The novelty of her poetics can be attributed to the syncretic nature of her subject matter. While she sought to preserve Afro-Cuban lore that she believed was destined to vanish, she also invented a new kind of prose in Castilian, one that drew from Cuban mulatto popular culture. The syncretic literature that Cabrera created involves more than just borrowing from discrete cultural realms; rather, it is a complex phenomenon involving the synthesis of cultural elements. Cabrera's *Cuentos* is an enterprise without precedent.

How, then, did Lydia Cabrera convey orality in writing? How did the fragmented outlines of her early conversations with her *tatas* find their way to the pages of these imaginative short stories? The extent of innovation on the part of the writer was greater in some instances than in others. Jorge and Isabel Castellanos, who conducted extensive studies of Cabrera's early ethnographic notes, contend that her creative effort varied significantly from story to story.[28] Where the intent was to preserve a given anecdote, the task of composition entailed combining fragments, clarifying the story line, and polishing the language. In others, even the underlying themes were the product of Cabrera's imagination, and she intertwined these creations with excerpts from Afro-Cuban folklore and allusions to universal lore.

The first story of *Cuentos*, "Bregantino, Bregantín," exemplifies Cabrera's ingenuity for inscribing the "oral," because it incorporates certain formulaic epithets associated with a storytelling tradition. For example, the story opens with an allusion to a mythic past. Lydia Cabrera mimics her *tatas* by setting the scene for a fabulous tale. "Bregantino, Bregantín" tells the story of a young black princess who for years lived timidly in silence. She finally breaks her silence to inform her father that she wishes to be married. Her meddlesome mother, the queen, intervenes to ensure that the young princess marries the finest suitor. The *babalao*—"father of secrets," or diviner—designates the date for a grand contest to take place. After a series of tests, Lombriz (Earthworm) is declared the victor and marries the young princess. This peculiar intermingling of humans and animals is commonplace in Cabrera's narratives and is characteristic of both African and Asian folklore. In this and other fiction by Cabrera, animals act like humans and even demonstrate a capacity for complex reasoning. This is especially patent in Cabrera's 1971 collection, *Ayapá: Cuentos de Jicotea* (Ayapá: Stories of Jicotea), a compilation of stories about the multifaceted and capricious protagonist, Jicotea, "a freshwater tortoise."

"Bregantino, Bregantín" exemplifies the dry, sarcastic wit that runs throughout Cabrera's narrative. Male protagonists frequently receive the brunt of the wry humor in an otherwise predominantly patriarchal African society that favors males as central figures. Lombriz finally abandons his bride and leaves the kingdom in the hands of his servant and good friend Toro. King Toro begins his reign in Cocozúmba by ordering the decapitation of all males and clamoring his glory cry, "¡Yo, yo, yo, yo, yo, yo!"[29] [I, I, I, I, I, I!]. This slaughter ultimately results in the elimination of the masculine gender from the spoken language (except, of course, when referring to Toro)! Little authorial winks like this are scattered throughout Cabrera's narrative works.

In an interesting moment in the story, Sanune, one of Toro's concubines, retreats into the *monte* to find solace in her protectors "Ogún y Ochosi (San Pedro y San Norberto)." Here ensues the internal tale of the two *orishas*, which parallels the framing anecdote. The Ogún and Ochosi tales most likely stem from Cabrera's contact with *santeros* during her 1930 visit to Havana. Their insertion into the text contrives the reality of a storytelling session and illustrates that there is always an interaction, a mutual shaping, between stories and framing device. In both the frame and the internal tale, verses and choruses in African languages are intercalated to form a linguistic collage. This technique reflects Cabrera's affinity for ethnographic surrealism and embellishes the syncretic nature of the text. Proverbs from the Iberian Peninsula are interspersed with Lucumí and Congo sayings, and these are mixed with more recent Creole creations. Cabrera's gesture of erasing boundaries by mixing linguistic traditions is repeated in her short collection *Refranes de negros viejos*, published in 1955. In a broad sense, her scientific work, consisting of this collection of proverbs, *Lucumí* and *Congo* vocabularies, and a detailed account of the "ashé" (virtue, secret force) of precious stones, complemented her literary creations.

In *Cuentos*, the incorporation of rhythmic choruses in African languages has a stylistic and musical effect, and also preserves the songs themselves.

The intended reader of the anecdotes would most likely be unfamiliar with the African lexicon and thus be unable to distinguish between one African language and another. Rhythmic and sonorous verses become linguistic instruments that re-create the moment of performance in which a tale might be heard. Lydia's experiences as an observer of storytelling jousts taught her the importance of the role played by songs that are intertwined with the action in African tales.[30] She reinvents these beats and repetitive syllables to heighten the African rhythms of the narrative. Some of the titles of her *Cuentos*, like "Chéggue" and "Eyá," announce the Yoruban sounds that resound throughout the text, and they establish an oral context for the collection. The syllabic chants and overflow of assonances, predominantly of *o* and *u*, spill into the Castilian prose to create an African tone. In this way, the writer's ingenious play with language effects an inventive rhythmic style that synthesizes African and Hispanic elements. She conveys oral language in writing by incorporating onomatopoeic expressions, interpolated songs, colloquial sayings, and punctuation and interjections reflecting oral narration.

The 1940 edition of *Cuentos* includes footnotes that clarify African words placed in quotations within the narrative. Some of these translations cite Fernando Ortiz's *Catauro de Afrocubanismos* (A Basket of Afro-Cuban Expressions) as a source. Although these notes appear to be somewhat haphazard and rather inconsistent, they are revealing because they shed light on some of the seams and strains of the text. Notes, quotation marks, and casual parentheses indicate that the writer is fumbling to grasp her material. The interspersed narration and commentary suggest that she uncomfortably straddles anthropological analysis and literary creation. Cabrera's suppression of the notes of commentary in the second edition demonstrates her desire to signal a distinction between her academic studies and her literary experiments. In subsequent editions of *Cuentos negros de Cuba*, as well as in her 1948 collection *Por qué... Cuentos negros de Cuba*, explicatory notes occupy the final pages, much like the glossaries found in regional novels like José Eustasio Rivera's *La vorágine* (*The Vortex*) and Ricardo Güiraldes's *Don Segundo Sombra* (*Shadows in the Pampas*).

In addition to being influenced by the Negritude writers, Cabrera followed in the steps of her Spanish contemporaries like Federico García Lorca and Rafael Alberti, in whose work she saw the synthesis of popular culture and a lyrical poetic style. García Lorca, in particular, penetrated the mysterious and magical forces that he saw inhabiting and tormenting man. The two writers first met in Madrid in 1926, and Lorca traveled to Havana in 1928. In *El monte*, Cabrera describes a Ñáñigo procession that she attended with García Lorca, and the verses that the event inspired for the Spanish poet.[31] Lorca's lyric poetry made a deep impression on Cabrera at a time when she was elaborating the stories that she had heard in her childhood. When he published *El romancero gitano* (*Gypsy Ballads*) in 1928, Lorca dedicated "La casada infiel" (The Unfaithful Bride) to "Lydia Cabrera y su negrita." The "negrita" was a young black girl raised in the house of Lydia's sister, Gracielle, about whom Lydia told García Lorca many stories. García Lorca's poetry, like Cabrera's narrative, seeks to evoke in writing the modulations and tonalities of the spoken and sung word. Both writers manipulated rhythm and language to enact a passage from the oral to the written.

Lydia Cabrera's travels to Spain in the twenties also brought her in contact with the founder of Spanish philology, Ramón Menéndez Pidal. At first glance, this meeting of minds may seem somewhat arbitrary. But the encounter had a profound impact on young Lydia, as the two were involved in intellectual pursuits that were strikingly similar. At the same time that Lydia Cabrera was "penetrating" (to use Ortiz's word) the *monte* of her native country, Don Ramón was combing the Spanish countryside, compiling songs to add to his immense archive, his personal collection of ballads. He even extended his quest to Spanish America, where he searched the hillsides for traces of Spanish ballads. Just as Cabrera's personal endeavor led to her *Cuentos negros de Cuba*, Menéndez Pidal's exhaustive investigations led to *Flor nueva de romances viejos* (New Flower of Old Ballads), which first appeared in 1928. This work contains a collection of old Spanish ballads that the collector feared were fading into oblivion. Menéndez Pidal makes the stunning poetic gesture of interspersing his own creations. His innovative collection includes old ballads, found in *romanceros* (collections of ballads) of the 1800s, some modern versions taken from Spanish oral tradition, and songs of Menéndez Pidal's own creation. In the introductory remarks he declares himself the modern *juglar* par excellence, proclaiming that each oral poet, whether ancient or modern, retouches and recasts the ballad he sings. The tradition, like all that lives, is transformed continuously; to live is to vary.[32] Both Menéndez Pidal and Cabrera sought to attribute cultural status to a an eclectic oral tradition, thereby expanding their respective national canons to include popular literature. They perceived an intrinsic link between orality and poetic invention.

LYDIA CABRERA AND WIFREDO LAM RETURN

Although Lydia did not publish another book until 1948, when her second collection of stories appeared, the literary project that directly followed her *Cuentos* was emblematic of her return to Cuba. Cabrera, like intellectuals who had flourished in Paris in the twenties and thirties, fled when war threatened the European capital. Soon after returning to Havana in 1938, she agreed to produce a Castilian version of Aimé Césaire's poem *Cahier d'un retour au pays natal*. Césaire's poem depicted the Negritude experience by making an emotional attempt to define a collective Caribbean spirit. The *Cahier*, an autobiographical treatise, also signaled Césaire's imminent return to his homeland, a return that would be shared by many of his Caribbean counterparts at the start of World War II. Cabrera, like Césaire, developed as an intellectual amid the radical climate of avant-garde France. Both writers then reentered their native lands and attempted to come to terms with their national identities.

Soon after Lydia returned to Havana, Wifredo Lam (1902–82), a Cuban artist born of a Chinese father and Afro-Cuban mother, arrived in the Americas with his companion, Helena Holzer Benítez. Césaire had originally requested that Wifredo and Helena collaborate on a translation of his poem. Helena, however, doubted her abilities to translate a poem of such imagistic complexity and passed the project on to Lydia. The publication of *Retorno* in 1943 was instrumental in bringing the Negritude movement to Cuba.

Cabrera's translation was accompanied by cover and interior illustrations designed by Lam and a preface by Benjamín Peret. The poem proclaims the symbolic nature of the collaboration of Cabrera and Lam: the traumatic return and adaptation to one's native land. Lam's return after nineteen years abroad meant a departure from a circle of European intellectuals and artists, Picasso among them, who had recently begun to praise his work. His artistic style was touched by the surrealist aesthetic, and the works he produced in Paris demonstrated his admiration of Cubism. Upon returning to his homeland, he found that there was little appreciation for these masters and even less for the artistic creations of Cubans of African descent. It became apparent to Lam that black intellectuals did not have a niche in the artistic community in Havana. He was met by a Cuban society that frowned upon his interracial relationship with a woman with whom he was not married. Despite these initial adversities, a group of intellectuals, Cabrera among them, befriended Lam and helped him to settle into Havana.

Like Lam, Lydia Cabrera did not enjoy a smooth reentry into Havana. Her mother died in 1932, and the Cabrera family home no longer existed. To make matters worse, her inheritance had been mishandled and Lydia found herself in a precarious financial position. Her desire to conduct research in black communities like Pogolotti and Regla could no longer be dismissed as hobbies, and the middle-aged upper-class woman was perceived as a curious anomaly. She quickly found support in her friendship and professional collaboration with María Teresa de Rojas ("Titina") who was to become her lifelong companion in exile. María Teresa had recently inherited a colonial home, La Quinta San José, from her first husband. The house was conveniently located near Pogolotti, the site of Lydia's early investigations.

The encounter of Cabrera and Lam profoundly affected both of their careers. They had previously come into contact with the African roots of their native Cuba in a Parisian intellectual setting steeped in surrealism and gripped by a fervor for ethnological studies. Their time in Paris allowed them to make a clean break with the Cuba of their respective childhoods. Now they found themselves in the unsettling position of being far removed from the French capital that had nurtured their intellectual and artistic development. Cabrera immediately recognized Lam's talent, and perhaps understood the impact that their different backgrounds had on their respective roles in the group of literati and artists in Havana. Some of her first publications in the early 1940s were aimed at introducing Lam to Cuba. In a review of his paintings, she cites famous Parisian artists and presents Lam as a potential link between Cuban and European art.

Lydia's description of Lam's art is virtually interchangeable with an assessment of her own creations. In a 1942 article published in the *Diario de la Marina*, Cabrera writes, "Dos viejas culturas —Asia y Africa— imprimen a su obra acento de veracidad entrañable, ancestral, y de ningún modo podría llamarse 'exótico' —en el vulgar sentido que ha ido cobrando la palabra— el lenguaje plástico que hablan sus formas exaltadas y depuradas." [33] [Two ancient cultures, Asia and Africa, imprint his work with an intimate truthfulness, ancestral but by no means "exotic," in the vulgar sense that the word has acquired, the language of a painting whose forms are impassioned and precise.] She concludes by harshly criticizing the Havana community that has ignored this universally renowned figure, claiming it inexcusable that his name remain silenced in Cuba. Lydia's thoughts on Lam suggest that she, too, was creating for a Western audience.

Two years later, Cabrera wrote a second article that detailed Lam's newfound passion for black cultural heritage. Her description perhaps also touches upon her own involvement with Afro-Cubanism: "De vuelta al país natal, esta tierra suya le despierta nuevas inquietudes estéticas: la cálida música de su armonía le suscita continuamente nuevos problemas que le punzan en la conciencia exigiendo la respuesta inmediata."[34] [When the artist returns to his native country, this land of his confronts him with new aesthetic challenges. The warm harmonies of its music insinuate themselves into his consciousness and provoke new uncertainties that clamor for immediate response.] Cabrera and Lam became engaged in analogous tasks of translating experiences—music, dance, and rituals—into their respective art forms, a process involving complex issues of medium, language, time, and space.

In the early 1940s, Lydia Cabrera and Wifredo Lam investigated the *monte* together, attending numerous Afro-Cuban religious ceremonies and probing the secrets of the sacred region. They collected materials fundamental to their culminating works: Cabrera's master ethnology *El monte* (1954) and Lam's milestone in contemporary painting, *La jungla* (1942–43) (*The Jungle*). Lam, like Cabrera, employed surrealist techniques to delve into the spiritual world of Afro-Cuban blacks. The painting depicts a rite of communion celebrated between an *orisha* and a practitioner. *La jungla* and *El monte* complement each other well. Their creators were drawn by the alluring otherness of a previously unexplored world at a moment when they sought to come to terms with their own identities in an unwelcoming homeland.

CONSTRUCTING *EL MONTE*

Upon renewing contact with her informants, Lydia Cabrera began to accumulate copious notes detailing her conversations and experiences as an observer of religious rites. She was particularly drawn to the songs, stories, sayings, myths and medicines of her black compatriots. By 1947, she had amassed sufficient material to publish an article entitled "Eggüe o Vichichi finda" in *Revista Bimestre Cubana*, a Havana bimonthly directed by Fernando Ortiz.[35] The title of the article, designating the Lucumí and Congo terms for medicinal plants, later assumes the position of subtitle in the lengthy heading of Lydia's masterwork: *El monte: Igbo finda, ewe orisha, vititi nfinda (Notas sobre las religiones, la magia, las supersticiones y el folklore de los negros criollos y del pueblo de Cuba)* (*El monte: Igbo finda, ewe orisha, vititi nfinda*; Notes concerning the Religions, Magic, Superstitions, and Folklore of Black Creoles and the Cuban People). Most of the information contained in the pages of this early article eventually appeared in *El monte*, although Cabrera chose to omit lengthy portions of the retelling of Omí Tomí's story, replete with dialogue and humor.

Curiously, Cabrera did not conceive the suggestive title of *El monte* until sometime after 1950, at which time she published a second fragment of the work under the title "La ceiba y la sociedad secreta Abakuá," which carried a note announcing the impending publication of the book "Vititi nfinda y Ewe-Orisha."[36] Despite the delay in deciding the book's title, the notion of *el monte* as the locus of a powerful and spiritual origin is omnipresent in the initial studies. "Eggüe o Vichichi finda" draws in the reader with the following introductory lines: "Un concepto ancestral que persiste profundamente en nuestros negros es el de la espiritualidad del bosque. En el monte, alienta, vive cuanto hay de sobrenatural y misterioso."[37] [An ancestral concept that profoundly persists in our blacks is that of the spirituality of the forest. In the *monte*, all that is supernatural and mysterious lives and breathes.] The *monte* connotes a spiritual region, an origin of songs and stories, akin to Santa Mónica in *Los pasos perdidos*. It reflects the author's longing for a coherent and authentic source of tradition. The term "monte" lacks a direct translation in English that adequately captures the transcendental powers that it possesses in Cuban Spanish. The title *El monte* alludes to a universal mother and fountain of life. This poetic title contrasts Cabrera's subsequent anthropological studies that carry either academic names or titles written in African languages, followed by their translations.

El monte represents the culmination of several prior publications. Of particular interest are Cabrera's numerous contributions to *Orígenes*, a Havana quarterly edited by José Lezama Lima and José Rodríguez Feo that was in print from 1944 to 1954. The magazine, which specialized in arts and literature, was motivated by nostalgia for a Cuban nation of the past. Its editors claimed to reject literary schools and tendencies, favoring instead works of pure creation.[38] Not surprisingly, Lydia Cabrera's first contributions to the magazine, accompanied by those of Paul Valéry, Lino Novás-Calvo, Wifredo Lam, and Aimé Césaire, were literary creations. Her short story "La virtud del árbol dagame" appeared in a 1945 issue, and "Jicotea esta noche fresca..." followed a year later. The latter was published much later in what is undeniably Cabrera's most creative collection of short stories, *Ayapá: Cuentos de Jicotea* (Ayapá: Stories of Jicotea). Both stories exemplify the writer's sharp wit and affinity for the beguiling characters of African lore. Jicotea, in particular, evolves significantly in Cabrera's later work into a motif for slavery and, more broadly, social repression.

While Lydia Cabrera consistently published in *Orígenes*, she remained ideologically on the periphery of the group that maintained a rather conservative and ethnocentric view of Cuban culture. In her opinion, African elements were embedded in all levels of a highly heterogeneous Cuban culture. Within the ideological context outlined by Lezama and his colleagues in the *Orígenes* group, the most striking magazine issue to appear was one in 1950 that boasted a cover decorated with symbols derived from the secret society Abakuá, very likely sketched by Cabrera. The designs clearly announce Lydia Cabrera's article "La ceiba y la sociedad secreta Abakuá," which later appeared as a chapter in *El monte* under the name given to the tree by Ñáñigos: "ukano beconsi." It is remarkable that this piece, which purports to be purely informative and free of interpretation, was published in *Orígenes*, a magazine that celebrates the freedom of poetic creation and is virtually devoid of this kind of ostensibly expository writing.

Even more perplexing, Lydia's article is preceded by a tribute to her as "poet of the metamorphosis," written by María Zambrano. This piece responded to the 1948 publication of Cabrera's *Por qué... Cuentos negros de Cuba* after a silence that lasted almost a decade. For Zambrano, Cabrera is a poet par excellence, embracing a nostalgic view of the past that transcends divisions between classes and races. In Cabrera's writing, fantasy and knowledge harmonize to the point of being indistinguishable, and constitute "poetic knowledge."[39] Zambrano argues that Cabrera's poetic voice stems from her actual participation in, rather than scientific investigation of, the magical world of Cuban blacks. This important review anticipates the poetic gestures that make *El monte* so richly complex. Zambrano's comments are just as pertinent to poetic moments in *El monte* and Cabrera's working articles as they are to *Por qué...*, her collection of stories. The side-by-side publication of a review of Lydia Cabrera the poet and a chapter of *El monte* in a magazine with an ideological bent like that of *Orígenes* is revealing, for clearly Cabrera's prose resisted easy categorization from the outset. Is she an ethnographer or a poet? How does she maneuver between the two realms? A progressive confluence of poetry and science leads up to the publication of her monumental work. Just as Cabrera's early short stories enriched her more academic articles, her transcriptions and vocabularies served as invaluable tools for reading her more creative literary productions.

EL MONTE: "LO QUE HE OÍDO Y LO QUE HE VISTO"
[WHAT I HAVE HEARD AND SEEN]

Although Lydia Cabrera's book is most commonly referred to as *El monte*, its complete title contains African words, "Igbo finda, ewe orisha, vititi nfinda," that announce the encounter of distinct languages and cultures that take place in the book's pages. The contents of the book promise to serve as a tool for deciphering its title. The subtitle is a Castilian explanation of the themes to be treated in the text: (Notes concerning the religions, magic, superstitions and folklore of black Creoles and the Cuban people). "Notes" seems a modest estimation of the book's contents: 564 pages of dense text, followed by 25 pages of photographs. However,

Cabrera's choice of subtitle is deliberate, for it signals her tendency to diminish and even discount her authorial role in the text's production. The book opens with a six-page preface, written by the author, in which she also refers to her work as a compilation of "notes." Cabrera's opening statements conspicuously lack any overarching purpose or authorial ambition:

> Las [notas] publico, no es necesario subrayarlo, sin asomo de pretensión científica. El método seguido, ¡si de método, aún vagamente, pudiera hablarse en el caso de este libro! lo han impuesto con sus explicaciones y digresiones, inseparables unas de otras, mis informantes, incapaces de ajustarse a ningún plan, y a quienes insensiblemente y por un afán de exactitud de mi parte, quizá excesivo, y que a ratos hará tediosa la lectura y confusa la comprensión de algunos párrafos, he seguido siempre estrechamente, cuidando de no alterar sus juicios ni sus palabras, aclarándolas sólo en aquellos puntos en que serían del todo ininteligibles al profano.[40]

> [I publish these notes (it goes without saying) without a trace of scientific pretension. The method I followed (if one can even remotely speak of a method to this book!) has been imposed by my informants through their explanations and digressions, one inseparable from the other and incapable of conforming to a single plan. Being insensibly driven by a desire for exactitude, perhaps excessive at times, I have followed them closely, though this may make their reading tedious and certain paragraphs confusing or difficult to comprehend. Nevertheless, I have taken care to alter neither their judgments nor their words, clarifying them on only those points that would be completely unintelligible to the uninitiated.]

So begins one of the most influential works of Afro-Cuban cultural history. Remarkably, Cabrera divests herself of all authorial responsibility; the informants are the driving force behind the text. What, then, is her conception of fieldwork, and how do the unruly transcriptions of spoken language, accumulated over decades, translate into textual form? How does Cabrera, who explicitly rejects being categorized as an ethnographer, anthropologist, or even a scholar, fashion herself as a researcher who produces an exhaustive interpretation of Afro-Cuban cultural practices?

James Clifford maintains that by the mid-1930s a new consensus among anthropologists had emerged: scholarly anthropological interpretations were to be founded on intensive cultural descriptions. He points out that ethnography, a process that is eminently enmeshed in writing, entails the textualization of experience. The anthropologist-writer responds to political and social constraints by fashioning herself as the source of truth.[41] Lydia

Cabrera's introductory disclaimer should not be taken literally. The process involved in translating dialogues, interactions, and observations into a coherent textual form includes manipulations that require the ethnographer to assume an authoritative position. Although Cabrera downplays her role as editor and author, her focus as ethnographer is to evoke a cultural totality. Holism in cultural representation is a cornerstone of twentieth-century ethnography. The anthropologist's desire to convey a realistic world has been labeled ethnographic realism, a term that alludes to nineteenth-century realist fiction.[42] Cabrera's claim to represent faithfully concrete Afro-Cuban reality is founded primarily on her position as a transcriber and translator of her informants' spoken language. She portrays oral discourse as indisputable and authentic truth.

In *El monte*, Lydia Cabrera strips herself of all authority by revealing the haphazardness of her fieldwork, and places responsibility for the text's production in the hands of her informants. She focuses on the "fuentes vivas" of Cuba's cultural history and repudiates her own role as interpreter, thereby inventing a generalized and collective author to dramatize an ongoing give-and-take of dialogues in the field. The introductory disclaimer attests to Cabrera's tendency to distance herself from the text and to imbue her black informants with authority. She asserts that her book records, objectively and without prejudice, what she heard and saw. Cabrera states that her black informants are the true authors of the book.[43] However, the notion of an idealistic plural authorship is problematic. In the end, the ethnographer is responsible for making editorial decisions and producing the physical text; the gesture of giving voice to the other is an act of authority.[44] This is not to say that the informant is outside the process. A certain amount of discretion and selection takes place on both ends of the intersubjective encounter. The informant, like the ethnographer, has a social and political agenda.

El monte is far more complex and intriguing than a mere compilation of notes. In the chapters that follow the introduction, stories proceeding from the mouths of informants intermingle with the anthropologist's explanations of Afro-Cuban rituals and beliefs. It is clear that the information stems from a collaboration based on mutual trust and interest. The ensemble of oral tradition, rites, behaviors and experiences is separated from its performative context and cast as a textualized "thick description."[45] This process of translation entails much more than the simple recasting of the Other's language. The inscription of dialogue and the shaping of voice imply an attempt to fix meaning and convey reality.

How, then, does Lydia Cabrera negotiate the continuum that includes both oral and literate modes? She construes writing as voice to give meaning to her subjects' expressions. In *El monte*, Cabrera contrives a textuality embedded with oral properties. The first step in inscribing the oral involves framing the multitude of voices. Titles and subtitles impose a certain hierarchy onto oral discourse. The anthropologist-writer then conveys the oral context by reproducing songs, stories, dialogues, and oral histories in writing.[46] Passage from the oral to the written essentially textualizes oral culture by creating the illusion of an oral reality.

As in her *Cuentos negros*, Lydia re-creates specific storytelling events in *El monte* by framing tales and providing multiple versions, without privileging one over another. There is a constant intermixing of descriptions of events and dialogic re-creations of them. For instance, Cabrera introduces the topic of "la bajada del Santo, o del fumbí o ngánda" [the descent of the Saint], which is immediately followed by an illustrative third-person narration of María G.'s first spiritual experience of this kind. Then, without transition, the voice shifts to a series of exclamations about drumming sounds, dramatizing an emotional exchange that recounts a young girl's spiritual union with Yemayá.[47] This textualization of voice and sound is representative of Cabrera's knack for combining anthropology and poetry to evoke the nuances of oral tradition.

Lydia Cabrera reenacts numerous storytelling sessions by essentially assuming the role of one of the black narrators that she observed so often. Her description of an African bard could almost be mistaken for an autobiographical account: "Con esa gracia tan característica y un don extraordinario de imitación, los negros narraban, cantaban y mimaban sus relatos, personificando con un arte que revelaba una observación asombrosa. [...]"[48] [With their characteristic grace, and an extraordinary gift for imitation, the blacks narrated, sang and acted out their tales, embodying their subjects with an art that revealed an astonishing sense of observation. . . .] This description appears in the preface of one of her literary publications, *Ayapá: Cuentos de Jicotea*. Nevertheless, it is equally revealing of Cabrera's capacity to contrive the atmosphere of a storytelling *justa* in *El monte*. Differing versions of stories coexist, demonstrating that truths are often multiple and variant. For Cabrera, like Ramón Menéndez Pidal, "to live is to vary."[49] Although she does not explicitly privilege one version over another, presumably the mere process of culling hundreds of note cards involves some editorial selection. How, then, does Lydia Cabrera convince us of the truthfulness of the fantastical stories she transcribes? At certain key points, a narrative voice interjects to address potentially skeptical readers.

During a series of interwoven anecdotes, Cabrera warns that a particular source may not be trustworthy. Before transcribing his story, she introduces him by relating yet another brief tale in which the informant, formerly a cook for an old Havana nobleman, went about his work so hastily that he prepared a chicken pie for the marquis and his guests that contained live chickens. The chickens burst out and wreaked havoc on the celebration. This humorous anecdote is immediately followed by the man's story regarding the spiritual powers of the deceased. Upon the conclusion of this story, Cabrera writes that the reader should be wary of the source of this tall tale, and believe what he or she deems appropriate. Nevertheless, as eyewitness to other seemingly improbable episodes, she herself is inclined to accept the story as truth.[50] Although Cabrera leaves the door open for interpretation, she subtly persuades the reader by masking her own interpretations. Her rhetorical interjections anticipate storytelling tactics that proliferate in testimonial novels like Miguel Barnet's *Biografía de un cimarrón* (*Autobiography of a Runaway Slave*).

The most compelling argument for the role of experience in cultural analysis is set forth by Wilhelm Dilthey, for whom experience is implicitly linked to interpretation. The theorist's description of this process sheds light on the ambiguity tied up in Cabrera's assessment of her own methods as participant-observer. In Dilthey's view, a "common sphere" shared by the researcher and subject is the beginning point for all studies of other cultures. According to Dilthey, understanding presupposes a "double relationship."[51] Lydia Cabrera, driven by personal inspiration, cultivates such a relationship with black individuals to build a meaningful common sphere. In the opening pages of *El monte*, Cabrera describes her entry into a world that was predominantly closed to whites. Omí Tomí was the first to have faith in Lydia's genuine curiosity. Once convinced that Lydia's interest in black culture was not disdainful, Omí Tomí introduced her to the great Oddedeí, who ultimately approved of Cabrera's presence in their community.[52] Thus, Cabrera bases her "method" on her own personal acceptance— her initiation, in a sense—into black communities and her unique rapport with her informants.

For Geertz, part of the ethnographer's task is to convince the reader that actually "being there"—seeing and hearing—grants the researcher access to the truth.[53] Lydia capitalizes on her exceptional relationships with black collaborators and uses the rhetorical strategy described by Geertz to validate the "notes" she puts forth. The construction of a common universe, to which she has privileged access, is also a mode of persuasion. This shared experiential world, founded on spoken language, has clearly defined boundaries, for the practice of fieldwork always presupposes the notion of an "inside" and an "outside." Although Cabrera may have felt at home in the Pogolotti neighborhood, she most likely conducted the majority of her analysis at the Quinta San José, where she would organize, order, translate, and edit her notes.

Cabrera's explicit denial of interpretive practices points to an underlying tension between interpretation and experience that marks all of her ethnographic works. She claims that her main objective has been to offer specialists material that has not passed through the "dangerous filter of interpretation."[54] It appears that she wants to distance herself from other ethnographers who possibly draw prejudicial conclusions from their contact with informants. Cabrera does not, however, clearly explain precisely what "interpretation" entails. Dilthey calls "exegesis" in cultural studies "the methodological understanding of permanently fixed expressions."[55] Through memory the researcher gives meaning to recollections of expressions contained in her experiences. Despite Cabrera's denial of methodical exegesis in *El monte*, even her understanding of oral expressions and personal experiences should be viewed as a form of interpretation. Herein lies the overall complexity of Cabrera's work: it purports to be a scientific report or recording while it derives its material from experiences that are chiefly biographical. To compensate for this ambiguity, Lydia Cabrera invokes oral properties as a way to enhance the veracity of her account.

Miguel Acosta Saignes, one of the first critics to review *El monte*, responds to the author's remarks about the arbitrariness of her investigative techniques in an interesting way. He interprets the book as a product of a rigid and meticulous method, thereby falling into the trap of Cabrera's rhetorical scheme. Acosta Saignes praises the book for its systematic ordering of information and faithful transcription of folkloric material. The critic reads *El monte* much as Lydia Cabrera intended. He says the virtue of the text is its fidelity to primary sources, as if the author were really a faithful scribe who transcribed only what she heard and saw.[56]

In striking juxtaposition is Francis de Miomandre's review, published in one of the final issues of *Orígenes*. For the French critic, who originally discovered Cabrera's *Cuentos negros* and translated them into French, *El monte* represents an extension of the poetic endeavor of the writer's first literary production. According to Miomandre, Lydia Cabrera is essentially a poet; and it is as a poet that she approaches folklore that scholars might study from the vantage point of sterile research.[57] He criticizes European intellectuals for too quickly dismissing customs of other cultures as irrational superstitions, and welcomes Cabrera's book as a sentimental illustration of a radical truth. Perceptively, Miomandre questions Cabrera's allusion to a plural authorship and points out that had the ethnographer not "been there," the traditions and experiences of this predominantly oral culture would have disappeared entirely.

Lino Novás-Calvo similarly praises *El monte* for its richly poetic prose. In a 1968 article announcing the appearance of a second edition, he advocates a broad readership of the book, which he argues is much more than a scholarly text. For Novás-Calvo, *El monte* is an intricate weaving of myths, stories, magic formulas, spells, legends, and mysteries of the blacks—and even whites—of Cuba.[58] Both critics struggle with the fact that Cabrera's monumental text, as its title suggests, straddles rigorous ethnographic research and a creative poetics. Perhaps the most fruitful approach to her work, then, is to suspend any dichotomizing concepts of science and literature and to think about *El monte*, and Cabrera's stories as well, as products of a complex process of cultural negotiation.

A comparative analysis of stories that appear in both *El monte* and her collections of short fiction shows that in her early works, Cabrera perceives a separation between literature and anthropology. Only later, in exile, does a full-blown fusion of poetry and ethnography, a new mode of cultural representation that transcends disciplinary boundaries, punctuate her writings. When confronted with an astonishingly rich archive of anecdotes and legends, Lydia Cabrera tends to select particular versions or combine several, embellishing them artistically to create a variant. The virtue of her creative process, a virtue that sheds considerable light on how one can begin to approach her literary works, is that it combines her childhood memories with adult investigations to produce stories that, in Ezra Pound's famous articulation, "make it new."

One story that exemplifies this process is the tale of Obbara. Versions of this story, which comes from Western African divination lore, are also told by Afro-Brazilians. In *El monte*, two versions of the Obbara tale are told in the final section of the book, which offers an "*a* to *z*" list of the rich vegetation that is indigenous to the mystical region. This "glossary" offers much more than concise descriptions of plants and their uses; it is also the place where Cabrera constructs a palimpsest of stories. Each plant, listed alphabetically, is the springboard for a series of tales that relate the histories of a pantheon of African spirits.

The legend of Obbara is categorized under the heading *calabaza* (pumpkin). The entry in *El monte* dedicated to *calabazas* explains that the vegetables are legitimate children of Changó. Two versions of the story follow. The second variant is the one that Cabrera embellishes in "Obbara miente y no miente" (Obbara Lies and Does Not Lie), one of the twenty-eight stories that make up *Por qué... Cuentos negros de Cuba*, which appeared six years prior to the publication of *El monte*. In *Por qué...*, each story provides a magical answer to great universal questions. A side-by-side comparison of the versions, one ethnographic and one literary, shows that the former is cast as the transcription of a monologue with very little descriptive imagery. One striking difference is that the *El monte* version includes words in African language, with parenthetical translations, whereas the version found in *Por qué...* is entirely in Spanish.

Both renderings narrate the tale of Obbara "the liar," who was invited by Olofi, "the Old Man of Eternity," to a party attended by all of the saints. Before setting out for the festivities, Obbara, an impoverished man, purified his body and clothes and made petitions to the gods. The evocation of this great scene is related in strikingly different ways in *Por qué...* and in *El monte*. In *El monte*, Cabrera writes, "Porque era Obbara, ni sucio ni andrajoso, sino vestido de blanco con unas alforjas grandísimas debajo de la montura del caballo. (¿De dónde habrá sacado ese caballo?)"[59] [Because it was Obbara, neither dirty nor ragged, but dressed in white, on a horse with an enormous saddlebag on each side. (Where had he gotten that horse?)] The same episode in *Por qué...,* in sharp contrast, appeals to all of the senses and demonstrates the writer's capacity to develop her own artful storytelling based on her ethnographic notes:

> Y a medida que Obbara, inmaculado, se allegaba, un olor de flores blancas, de azucenas, de campanas, se hacía más penetrante. Se desprendía de Obbara la claridad, la albura que es de Olofi y agrada a Olofi. Así cuando Obbara, resplandeciente de blancura, saltó de su caballo y vino a postrarse a los pies de Olofi, éste se volvió a los Santos, severo, y les mostró a Obbara, su pureza fundida en su pureza.[60]

> [And as the immaculate Obbara approached, a fragrance of white flowers, of lilies, of bells, became stronger. A whiteness emanated from Obbara, the whiteness of Olofi that pleases Olofi. So when Obbara, resplendent in his whiteness, jumped from his horse and came to kneel at the feet of Olofi, Olofi turned to the saints severely, and showed them Obbara's purity united with his own.]

Olofi decides to give each of the attendees a pumpkin. The other saints, displeased with this gift, throw their pumpkins into a gully. Their exclamations are practically identical in the two renditions of the story. In both, Obbara collects the discarded pumpkins and later realizes that his is filled with gold coins. Upon reuniting with Olofi and the other saints, he tells his story and reprimands the others for their disdainful attitudes. In *El monte*, the story ends with the advice of Capetillo, one of Cabrera's informants, who warns that the unfortunate children of Changó should sleep with a pumpkin under their pillows. In *Por qué...*, Cabrera opts for a more poetic conclusion, and writes, "La blancura de Obbara se confundía con la blancura de Olofi. Los Santos humillaron sus frentes."[61] [The whiteness of Obbara became confused with the whiteness of Olofi. The saints bowed their heads.] By the end of Cabrera's writing career, a lyrical poetics pervades her ethnographic texts completely, making her literary and anthropological works virtually interchangeable.

The first portion of *El monte* is cast as the representation of multiple language events. Lydia weaves her account together by interjecting brief descriptions of her personal reactions to what she heard and saw. The pages following the introduction are devoted to setting the scene by evoking the supernatural and mystical region of *el monte*. Cabrera traces the spiritual realm back to its African origins, and insists that its Cuban counterpart is equally powerful and meaningful. She essentially designates *el monte* as the origin of spoken language and song. The expository section of the book is a collage of direct quotations from black Cubans. Cabrera's tendency to superimpose voices creates the effect of a polyvocality that enacts the performative and oral context of the original enunciations.

El monte, which begins as the story of the ethnographer's learning process, transforms into a poetic journey into the mysterious realm introduced by the title. The start of this ritualistic journey takes place in the fourth chapter, "El tributo al dueño del Monte" (The Tribute to the Owner of the *monte*). Here Cabrera describes the appropriate greetings and solicitations that should be performed upon entering the forest in search of sacred plants. She assumes the role as guide, and her text becomes a metaphor for the complex world it seeks to represent. In order to textualize the utterances that render acceptance into *el monte*, Cabrera evokes an ensemble of voices in various languages. The rhythmic greetings in African language are inscribed in the text. These orations are not translated, but are set apart from the text, and the reader is left to infer their meaning. The reader is thus doubly displaced from the *viejo mayombero,* the guide who leads Lydia into the spiritual universe that resonates with songs and voices.

Throughout *El monte*, Lydia Cabrera subtly alludes to her relationships with informants. Interspersed, and set apart from monologues and conversations by means of parentheses, are brief explanations set forth by the author. For instance, she refers to José de Calazán Herrera as "my dear teacher," and employs tactics to "give" voice to collaborators by interjecting, "I hand over the word."[62] By the end of the first chapter, Lydia finds her own poetic voice and slips out of the pattern of fragmented quotations that characterizes the early pages. The first chapter ends with the evocation of the musical sounds of African languages, both Lucumí and Congo, to enhance the mystery of the ciphered world of *el monte*.

Cabrera creates a distinct oral register by endeavoring to reproduce her informants' words, writing their accounts in her own invented phonetic shorthand. She incorporates songs and prayers, thereby gaining access to *el monte*. Cabrera pauses here to include a two-page chapter that constitutes a moment of passage into the magical vegetation of *el monte*. The chapter is entitled "El tesoro mágico y medicinal de Osain y Tata Nfindo" (The Magical and Medicinal Treasure of Osain and Tata Nfindo) and opens by inviting the reader on a small journey through the plant world, with faithful followers of the Lucumí and Congo traditions as guides. The introductory passage marks a critical turning point in the text. Lydia positions herself and the reader as participants in a tour guided by her collaborators. She invites the reader on an excursion through the revered *monte*. Cabrera acknowledges that this metaphorical journey is really a construction, made possible by meticulous research and the organization of copious notes:

> A la entrada del monte, donde idealmente hemos pagado nuestro tributo acompañándolo de unos granos de maíz y encendido una vela, o para ser más verídicos, ante el montón de tarjetas en que anoto las informaciones de los que saben propiciarse al dios Osain y comprar efectivamente la voluntad inteligente de las plantas. [...][63]

> [At the entrance to the *monte,* where ideally we have paid our tribute, left some kernels of corn, and lit a candle, or to be more truthful, before the mountain of file cards on which I jot down information about those who know how to ingratiate themselves with the god Osain and to purchase the wisdom and good intentions of the plants. . . .]

The figurative journey into *el monte*, which is the story told over the course of the book, mimics the interpretive process undertaken by Cabrera.

In this brief middle chapter, the mosaic of languages revealed in the earlier sections is suspended, and a narrative voice that aims to orient the reader is inserted. Here Cabrera underlines important parallels between blacks and whites, and implicitly requests that the reader not draw naive and prejudicial conclusions from the accounts related by her black informants. She argues that all Christians, black and white, represent a mixture of good and evil; and that blacks' conceit of morality reflects their natural conception of life. Cabrera's apprehension most likely responds to previous prejudicial accounts of the immorality of Afro-Cuban rituals, and perhaps alludes to works like Fernando Ortiz's *Hampa afro-cubana: Los negros brujos* (The Afro-Cuban Underworld: The Black Shamans). Although Cabrera's intentions are good, the flaw lies in her attempt to propose a broader conception of morality while she herself writes from a mentality that already has fixed notions of what is moral and what is immoral. The anthropologist, whose credibility rests on "being there," must also step out of the figured "inside" to inscribe it. Cabrera employs rhetorical and discursive tools that enable her to be both "there" and "outside." Authorial exclamations in Lucumí reveal how the author straddles two worlds, linguistic and cultural. They signal that Lydia is enough of an "insider" to express herself in the native language.

The introductory remarks set the stage for a collective excursion into the complex jungle of ceiba trees. The four chapters that conclude the first section of *El monte* discuss the sacred meanings of the trees in both Lucumí and Carabalí traditions. Cabrera apologizes for the digressions that lead the reader on a winding tour of *el monte*. Those who have had the patience to follow the explanations and digressions of "our guides," she writes, will remember the ceiba tree as the perfect type of a sacred tree.[64]

Not surprisingly, Cabrera opts to conclude the expository portion of *El monte* with a poetic image of Ukano Mambré, the sacred royal palm of Abakuás. The understated narrative voice of Lydia the interpreter interrupts briefly to signal the end of the exhaustive information that constitutes the book. The final oration complements the poetic description of *el monte* that concluded the initial chapter:

> Ukano Mambré eleva su tronco de esbeltez incomparable, mece su lánguido penacho en el cielo abakuá, fija en un eterno presente mítico, evocando al abanekue los hechos capitales de su historia: la revelación de Ekue [...] ; el sacrificio de Sikán [...]; y el nacimiento de Abakuá, pues en torno al árbol venerado se reúnen los primeros obones y se organiza la sociedad.[65]

> [Ukano Mambré lifts its incomparably slender trunk, shakes its languid crest in the Abakuá sky, settles on an eternal mythic present, evoking to the Abanekue the essential facts of its history: the revelation of Ekue . . . ; the sacrifice of Sikán . . . ; and the birth of Abakuá, for the first *obones* gathered around this sacred tree and around it the society was organized.]

This powerful description illustrates how Cabrera decodes and poetically recodes the voices of her informants. The process of transcription entails the invention of an "eternal mythic present," a paradox that exemplifies the dilemma of ethnography, a practice that is based on an experiential oral present, yet fixed eternally in written form.

Although Lydia Cabrera received no formal training as an anthropologist, and explicitly refused to be categorized as one, she was an ethnographer by method and practice. Perhaps her tendency to diminish her role as author can be attributed to her lack of formal instruction. Clifford argues that a new kind of professional fieldworker-theorist appeared in the early

1920s. This new-style researcher aimed at mastering particular themes or institutions in order to describe a broader cultural whole. Cabrera's fieldwork practices coincide with those of this new breed of researcher. Curiously, she denied proficiency in Lucumí, and yet was able to produce exhaustive glossaries of several African languages.

In all of her writings, Cabrera assumes an uninformed position and exaggerates her lack of scientific knowledge as a tactic to convince the reading public of just the opposite. For instance, the introduction to her publication *Anagó: Vocabulario lucumí (el yoruba que se habla en Cuba)* (Anagó: Lucumí Vocabulary and Spoken Yoruba in Cuba) begins with false modesty. Cabrera acknowledges that she is not a linguist, and is ignorant of African languages.[66] This is one of several instances in which she subordinates herself to "specialists" in the field. Very early on in her investigations, Lydia recognized the utility of language as a means of gaining the confidence of her African collaborators. She began to take down Lucumí words in the late 1920s, and realized that memorizing them and using them in conversation granted her important access to the world of black storytelling.[67] Artful use of spoken language was one of Cabrera's key stratagems for attaining access to the world she endeavored to decipher.

Although she does not explicitly outline her research techniques in *El monte*, we can infer from several passages that her ethnographic texts rely heavily on data synthesized from her copious, and somewhat fragmented, notes. Not only did Cabrera interview in the field, in Pogolotti and Matanzas for instance, but she also invited her collaborators, referred to affectionately as "amigos," to the Quinta San José. Lydia recalls that in meetings with Nino de Cárdenas, the old man would inevitably elaborate at length Congo traditions. He would forget about Cabrera's presence, becoming wholly drawn into the scene he was describing. At times, she could not understand his words, but his gestures and sign language enabled her to follow the story.[68] It is clear that both parties had a stake in the act of textual production. The process of translation that Cabrera ultimately performed included the formulation of a language that could adequately transmit the nuances and gestures tied up in such piecemeal information. As an ethnographer, she relied on her own memory and intuition when she attempted to re-create these language events. She recalls experimenting with a tape recorder when she met with an informant who intended to explain the process by which the voice (soul) of a person is stolen and bottled up. When the man heard his own voice on the machine, he became frightened and fled. At that moment, she decided not to tape her conversations mechanically, but instead to transform herself into a tape recorder.

Cabrera aspired to produce a written memory of Cuban blacks for whom the powers of recollection united generations. She respected her black compatriots for passing oral traditions from generation to generation. In *El monte* Lydia commends members of the secret society Abakuá for their ability to integrate their present with their ancestors' past.[69] Implicit in Cabrera's profound respect for the Afro-Cubans' capacity to preserve sacred oral history is a bitter critique of other Cubans' inability to do so. In fact, she is shocked and amused to discover that blacks have been the ones to salvage much of the folklore and history transmitted by the early Spaniards.[70]

In part, Cabrera's quest to preserve Afro-Cuban culture and to incorporate it into Cuban national history represented a personal attack on her own social class. This critique becomes even more pronounced in her later productions, both literary and ethnographic, published in exile. In all of her writing, she praises Cuban blacks for the integrity of their communities, enhanced by the memory of a common history. Cabrera's works are founded on the premise that a link exists between oral memory and authentic cultural expression. Eugene Vance refers to cultures that grant special importance to the faculty of memory as "commemorative." By "commemoration" he means "any gesture, ritualized or not, whose end is to recover, in the name of a collectivity, some being or event either anterior in time or outside of time in order to fecundate, animate, or make meaningful a moment in the present."[71] She undertook a commemorative process in her efforts to give meaning to the expressions of her collaborators. Her texts are punctuated by an underlying political agenda that dichotomizes Cuban culture in terms of we/they, oral/literate. By privileging black oral culture, she subtly criticizes the public for which she writes.

After reading *El monte*, one might erroneously conclude that the African cultures with which Lydia Cabrera came into contact depended solely on oral communication. Generally speaking, however, the influence of literacy varies from one subgroup to another, and literacy constantly interacts with oral discourses and registers. In some respects, Cabrera, as did Ortiz, associated literacy development with progress and social mobility. Over the course of her investigations, she came across *libretas de los santeros*, manuscripts or typed notebooks, used by Lucumí devotees to collect and record legends. Some of the entries inscribed in the booklets have little to do with the Lucumí religion, but rather recount popular sayings, anecdotes, and pieces of advice.

Cabrera became fascinated with the points of contact and discrepancies between the stories compiled in the *libretas* and their oral versions. Her analysis reveals her own notetaking techniques. The authors of the notebooks pronounce and transcribe the words they heard from their elders. She explains that the notebooks are fragmented and incomplete, since they mainly serve as mnemonic devices for *santeros* who use them. Cabrera idealizes the purity and authenticity of a mentality untouched by literacy, implicitly casting writing as a supplement associated with progress and modernization. She speaks somewhat nostalgically of the days when *santeros* passed on knowledge orally, drawing a clear distinction between the inscription of a text in one's memory and the physical writing of it on paper.[72]

For Cabrera, the process of inscription, or figuratively writing-in-the-memory, is preferable to its literary counterpart. Both instances, however, exemplify "writerly" moments. Lydia justifies the necessity to preserve the legends on paper by arguing that oral tradition is destined to disappear. Herein lies the predicament that subtends all of her work: Cabrera's ethnographic authority is contingent on her ability to understand the expressions of her subjects who, she claims, are embedded in an oral world, while she inescapably writes from within a literate culture. This construct enables Cabrera to present herself as the key mediator between seemingly incongruous worlds. On a theoretical level, Cabrera fails to realize that the fundamental difference between the spoken and written word that she encounters stems from her own literate mentality. The abyss or "great divide" she perceives is a construction that does not correspond to social reality.

Cabrera asserts that, given the inaccuracy of the notebooks, she has consulted individuals to clarify the meanings of words rather than used a dictionary; her only dictionaries have been her black informants.[73] Implicit in her statement is a critique of the mechanical and scientific nature of writing. She chose not to use tape recorders or dictionaries, so as not to inhibit her native collaborators. Her conceit consisted in affecting to have experienced language in its most "authentic" and oral form. At the same time, she meticulously recorded what she heard, inscribing it in her memory like the *oluko* (teachers), and later spliced it with what she perceived to be imperfect written records from the notebooks to generate a text that only she could produce.

What becomes clear is that writing permeates the Lucumí expressions that compose the text, and Cabrera is not just a listener, but also a reader of "writerly" moments in *santería*. In this context, it is critical to expand the notion of writing from its narrow definition as phonetic notation that Cabrera implies in her description of the Lucumí notebooks. Although the *libretas* indeed represent a form of physical writing, unwritten beliefs and traditions are also part of the corpus of events textualized by the ethnographer. Interpretation, as has been seen, presupposes textualization.

A Lucumí tradition that calls for the reading of signs is the *dilogún*, or *caracoles* (shells), the most widespread method of divination. In this ritual, a *santero* breathes on a handful of small conch shells to give them *aché* (spiritual power), and asks that the devotee do the same. He then tosses them onto the floor, and the shells land with their openings facing either downward or upward. The configurations of each toss (there are sixteen possibilities) determine the *odus* (figures or letters) of the *dilogún*. Each of these *odus* corresponds to a certain number of legends, proceeding from oral tradition, that provide advice, predictions, and sayings appropriate to the problem at hand.

Two classes of *odus* exist: one group that can be read by *santeros,* and a second group that can only be interpreted by a *babalao*, a diviner or priest of the *ifá* oracle, the great *orisha* of divination. Similarly, the tossing of pieces of coconut, *dar coco*, a ritual that is not as complex as *dilogún*, represents yet another ritualistic language of signs that Cabrera, like the *santero*, seeks to decipher. Cabrera's transcriptions of *dilogún* reflect her privileged access to the secret language. Each variant of a *pataki* that she incorporates into *El monte* represents a different toss of the shells.

This arbitrary, and yet fundamentally scientific, practice is analogous to Cabrera's true method. It points to her penchant for an oral culture that values variation. By incorporating multiple versions of stories, she sought to convey this aesthetic in writing. The shell toss is emblematic of the text's composition. The ritual symbolizes the activities of reading and interpretation involved in the complex process of transcribing *patakíes*.

Lydia Cabrera asserts that the notes that constitute *El monte* follow no comprehensive plan. What she means, of course, is that the text lacks the scientific organization that might be characteristic of ethnographies published by anthropologists like Fernando Ortiz, Pierre Verger, or Alfred Métraux. But, in spite of the distinction that Cabrera attempts to draw between her text and other ethnographies, the fact remains that *El monte* is driven by an overriding plan. The early chapters constitute a justification of Cabrera's role as participant-observer, an account of her privileged access to the black point of view and oral histories, and a poetic description of the complex and powerful term *el monte*. These segments contain numerous versions of narratives spliced together to form a collage of tales that Cabrera has wrought with a great deal of specificity. However, in spite of her best attempts to provide faithful transcriptions, the text is still a representation of various dialogues. Cabrera resists tendencies to impose coherence on a process of textualization that is by nature unruly. She uses few transitions and incorporates multiple versions to portray the predominantly oral culture in writing.

Because *El monte* came together as a series of articles written over the period of several years, the text reflects the evolution of Cabrera's fieldwork techniques and a diversification of her relationships with her informants. In the second chapter, "Bilongo," a large portion of which was published in a 1947 issue of *Revista Bimestre Cubana*, Cabrera focuses on a single "privileged" informant, Omí Tomí, and essentially creates an ethnographic monograph. Here she risks typifying black culture by recounting the biography and stories of an individual descendant of African slaves. However, subsequent chapters show a divergence from this tendency. Omí-Tomí's biography is the only one specifically delineated in *El monte*; she is joined by a multitude of representatives from both Lucumí and Congo cultures. The episodes recounted by these actors are pieced together to form a palimpsest of experiences, observations and stories.

James Clifford regards ethnography as a type of performance that is comprised of stories. He finds that the fact that ethnographies are inescapably allegorical strongly affects the way that they are written and even read. For Clifford, "the very activity of ethnographic *writing*–seen as inscription or textualization–enacts a redemptive Western allegory."[74] Thus, we can read the initial portions of *El monte* as a fiction of learning, a *Bildungsroman* that entails Cabrera's acceptance into another culture, and finally the acquisition of authority to portray that culture. The text seeks to vindicate and salvage what seems to be a vanishing oral culture, one that is threatened by forces of modernization. The struggle between urbanization and preservation of traditions became an important theme in Cabrera's writings in Miami, where she resumed her studies of Afro-Cuban culture after a period of silence.

It is, however, problematic to think that a culture, perceived as an essentialized entity, disappears after the onset of modernization. This kind of redemptive work assumes that the "primitive" society is weak and requires the intervention by an outsider to salvage it. Interestingly, the fragile culture to be preserved is cast as the true, authentic and oral culture. Quite possibly, Cabrera understands this modern anthropological dilemma and opts to divest herself of authoritative responsibility as a way to bypass the predicament. She cannot, however, erase herself entirely from the book she ultimately produces.

Another humanist allegory underlies the act of salvaging "authentic" discourse: the passage from an oral mode into a written one. Clifford argues that this issue has charged historical and ethnographic writing for ages: "Every ethnography enacts such a movement, and this is one source of the peculiar authority that finds both rescue and irretrievable loss–a kind of death in life–in the making of texts from events and dialogues. Words and deeds are transient (and authentic), writing endures (as supplementary and artifice)." Clifford acknowledges that the "most subversive challenge" to his notion of this particular allegorical dimension is found in Derrida's *Of Grammatology*.[75] But, even subscribing to Derrida's "grammatology," which expands the definition of writing to the point that all humans are inescapably committed to writing, it is important to recognize specific ways in which ethnographers textualize oral discourse. Instead of accepting the cliché of irretrievable loss that subtends Western discourse by treating books like *El monte* as keepers of tradition, these texts are instead a new beginning, an invention of an oral aesthetic that illustrates the poetic capacity of non-Western forms of discourse. Faced with the crucial predicament of how to achieve in writing what speech evokes, Lydia Cabrera created a polyvocal text that represents the complex nuances of Afro-Cuban culture.

A POETICS OF EXILE

The second edition of *El monte* was not printed until 1968 in Miami, when Lydia's friend Amalia Bacardí offered financial assistance. This publication ended a decade of prolonged silence. It is an important gesture that she would consent to rework a monumental book that sought to define the culture of a nation now become odious under its new regime. On July 24, 1960, when Lydia Cabrera and María Teresa de Rojas joined other Cuban intellectuals who left their native island to live in exile, they were unaware that they would never return. Before fleeing Cuba, Lydia filled a trunk with all of her precious notes. These notes became the only tangible reminder of her years of conversations with descendants of African slaves. Ultimately, they enabled her to continue writing. In her apartment in Miami, Cabrera attempted to reconstruct her Cuba. She hung a *Virgen de Regla* and old maps on her walls, and decorated with figurines of *jicoteas* (tortoises) in all shapes and sizes, precious stones, and her collection of *chicherekú* dolls. She did not regain the spirit and motivation to resume her writing until 1968. In this year, she reedited *El monte* and took an important trip to Paris, where she reunited with some of her colleagues at a conference on cults to deliver a talk entitled "Le guérisseur noir de Cuba," a theme which would ultimately be treated in her book *La medicina popular en Cuba* (1984).

In the late 1960s, Lydia rekindled relationships with Miami intellectuals who shared her interest in Afro-Caribbean culture. She learned from Isabel Castellanos, whose Georgetown University doctoral thesis was entitled "The Use of Language in Afro-Cuban Religion," that Abakuá members of the Regla Kimbisa practiced in exile. Cabrera became interested in how *santería* manifested itself in the United States. Her first three publications in exile represent some of her best, and least appreciated, literary and ethnographic works. These include *Otán Iyebiyé: Las piedras preciosas* (1970) (*Otán Iyebiyé*: The Precious Stones), *Ayapá: Cuentos de Jicotea* (1971), and *La laguna sagrada de San Joaquín* (1973). The subject matter is the same as that of her previous works, but these books are punctuated by the pains of exile—the displacement of the writer into an alien and unforgiving world, and a yearning for a distant past.

What concerns us here is how this distance is brought to bear on Cabrera's works, which paradoxically derive their authoritative truth from the evocation of an experiential and oral present. The tone of her post-diaspora writings is strikingly aggressive, in sharp contrast with the modest and unassertive attitude that marks her early works. The political situation of her homeland raised the stakes of her quest to rescue and preserve Cuba's heterogeneous cultural elements. Now her project was somewhat altered; her readership consisted predominantly of Cuban exiles, and funds for publishing were scarce. She fought her battle on two fronts: she condemned Castro's authoritarian regime, and she denounced the evils of modernization that plagued the United States.

In 1979, Cabrera delivered a speech called "Religious Syncretism in Cuba" to a Miami public. It bears mentioning that she had previously written an illuminating article with the title "El sincretismo religioso de Cuba. Santos, orishas, ngangas, lucumís y congos," which was published in a 1954 issue of *Orígenes* dedicated to her good friend José Lezama Lima. In the conference, Cabrera poignantly explains that the African slaves who were brought to Cuba could only comprehend the Christianity of whites from their own perspectives, which conceived of a reality determined by natural forces. She maintains that it was important for blacks to feel that their gods had accompanied them in their tragic voyages of diaspora. The religious syncretism to which Cabrera ultimately refers in the concluding remarks of her Miami talk is one that defines the exilic culture surrounding her:

> We ask ourselves: What will be the future of the Regla of Ochá in this foreign country, without happiness? . . . Are the Orichás happy beneath the sun under which the skies do not shine, and the drums have to remain silent? I am afraid that in the long run what we call Santería will be transformed. Here everything changes, but as long as a certain species of Cubans are not converted into machines and totally dehumanized, or as long as some modern men and women still keep the primitive deep within themselves, there will not be a lack of those who solicit help of gods, nor clients for magic.[76]

Thus, reconceiving her purpose, Lydia Cabrera vowed to study Afro-Cuban culture that had been doubly displaced from its African roots. The Cuban past she longed to regain was almost exclusively African in origin. Cabrera's prolific writings, published during the final three decades of her life in the Colección del Chicherekú en el Exilio, are shaped by her passionate reactions to life in exile.

Her first major publication in the United States was a collection of short stories, the third of her career, entitled *Ayapá: Cuentos de Jicotea*. This is the most animated and playful of Cabera's literary productions and, given the circumstances of exile, the most inventive. Whereas *Cuentos negros* did not contain an author's introduction, Cabrera's lengthy prologue in *Ayapá* discusses both slavery in Cuba and the resilience of oral tradition among black cultures. The opening remarks suggest her underlying political agenda for the seemingly lighthearted collection of stories. Jicotea is not only the crafty protagonist of the collection's twenty-one stories, but also symbolizes the plight of the African slave, both historically and under Castro's repressive regime. The small turtle is perhaps also the personification of the exiled Cuban, trapped in an alien world. In this dynamic collection, we see the full-fledged manifestation of Lydia's ironic and playful humor, which we caught glimpses of in *Cuentos negros* and even earlier in her columns published under the pseudonym "Young Woman in Society." She, like her cunning protagonist, is a trickster who employs twists of language cunningly to deceive and seek revenge.

Within the context of slavery in Cuba, Cabrera maintains that stories served to distract slaves from their daily hardships and, as in Africa, it was essentially their form of theater. She persuades readers of the truthfulness of these anecdotes in much the same way that she persuaded readers of *El monte* that the words from her informants' mouths came from generations of authentic oral tradition. In both texts, Cabrera privileges the spoken word as the mainstay of collective lore. Her "old friends," the descendants of African slaves, are figured as the conveyers of truth in *Ayapá*; community elders had repeated stories about Jicotea with "reliable authority" since remote times.[77]

In order to conjure up the oral context in which the stories were performed, the text is embedded with oral properties. Through her exhaustive research that culminated in the publication of *El monte*, Cabrera gained insight into aspects of oral culture. The first step in re-creating a collective storytelling event entails a detailed description of the performance itself. In a key passage of the introduction, Cabrera tells us clearly, in what is perhaps her most lyrical piece of writing, of the nuances of black oral tradition and the mystical powers of the storyteller:

Desarrollando la trama fantasmagórica de sus cuentos, este viejo, que al fin tuvo que cederle a la muerte, se convertía en cuadrúpedo, en ave, en insecto, en árbol o en río. ¡Era admirable! Su cuerpo ondulaba como el majá de Santa María o como el río; sus brazos sugerían las llamas de un incendio; los tonos de su voz, todos los ruidos. [...] Sabía desfigurarse como un ente horroroso del otro mundo. [...] Para él, poeta sin sospecharlo, todo en el mundo y cuanto a él le pertenecía [...] vivía conscientemente, tenía un alma [...] que podía traducir lo que el silencio de cada cosa expresaba.[78]

[Developing the phantasmagoric plot of his stories, this old man, who ultimately yielded to death, transformed himself into a quadruped, a bird, an insect, a tree or a river. It was remarkable! His body undulated like that of a boa or like the river; his arms suggested dancing flames; the tones of his voice, all possible sounds. . . . He knew how to reconfigure himself as a horrifying being from the other world. . . . For him, a poet without suspecting as much, everything in the world . . . lived consciously, and had a soul . . . and he could translate what the silence of each thing expressed.]

Cabrera's description recalls the wandering bard and keeper of lore, a unique character who frequents the pages of Spanish American narrative. In Carpentier's *El reino de este mundo* (*The Kingdom of This World*), Mackandal, the powerful black storyteller, magically transforms himself into animals to elude slave owners. This archetypal figure is revisited in the works of several other writers, including Gabriel García Márquez, Mario Vargas Llosa, and Augusto Roa Bastos. In Cabrera's version, the oral poet's gestures and grimaces pervade the text so completely as to lend perfect verisimilitude to the story. Her task as "transcriber" is to re-create this unique storytelling event in written language. The Afro-Cuban oral tradition, of which she is a fervent admirer, becomes fictionalized in her collections of short stories. This process entails the literalization of the dynamic and fantastical performance described above.

Ayapá opens with a rhythmic verse in African language, "Tururú yagüero, tururú tururúm," which resonates throughout the first story depicting a mythical past when "everything was present."[79] The song inaugurates a magnificent interplay of stories about the wiles of Jicotea. The disposition of the capricious and humanlike turtle undergoes dramatic metamorphoses in each of his many adventures. However, a thematic thread ties the stories together: Jicotea uses the power of language to enchant, deceive, and seek revenge. In "Ncharriri," a word is like a "spark of fire" that is capable of transforming the universe.[80] Popular sayings and truisms, as well as different dialects, are sprinkled throughout the narrative to enhance the colloquial nature of the text. Cabrera most likely made ample use of her own collection of *Refranes de negros viejos*, of which a second edition appeared in 1970, a year prior to the publication of *Ayapá*. She formulates a literary language that is undeniably poetic and teems with alliterations, assonances, and onomatopoeic words. Lydia mimics the animated story-teller of her introduction; she too is a "poet without suspecting as much." In its entirety, *Ayapá* attempts to reinvent, in literary form, the art of storytelling, a tradition displaced from its African origin by two diasporas.

Although Lydia Cabrera did not publish another literary work until 1983, when her *Cuentos para adultos, niños y retrasados mentales* (Stories for Adults, Children, and the Mentally Retarded) appeared, she wrote several ethnographic texts during the seventies. If *El monte* marks the starting point of her ethnographic oeuvre, the investigative work that follows breaks with convention and embraces new regions previously unexplored by anthropologists. Cabrera's post-1960 publications range from collections of Cuban superstitions or of animals in Cuban folklore, to detailed essays on Reglas de Congo and the Regla Kimbisa and numerous entries in the *Enciclopedia de Cuba*, published in San Juan and Madrid. These works reflect an almost obsessive preoccupation with the preservation of a tradition that the writer fears is vanishing. To counter this loss, she explores her memory as a means of returning to the poetic and marvelous world of her childhood, in which men, animals and things spoke the same language.[81] The language of diaspora is invoked with a twofold intention. Cabrera's nostalgic desire to return to a collective past goes hand in hand with a personal political agenda to denounce Cubans, most likely of her social class, for disregarding their own culture. Cabrera uses blacks' capacity to maintain a sense of connection with their ancestors as grounds for condemning Cuban exiles' inability to do so.

At certain vital moments, there is a drastic deviation from the language of nostalgia and reverence found in her earlier works. She acknowledges her jealousy of descendants of black slaves who have resisted white oppressors and managed to celebrate the oral traditions—music, language, dance, and literature—of their forefathers. Cabrera's most bitter indictment, rooted in the conditions of her exile, appears in the prologue of Mercedes Cros Sandoval's book *La religión afrocubana*, where she implores Cuban exiles, living in the supposed "bastion of liberty," to preserve their identities and souls.[82]

In 1972, Lydia and María Teresa sought refuge from the United States to spend two years abroad in Madrid. There Cabrera produced what is perhaps her most poetic and personal piece, *La laguna sagrada de San Joaquín*, published in Madrid in 1973 and dedicated to Cabrera's compatriot in exile,

Lino Novás-Calvo. In many ways, the text parallels her metaphysical return to Cuba in the 1930s that resulted in the production of her *Contes nègres de Cuba*. It is when abroad that she is most capable of researching a distant time and place. *La laguna* remembers and recounts a 1956 excursion into the hinterlands of Matanzas shared by Cabrera, the anthropologists Alfred Métraux and Pierre Verger, and the photographer Josefina Tarafa. It is the most aesthetic and lyrical of Lydia's ethnographic treatises.

The 1973 publication defies categorization; it represents the melding of a travel journal, a collection of fantastical stories and songs, a personal diary, a study of sacred traditions, and the transcription of numerous interviews. Again there is the complete fusion of the literary and the ethnographic that, as was seen, marked certain key moments of *El monte*. In *La laguna*, Cabrera poetically invokes the image of the sacred ceiba tree to describe the unique scenery of Matanzas: "Al fondo de la laguna en puro horizonte de cielo unas ceibas solemnes, majestuosamente indulgentes, guardan su soledad."[83] [At the far end of the lagoon, at the very horizon and against the sky, the solemn ceibas, majestically indulgent, maintain their solitude.] At the time Cabrera put this passage into writing, she was miles and decades away, contemplating where she once had been and could no longer return.

The distance of retrospect makes the book a tribute to her "old friends" of Matanzas. It is a book written in the painful language of diaspora. Poetry and ethnography are linked together by a yearning for an irretrievable world. A sense of alienation and a desire for eventual return are the motivating forces behind *La laguna*. What alleges to be an analysis of an African man's attitude toward the lagoon waters is really a poetic quest, on the part of the anthropologist-writer, for an estranged identity.[84]

Cabrera's ethnographic work of the seventies and eighties is distinguishable from her earlier production by a marked evolution in the narrative voice. In *La laguna*, the allegorical return is narrated by a more authoritative and confident ethnographic "I." Whereas previously, Cabrera inscribed a self-conscious distance from the interpretive process, here the participant-observer weaves herself into the text as one of many collaborators. The absence of an introduction is revealing in this regard. The story unfolds as a series of personal encounters over the course of a collective excursion. In *El monte*, the conscious explanation of a lack of precise method pointed to just the opposite. In *La laguna*, Lydia Cabrera does not try to convince us of "being there," since the experience is actually a remote memory. Her task is rather to convince the reader of "having been there," an endeavor that is aided by the incorporation of photographs of Cabrera and her informants.

Cabrera re-creates conversations that took place almost thirty years prior, describing the gestures and exclamations as if they had occurred yesterday. These oral moments aim to lend an air of presentness and authenticity to the text. She remembers the expressions of Ma Francisquilla, one of her most cherished collaborators, whose shouts of astonishment and smiles of satisfaction would reveal her strong, toothless gums. In this way, Cabrera's own ability, like that of the ancestors of slaves, to remember minuscule details of anecdotes, songs, and traditions enables her to fix a moment in the past that she fears no longer exists.

The oral takes on new meaning in Cabrera's exilic writings. Whereas in *El monte* and her articles published in the forties and fifties, songs and dialogues were invoked to create the effect of an "eternal mythic present" and to convince readers of the important and unrecognized role played by blacks in the Cuban culture of their day, works like *La laguna* bring the oral into play as a means of nostalgically grasping for a source that is irretrievably lost. Throughout her career as an anthropologist-writer, Cabrera experienced an anxiety about origins that subtends Spanish American narrative discourse. By poetically transposing what she heard and what she saw, Cabrera rewrote Cuban cultural history in both her ethnographic studies as well as her literary creations.

Lydia Cabrera explored Cuba's heterogeneous cultural history by delving into the complex world of black oral history. Her writings indicate that she perceived orality as an authentic expression of communal culture. Like José María Arguedas and Miguel Barnet, anthropologist-writers who were similarly fascinated with other voices and other traditions, her desire to preserve oral lore stemmed from dissatisfaction with hegemonic forms of discourse. Although she downplayed her role as author in both her ethnographic and literary texts, Cabrera fashioned herself as a mediator between Cuba's oral and literate communities. By the final decade of her life, her desire to preserve Afro-Cuban culture was as much intellectual as it was personal. The songs and stories that captivated her as a child and intrigued her as an anthropologist and writer were memories belonging to a displaced homeland. By allowing these oral memories to speak in her texts, Lydia was inscribing her own traditions and preserving those of her black compatriots.

3

Echoes from
Los ríos profundos

José María Arguedas and Lydia Cabrera undertook strikingly similar personal quests: they both sought to revitalize nonhegemonic cultures that were part of their individual identities. Both undertook to expand notions of national culture to include marginalized groups whose predominantly oral traditions they feared were under threat. Ultimately, both writers were concerned with creating within and for Western written culture, rather than for the cultures whose traditions they defended.

Arguedas simultaneously affirmed his authority as a native speaker of Quechua who experienced Andean life firsthand and as an eyewitness to the events he portrayed. He attributed his personal and intellectual formation to the Andean Indians who nurtured him, imparting their language, traditions, and songs.

Arguedas was born in Andahuaylas, in the sierra province of Apurímac in 1911. His father, Víctor Manuel Arguedas Arellano, a lawyer, was a native of Cuzco. After his mother died in 1914, Arguedas saw little of his father and lived among the Indians who worked on his stepmother's estate in San Juan de Lucanas. In his early adolescence, Arguedas suffered abuse from his stepbrother Pablos and finally managed to escape in 1921 to live in Viseca, a rural hacienda belonging to his uncle José Manuel Perea Arellano. It was in Viseca that Arguedas first came into contact with the Indian community of Utek'. With these Indians he forged his happiest memories, nurtured by father figures like Felipe Maywa and Victo Pusa, who later inhabited the most personal moments of his narrative texts.

The early 1920s marked a turning point in Arguedas's personal and intellectual development. During this period, he became aware of his unique position as both Spanish and Andean. Arguedas's first attempts at literary creation, published collectively in *Agua* (Water) in 1935, were dedicated to the indigenous peoples of Viseca, with whom he trembled with cold in the fields, and danced with happiness at the carnivals.[1] In the three stories compiled in *Agua*, one first senses Arguedas's struggle with issues of language and translation, a dilemma he faced throughout his career.

Arguedas wrote in Spanish. Only in his poetry published during the final decade of his life did he experiment with written Quechua. For this reason, there is some debate regarding Arguedas's claims to be a native speaker of Quechua. His parents were bilingual, as were most inhabitants of Apurímac. In a 1966 interview, Arguedas clarified that, until he was nine years old, his predominant language was always Quechua. The fact that he could never write poetry in Spanish revealed to him that his mother tongue was Quechua.[2] Arguedas insisted on a clear distinction between Quechua, a poetic language, and Spanish, a literary and academic language.

Although Arguedas's goals were primarily concerned with Western written culture, he profoundly identified with Quechua as a source of artistic inspiration. Arguedas's sense of off-centeredness in a world of opposing cultural systems powerfully shaped his discourse as a writer of fiction and ethnographies. He responded to the ambiguities that also subtend Lydia Cabrera's writings by contriving a narrative voice that stands both inside and outside the realm he sought to describe.

Like Cabrera, Arguedas was enchanted by the songs and stories he heard in his childhood. As an adult, he sought to revitalize Andean oral traditions by inscribing Quechua lore in literary form. Ultimately, his studies in ethnography enabled him to "write" Quechua orality by mediating between the opposing halves of his bicultural identity. His texts, both anthropological and narrative, stage his contradictory insider/outsider position with regard to both the Andean and Hispanic worlds.

José María Arguedas: "Mak'tillo falsificado"
[Phony young man]

Arguedas's early writings indicate that he engaged in anthropological reflection long before he received formal training as an ethnographer. These texts reflect his initial attempts to interpret faithfully Peruvian reality. Unpublished works indicate that, from early on, his writing focused on Andean culture from the perspective of the Spanish-speaking world. In a 1929 sociological essay, Arguedas described the expression of Indians of the sierra as filled with fear, admiration, and shyness, emotions embedded in their souls over countless years.[3] Arguedas's first literary publications reflect a dramatic revision of this representation of Andeans. Driven by the desire to correct erroneous portrayals of Peruvian reality, he increasingly strove to express the interiority of the indigenous world that nurtured him. One strategy he employed was the exaltation of Quechua as a vehicle to evoke a poetic and lyrical realm.

In his early short stories, which describe the injuries inflicted on Indians by white landowners, Arguedas resolved the stylistic question of perspective by creating the motif of the young narrator-protagonist, a figure that fully evolves in *Los ríos profundos* (*Deep Rivers*). This voice feels the awkward pains of alienation most certainly experienced by Arguedas, who straddled Peru's Quechua-speaking and Hispanic worlds. Juan, the narrator-protagonist of "Los escoleros" is conscious of his difference, of being a "mak'tillo falsificado" [phony young man]. The young man of the story undergoes symbolic tests to prove his strength and thus ensure his acceptance into the Indian community. Nonetheless, the youth is unable to enter completely into the cultural realm of his Indian friends, and he is ultimately relegated to the position of an outsider. The trilogy concludes with "Warma kuyay (Amor de niño)," the most personal and autobiographical of the three stories in *Agua*. The final scene sees the exodus of Ernesto, the narrator-protagonist, from the nurturing world of the Andean peoples, and his entry into the repudiated white world.

The strict division between the Indian and white worlds, characteristic of Arguedas's early works, recalls the traditional theories of *indigenismo* (indigenism) outlined by Peruvian theorist and politician José Carlos Mariátegui, an articulate exponent of indigenous topics. Mariátegui, influenced by European contemporary movements and by indigenous uprisings in Mexico, saw the Inca empire as an early example of the socialist model. In his *Siete ensayos de interpretación de la realidad peruana* (1928) (Seven Essays of Interpretation of Peruvian Reality), the cornerstone of *indigenista* thought, Mariátegui emphasized the dualistic nature of Peruvian society, a notion that *indigenista* writers directly applied to their literary creations. Before his death in 1930, he had firmly established the beginnings of the Peruvian Communist Party (el Partido Comunista Peruano), and two workers' unions: one urban (la Confederación General de Trabajadores), and one rural (la Confederación de Yanaconas y Campesinos). For Mariátegui, the Indian was inextricably linked to all notions of Peruvian nationalism.

Unlike Lydia Cabrera, who was an avid reader of Western literature from an early age, Arguedas's initial experience was with highly politicized writings. Although Arguedas was not an active member of the left-wing party Alianza Popular Revolucionaria Americana (American Popular Revolutionary Alliance), his ideas were certainly influenced by its anti-capitalist and regionalist tendencies and by the treatises of Mariátegui, Victor

Raúl Haya de la Torre, Dr. Luis E. Valcárcel, and other Peruvian politicians and theorists. Arguedas's early experiments with narrative discourse echo Mariátegui's conception of a divided nation. But Arguedas consistently maintained that Mariátegui's ideas verged on racism insofar as they stemmed from an uninformed perception of indigenous realities. In this sense, Arguedas practiced an Andeanism akin to that put forward by the sociologist José Uriel García.[4] In his 1930 book *El nuevo indio* (The New Indian), Uriel García advocated a new appreciation for the assimilative capacities of Peru's Indians. For him, as for Arguedas, the integration of indigenous cultures should entail the preservation of the groups' integrity and traditions. In all of his writings, both anthropological and narrative, Arguedas sought to preserve the voices of Peru's disenfranchised peoples. Over the course of his career as a writer and ethnologist, Arguedas's contributions to *indigenista* thought diverged from Mariátegui's. Arguedas moved beyond Mariátegui's description of Peru's social binarisms and embraced the polyvocalities of Peru's heterogeneous society.

The evolution of Arguedas's vision of Peruvian culture parallels the sociologist and historian Alberto Flores Galindo's influential study *Buscando un inca: Identidad y utopía en los Andes* (Searching for an Inca: Identity and Utopia in the Andes), published in 1986. Like Arguedas, he recognized popular culture as complex and heterogenous. Flores Galindo contends that, in the Andes, the collective imagination has traditionally defined an ideal society as a return to a past that preceded the arrival of the Europeans. His book traces the ideological projects of various Peruvian intellectuals, like Arguedas, who sought to alter the present by reclaiming the past. Flores Galindo cautions against focusing solely on the past. He calls for an end to the "search for an Inca," and argues for a type of socialism that is open to progress, modernization, and the future.[5] Flores Galindo draws a compelling analogy between the diverse history of ideas regarding Andean utopia and the conflictive personal history of Arguedas. He finds an interesting distinction between Arguedas's scientific and literary projects, affirming that Arguedas's texts about communities and popular art deal with themes of progress, modernization, and harmonious change, in which the mestizos of the Mantaro Valley are converted into a prototype of the future country. But in the fictional texts, where the narrator lets himself be carried away by the imaginary, the mestizos seem weakened, leaving the Indians and whites in opposition, with violence as the only language. In Arguedas's narrative, no change—that is, no true social cataclysm—is possible.[6]

In his fiction, Arguedas struggled with the theoretical issue of conveying Quechua voices in written Spanish. The confrontation between two social and language groups that Arguedas experienced personally led him to contend with this linguistic dilemma. Arguedas, like Flores Galindo, recognized ancient Andean traditions as an important source of future definitions of Peruvian national identity. In Arguedas's version of an Andean utopia, the Andean world and the West would unite.

Like previous generations of *indigenista* writers, Arguedas opted to compose his texts primarily in Spanish, not in the native Quechua of the oral narratives that originally inspired him. In the stories in *Agua*, he constructed a tidy linguistic division, incorporating Quechua in the form of interjections and verses of songs. The resulting disjunctions in textuality prompt one to ask in what language the author was consistently thinking. The distinction between languages is too neat in these early writings, as were Mariátegui's simplified oppositions between *ladinos* (non-Indians) and Indians. As Arguedas's writing matured, his stylistic innovations reflect a more complete understanding of the complexities of Peru's social relationships. His early attempts to create personal and realistic fictions of Quechua culture corresponded to the limitations imposed by *indigenistas* like Mariátegui and Valcárcel. In the 1940s, Arguedas gradually transcended the contradictions that marked early theories of *indigenismo* to forge a new kind of thinking, commonly known as *neoindigenismo*, in which he championed mestizo culture as the key to Peru's development.

In 1931, Arguedas reunited with his brother, Arístides, at the Universidad de San Marcos, where he decided to major in literature. At that time, he was an avid reader of *Amauta* and other political treatises that had been in circulation since the end of World War I. Intellectuals who wrote for *Amauta* argued that Peruvian class struggles resulted from the end of the feudal system combined with communal efforts to institute a socialist system. The Peruvian linguist and critic Alberto Escobar, a close friend of Arguedas, describes the *indigenismo* presented in the magazine as the intersection of a literary project and a social program.[7] This blending of art and politics appealed to the young Arguedas as he attempted to interpret Peruvian reality in narrative form.

In addition to composing the three stories that later appeared in *Agua*, Arguedas joined his university colleagues as a political activist, collaborating in the publication of the magazine *Palabra* in 1936 and participating in CODRE (Comité de amigos para la defensa de la República) in 1937. During the same period, he met Celia and Alicia Bustamante, members of Lima's artistic elite and founders of Pancho Fierro, a club of intellectuals dedicated to the collection of folklore and popular art to which Arguedas contributed compilations and translations of Quechua songs. In 1939, Arguedas married Celia Bustamante Vernal.

Arguedas's first studies of folkloric material were inspired by an elitist environment heavily influenced by Mariátegui's theories and the repercussions of the Mexican revolution. Alicia, convinced of the intrinsic values of indigenous art, was the first to grace Lima with an exhibit of Peruvian popular art in 1939, which traveled to Europe in the decades that followed. In an article published in a 1969 issue of *El Comercio*, Arguedas reflected on the important contributions of Alicia and other members of Lima's intellectual elite, claiming that the most difficult task was to extend an understanding of indigenous art (music, oral literature, visual arts) to an urban, Creole public.[8] Arguedas praised Alicia's catalogued collection of handicrafts as a vital document. His encounters with Lima's intellectual elite in the 1930s were crucial to the development of skills as an expert in Peruvian folklore. Arguedas followed closely in Alicia's footsteps as what he called a "puente vivo" [living bridge] between two distinct cultural worlds.

Like Alicia Bustamante, Arguedas was an avid collector. Until his death, he worked diligently to collect songs and stories and to integrate these art forms into mainstream popular culture. He was committed to bringing music of the sierra to urban radio stations and to creating a comprehensive archive of Andean oral literature. This quest was as much professional as it was personal. As James Clifford perceptively notes, "In the West . . . collecting has long been a strategy for the deployment of a possessive self, culture and authenticity." Furthermore, "To see ethnography as a form of culture collection (not, of course, the *only* way to see it) highlights the ways that diverse experiences and facts are selected, gathered, detached from the original temporal occasions, and given enduring value in a new arrangement."[9] Expectations of pureness and essence are built into "culture collection," a practice based on the assumption that artistic production can coherently represent another culture. Fearing that it was threatened by modernization, Arguedas was committed to the salvation of Quechua oral tradition. His interest in Quechua orality stemmed from his deep concern with the social and political discrimination of Andean peoples.

CANTO KECHWA: A MUSICAL TOUR

At San Marcos, Arguedas began work on a thesis entitled "La canción popular mestiza, su valor poético y sus posibilidades" (The Mestizo Popular Song, Its Poetic Value and Its Possibilities). His university study was interrupted, however, by a brief period of imprisonment resulting from his participation in a protest staged by students in response to the Italian general Camarotta's visit to Peru. More than two decades later, Arguedas recounted his experiences in a novella called *El Sexto* (1961), after the name of the prison.

During his imprisonment Arguedas composed his second book, *Canto kechwa* (Quechua Song), an important text published in 1938 that demonstrates his talent as a compiler and translator of Indian folklore. As the title suggests, the book contains the Spanish translations of twenty-one Quechua songs, and several illustrations by Alicia Bustamante decorate its pages. Of particular interest is the prologue to the collection. This essay, a nostalgic confession by the author, has been largely overlooked by critics. It merits attention, however, for it is here that Arguedas first expressed his fascination with Quechua oral tradition and broached themes that he revisited in his later publications, both literary and ethnographic. The essay represents a stylistic experiment: the first example of Arguedas's hallmark synthesis of expository document and poetic narration.

For Arguedas, personal experience and scientific observation comingled in a unique dialectic.[10] John V. Murra, a Cornell University anthropologist and Arguedas's friend and colleague, remarks that one of the shortcomings of Arguedas literary criticism has been that it largely fails to address his scientific production.[11] By examining the layers of discourse in Arguedas's hybrid texts, we can better understand the forces that shaped his rhetoric. Like Cabrera, Arguedas began writing essays based on scientific observation before he received formal training as an ethnographer. In his early work, and throughout his writings, experience outweighs theory as a source of authority.

In the prologue of *Canto kechwa*, Arguedas experimented with narrational viewpoint and conceived two particular voices that anticipated the technique employed two decades later in *Los ríos profundos*. A similar stratification of discourses marks all of his writings. The essay opens with the evocation of a remote and sonorous past, recalling the women and young children who sang in the patio of the Viseca hacienda.[12] The text that unfolds is essentially a reconstructed excursion of Arguedas, the young protagonist, through various regions of Peru. Music motivates this journey that re-creates the songs and stories Arguedas heard in his childhood.

At the age of twelve, Arguedas was taken from the nurturing environment of Viseca by his father, whom he joined on his travels through the Peruvian countryside. The regions that the narrator-musicologist visits in his tour of Peru in *Canto kechwa* anticipate the various settings that Ernesto of *Los ríos profundos* encounters in his travels with his father. The introduction of *Canto kechwa* recalls that, in the valley of Apurímac, José María and his father came across a community of Indians silenced by an authoritarian landholder, an episode that he later incorporated into "La hacienda," the fourth chapter of *Los ríos profundos*. In the coastal cities, in contrast, the public regarded those who sang *waynos* (Quechua songs), as inferior, and treated them as objects of ridicule.[13] In Lima, however, where movements to defend native culture were already underway, the young traveler encountered artists and writers who advocated the preservation of indigenous art forms.

What better form to express the progressive collection of songs and traditions, a hobby that intrigued Arguedas throughout his lifetime, than an autobiographical account of travels? The journey emerges as the story of Arguedas's quest to pin down an appropriate ethnographic voice. He was constantly negotiating his position vis-à-vis the events and characters of his past. Arguedas's prologue to *Canto kechwa* demonstrates some preliminary experimentation with personal testimony, a style that suited his needs both as an ethnographer and as a creator of literary works. An autobiographical style allows for a narrative voice that portrays a participant-observer who is at once united with and apart from the world he describes.

In the prologue of *Canto kechwa*, the narrator-protagonist's arrival in Lima marks a shift from a personal narrational voice to a more objective and analytical one. Arguedas articulated a thesis that distinguishes all of his subsequent ethnologic and literary work: he recognized the value of mestizo culture and conceived popular mestizo culture as extending directly from indigenous traditions. For Arguedas, the *wayno* was an emblem of mestizo art. He envisioned a future in which indigenous art forms, symbols of his Peruvian nation, would be regarded as a source of pride rather than shame, and would be appreciated as on a par with their European counterparts. Arguedas insisted that the songs compiled in *Canto kechwa* were not ancient; rather, they reflected the artistic expression of present-day Indians and mestizos. He sought to preserve traditions by reviving and reinventing them in the oppositional world in which he lived. The compilation of translated songs, and the crucial prologue that introduces them, set the groundwork for a project and personal quest that engaged him throughout his lifetime.

Arguedas articulated a twofold plan for his translations in *Canto kechwa*: first, he aimed to demonstrate that indigenous cultures possess the capacity to create expressive and poetic language; and, second, he proposed that native creations be recognized as legitimate and valuable art forms. In order that his collection be received by a reading public with faith in its authenticity, Arguedas needed to establish his authority as a purveyor of Andean truths. To do this, he insisted on his status as a native Andean participant with firsthand experience of the transcribed songs. The first half of the prologue, a literary excursion guided by the narrator-musicologist, is devoted to this objective. This narrative persona positions himself as an expert, and warns against the dangers of composers who claim to create a "true work," but who fall short of producing authentic art. How, then, is one granted access to a realm deemed authentic? According to Arguedas, coexistence with a native culture enables one to faithfully interpret its nuances.

Ironically, Arguedas, who presented himself as a qualified informant on Andean culture, did not explicitly claim to belong to the world that he interpreted. In his estimation, intimate knowledge of Quechua was the key to understanding the music of the sierra. Arguedas exalted his native language, arguing that Quechua was a perfect language for the "superior man," and could produce great literature.[14] Simultaneously, however, he played down his role as a native speaker of Quechua to avoid alienating his Spanish-speaking audience.

The prologue to *Canto kechwa* was one of Arguedas's first efforts to come to terms with a narrational voice appropriate for conveying both ethnographic knowledge and personal experience. He created the illusion of being both an insider, a native of Peru's sierra, and an outsider, an objective observer of the Andean oral traditions he sought to portray. This confluence of vantage points is characteristic of ethnographic experience. The contradictory insider/outsider position strikes at the heart of the problem of writing the oral. Anthropologist-writers like Arguedas and Cabrera faced an interesting dilemma: both wrote from within a Western literate culture that they believed threatened oral traditions.

Arguedas's need to manipulate his position and to mediate between two languages is typical of ethnographic subjectivity. Any attempt to interpret the Other's identity entails an effort to control one's own identity. Clifford adapts Stephen Greenblatt's concept of literary self-fashioning to ethnography, arguing that although ethnographic discourse "portrays other selves as culturally constituted, it also fashions an identity authorized to represent, to interpret, even to believe—but always with some irony—the truths of discrepant worlds."[15] Arguedas's solution, creating cultural fictions to describe his personal past and Peru's present and future, carries over into his literary works as well.

In contrast to the fieldwork techniques employed by Lydia Cabrera, Arguedas portrayed himself as both a privileged informant and an interpreter. Alejandro Ortiz Rescaniere, Arguedas's most accomplished student and colleague in the 1960s, referred to his mentor's peculiar status in a 1967 letter: aside from being an ethnologist, a man of Western science who studies other cultures, Arguedas could live and think from within that culture. José María the ethnologist could study José María the informant.[16]

However, the virtue described by Ortiz as a marvel was ultimately a source of Arguedas's desperate emotional conflict. Arguedas was motivated to write by his personal experiences and compassion for Peru's oppressed cultures. But he could only express this part of himself by invoking anthropological knowledge, a discourse he struggled to master and one that necessitated displacement from the world of the sierra.

Arguedas's early efforts as an ethnographer and folklorist relied heavily on a personal history of collective experiences. He fashioned himself as an ardent listener and singer of Quechua tales and songs. His rapport with indigenous cultures differed from Cabrera's relationships with her Afro-Cuban informants. Arguedas based his findings on a lifetime of personal experiences. Even after he graduated from the Universidad de San Marcos with a degree in ethnology, Arguedas still depended primarily on the credibility conferred by his experiences. In letters to Murra, he confessed that he had very poor theoretical training, and relied primarily on his intuition.[17]

Arguedas's writings in the 1930s demonstrate that he was a practicing ethnographer long before he received any formal training. He attempted to make Andean folklore readable for a Western public. Arguedas offered his interpretive translations of *Canto kechwa* as expressions of Indian and mestizo culture. In the prologue, he insists that the translations are interpretative, rather than literal; and admits that someone who felt more "authentically" Indian might be able to offer purer versions of the songs.[18]

Arguedas's task in his first book of ethnologic material was one of translation of songs from the oral to the written form; his goal was to incorporate Andean tradition into the realm of valued art. As in Cabrera's writings, orality was associated with an important source of national culture. That Arguedas wrote eloquently in Spanish speaks to the fact that he was writing for and within Western culture. At the same time, he posited that the intimate knowledge of Quechua granted him privileged access to interpret Andean culture.

COLLECTIONS: ARGUEDAS THE FOLKLORIST AND THE TRANSLATOR

After his liberation from El Sexto in October of 1938, Arguedas became committed to the investigation of Andean folklore. Between 1938 and 1957 he was primarily interested in anthropological themes. For the first time, his writings entered international circles, and he published a series of articles in *La Prensa*, a Buenos Aires periodical. Over the next decade, he published approximately thirty-four articles, several of which appear in Angel Rama's 1976 edition of *Señores e indios. Acerca de la cultura quechua*

(Gentlemen and Indians: About the Quechua Culture), a compilation that was expanded and republished under the title *Indios, mestizos y señores* (Indians, Mestizos, and Gentlemen). These articles include compilations of folkloric material—Quechua legends, songs, and poems—translated by Arguedas, as well as ethnologic and sociological essays that formed the basis of his more extensive projects in the decades that followed. It was in *La Prensa* that he first formulated theories on orality and translation that significantly influenced his rhetorical strategies for expressing the oral in narrative discourse.

Between 1939 and 1941, Arguedas used Sicuani, a town between Puno and Cuzco, as his field of study. This stay in Sicuani was instrumental in his development as an anthropologist-writer. Like Cabrera, Arguedas was motivated to collect native folklore by a sense of urgency. He endeavored to extend Peru's national perception of culture to include Andean practices. Arguedas compiled accounts from informants who were essentially mestizos, thereby privileging their experiences and traditions over those of Peru's pure Indians. He was fascinated with contemporary oral traditions, and made very clear in *Canto kechwa* that the songs of his compilation belonged to present-day, and ideally the future, Peru.

Conscious of the shortcomings of earlier *indigenista* writers, Arguedas sought to revise the poorly informed accounts of *indigenistas* regarding the Andean experience by gaining insight into the mestizo population that he was helping to educate. His role as a Spanish teacher in Sicuani was crucial to this project; Arguedas taught mestizo youths the language that would grant them access to the world of white Peruvians while simultaneously celebrating the Quechua language that, for him, was an unparalleled medium of poetic and creative expression.

Arguedas's first article published in *La Prensa*, "Simbolismo y poesía de dos canciones populares quechuas" (Symbolism and Poetry of Two Popular Quechua Songs), appeared in 1938. His treatment of folkloric material as a personal memory recalls the intermingling of autobiography and investigation manifested in *Canto kechwa*. Arguedas distanced himself from theorists like Mariátegui who intellectualized Andean culture from a very objective standpoint. A personal and nostalgic tone permeates all of Arguedas's publications in *La Prensa*, establishing a poetic synthesis of scientific observation and artistic narration characteristic of all his writings.[19] For example, upon analyzing a Quechua song, he recalled that he would close his eyes and imagine the stars flickering in the heavens.[20] Orality is linked to memory in all of Arguedas's writings. Like Lydia Cabrera, he associated songs and stories with lighthearted moments of his childhood.

It is not surprising to find that Arguedas struggled with the conventions and necessities of linguistic expression throughout his career. His constant efforts to polish his written Spanish offer an example of the cultural dualism that he frequently described. In a significant *La Prensa* article, "Entre el kechwa y el castellano la angustia del mestizo" (Between Quechua and Spanish, the Anguish of the Mestizo), Arguedas posited his linguistic dilemma clearly. He noted that in César Vallejo's writings one can first sense the tremendous conflict of the mestizo: a constant battle between an interior world, with Quechua as its primary referent, and Spanish, the official language of Peru. Although he traced the internal conflict back to the writings of Felipe Guaman Poma de Ayala, Arguedas argued that he was dealing with a modern-day predicament, one that he experienced firsthand: the authentic man of his land who felt the need to express himself in a foreign language would learn that Spanish could not express his soul or the landscape where he was raised. For Arguedas, Quechua, the language of his soul, lacked universal value.[21] Arguedas contended that anguish provoked by this linguistic conflict would drive the mestizo to achieve full command of Spanish. Nevertheless, because the mestizo perceived the subject's spirit to be transcendentally linked to a poetic and picturesque world that could only be expressed in Quechua, pure Spanish could never be his exclusive means of expression.

Had Arguedas ended the article here, however, he would have jeopardized the legitimacy of his own writings. Arguedas qualified his argument by adding that written Quechua was destined to be forgotten. The dilemma described by Arguedas was both personal and collective. He insisted that Quechua was a legitimate and poetic language, but endorsed Spanish as the official language of written expression. Arguedas, like Cabrera, saw oral discourse and written discourse as distinct forms of expression. In his writing, he sidestepped the predicament posed by writing the oral by creating an oral poetics that could convey Quechua orality in written Spanish.

Alberto Escobar has studied extensively the question of language in Arguedas's narrative. He finds a strong correlation between the use of language and a conceptualization of Peruvian culture throughout Arguedas's writings. According to Escobar, Arguedas conceived Peru's plurality of languages as diverse creative manifestations, belonging to distinct human societies.[22] The representation of Peru's linguistic complexity in Arguedas's texts highlights the author's preoccupation with questions of personal and cultural identity. For Arguedas, language and culture are always interwoven.

Throughout his life, Arguedas sought to comprehend and interpret Andean traditions, with the hope that these traditions might be incorporated into contemporary Peruvian culture. Escobar describes an interesting parallel between Arguedas and Dante. Both intellectuals propose the coexistence of two distinct linguistic systems, highlighting the contrast between the social prestige of one and the expressive lyricism of the other. Arguedas, like Dante, believed he was personally witnessing the extinction of a past world and the emergence of a new, distinct society. Escobar concludes that language was an essential instrument in each one's quest to interpret and express a mixed identity, both personal and collective.[23]

Arguedas's texts exemplify his idea that Spanish and Quechua are distinct forms of literary expression. They re-create the personal challenges the author encountered as a bilingual speaker and a member of two cultural worlds. Escobar describes the coexistence of languages in Arguedas's writing as "copresencia": a tense relationship between Quechua and Spanish that one can detect in the presence of certain expressions in both languages, or their absence in one of them.[24] Through the manipulation of spoken language in literary discourse, Arguedas sought to reconcile the contradictions inherent in his bicultural identity.

Arguedas applied his theory of linguistic dualism to his analysis of various aspects of Andean culture. For example, in an article published in *La Prensa*, he declared Gabriel Aragón the most accomplished musician of popular song in southern Peru and praised his ability to compose *waynos* in which the mestizo spirit resonated. According to Arguedas, Aragón's most sublime songs, those possessing the signature of the southern ravines of Peru, were the musical pieces written in Castilian. By celebrating musicians like Aragón, who interpreted popular songs in Spanish without sacrificing native artistic integrity, Arguedas opened a new space for his own artistic creation. In articles like this one, Arguedas introduced his conception of *mestizaje* as something more complex than a cultural mixing; rather, he envisioned a dynamic process resulting in the production of new artistic forms.

Arguedas's early writings in *La Prensa* show his ardent passion for music. Several articles broach themes that were later incorporated into the sonorous world of *Los ríos profundos*. During his stay in Sicuani, and over the course of the decade that followed, he became an accomplished musicologist. The articles he published tended to focus on mestizo manifestations of music: for instance, his essay on the *charango*, the most expressive instrument of Indians and mestizos alike, praised the *wayno* by exclaiming that it is the strength, the voice, and the eternal blood of all Andean celebrations.[25]

Between 1940 and 1941, Arguedas published three articles bearing the title "La canción popular mestiza en el Perú, su valor documental y poético" (The Popular Mestizo Song in Peru: Its Documentary and Poetic Value). The first of the series focuses on the *wayno*, a constant theme in Arguedas's folkloric investigations. The article uses music as a way of thinking about

Peruvian culture. For Arguedas, a song was like an indestructible memory. He explained that the history of Peru mirrors the history of the *wayno*; by reflecting on the evolution of the popular song, one can comprehend the nation's process of *mestizaje*. Arguedas invoked the striking image of a geologic palimpsest, suggesting that in a musical piece, as in a geologic formation, traces of past eras exist simultaneously with the present. He made the important distinction that *waynos* speak for themselves, narrating the spiritual history of the mestizo community.[26]

This metaphor encompassed his own narrative: Arguedas reconstructed a similar palimpsest in the first chapters of *Los ríos profundos*, in which Ernesto embarks on a poetic journey through the levels of history encrusted in the walls of Cuzco. Arguedas's fascination with the *wayno* informed the rich textuality he wove in his most celebrated novel. The text of *Los ríos profundos*, as a synchronic entity, seeks to harmonize a succession of latent songs, sounds and events.

In the series of articles dedicated to Peru's popular song, as in *Canto kechwa*, Arguedas experimented with poetic discourse and discovered that descriptions of natural images conveyed the cosmic and dynamic Quechua oral culture he experienced in his childhood. For Arguedas, Quechua words, as evidenced by the proliferation of onomatopoeia, were saturated by the natural world they represent. He put this theory into practice in *Los ríos profundos*, a novel in which he contrived a literary discourse permeated by sound. In this acclaimed novel, sound and music embody an alternative to Western culture.

While in Sicuani, Arguedas had an encounter that had a profound impact on his work as a translator. He met Father Jorge A. Lira, the parish priest of Maranganí, who was preaching to a group of Indians in the town's plaza. Arguedas implored Lira to put living Andean culture into writing before it vanished, and suggested that he compile a dictionary of the Quechua language. The two folklorists collected Quechua stories and songs from Indian informants, and together they transposed this oral tradition into written Spanish. Their greatest challenge was to express in Spanish the rhythmic and singing quality intrinsic to Quechua.

Arguedas's collaboration with Lira marked a second phase of his career as a translator. As in *Canto kechwa*, he struggled to communicate the intention and true content of a language he perceived as purely phonetic. In the introductory remarks to a compilation of tales published in *Canciones y cuentos del pueblo quechua* (Songs and Stories of the Quechua People) in 1949, Arguedas tells us that he and Father Lira developed what he termed "the oral method," whereby Lira read stories out loud and Arguedas composed written translations, at times preserving Quechua sounds because of their onomatopoeic qualities. Arguedas insisted on his experience as a native speaker of Quechua, but also claimed that he possessed an equal command of Spanish "in form and spirit."[27] He subtly distinguished his authority from that of Lira, insisting that his own experience provided him with the ability to penetrate the complex linguistic world of Quechua orality.

Arguedas praised the care Father Lira took to produce faithful transpositions of lore he collected in Maranganí. He affirmed that the voices of the tales, typical of the Quechua peoples, were distinct from the Quechua practiced by literate missionaries and experts in Quechua literary history. Arguedas tells us that, though such a thing as literary Quechua exists, only someone who has experienced the language since childhood can truly comprehend the richness and subtlety of the complex oral language. In the short essay, Arguedas explained that, for Father Lira, even approaching such an intimate comprehension of the richness of Quechua phonetics required significant effort.

In a letter sent to his friend Manuel Moreno in 1941, he cast Lira's work in a still less positive light. Arguedas criticized Lira for suffering from the "fever of *indigenismo*," by defining *indigenismo* as blindly defending the Inca period, and simultaneously treating present-day Indians with scorn.[28] One decade later, when Arguedas learned that Father Lira had eliminated all words of Spanish origin from his collections of indigenous songs, he criticized him for failing to appreciate the words of Spanish origin that the Quechua-speaking population had incorporated into its vocabulary since the Conquest.[29]

Arguedas rejected Lira's and other *indigenista* claims that Indian identity should be defined solely within the context of the history forged by Inca ancestors. On the contrary, he advocated an *indigenismo* that appreciated Peru's heterogeneous population, and urged Indians to subscribe to Western culture to a certain degree, without sacrificing their own traditions. Herein lies the paradox that subtends all of Arguedas's writings: it was precisely with the archaic and ephemeral Indian traditions that Arguedas felt profound solidarity, a link to a personal and collective past. But while he advocated the preservation of these traditions, he recognized that revitalization could ultimately lead to abuse and destruction.

The publication that resulted from Arguedas's collaborative work with Father Lira, *Canciones y cuentos del pueblo quechua*, demonstrates that, in Arguedas's estimation, a synthesis of Western and Andean cultures was not only possible, but desirable. The compilation includes the same songs originally published in *Canto kechwa*, as well as some new ones. All of the *waynos* of the collection are Indian, and Arguedas demonstrated that Spanish terms had been successfully incorporated into the Quechua lexicon. Unlike

Lira, he celebrated these linguistic phenomena and maintained that, whereas the Quechua context remained intact, the Spanish words had been transformed to serve a new function, a process referred to as "integration and retranslation" by ethnologists.[30]

Arguedas's argument in favor of a Quechua poetic language, infused with the Spanish lexicon, strengthened his defense of the virtues of mestizo culture. He triumphantly concluded the introduction to *Canciones y cuentos* by stating that the songs and stories were a testimony to the creative capacity of Peru's native peoples. The Quechua oral tradition Arguedas engaged did not exist as a timeless, pure entity. Rather, he felt it essential to incorporate it into contemporary national culture. In his view, modernization should not bring the loss of one language or the other, but rather a productive mixing. Arguedas criticized intellectual projects that proposed a Peruvian utopia by calling for a return to an idealized historical moment, thereby rejecting processes of modernization.[31] On the contrary, he aimed to understand Andean traditions from a contemporary perspective.

YAWAR FIESTA AND PUQUIO REDISCOVERED

At the same time that Arguedas worked with Father Lira to translate oral texts, he fought a similar linguistic battle writing his first novel, *Yawar fiesta*, published in Lima in 1941. In an essay originally published in 1950, and now an introduction to *Yawar fiesta*, Arguedas described how he struggled for years to banish Quechuisms from his written language and to convert literary Spanish into the sole mode of expression. Ultimately, upon determining that specific Quechua rhythms and words were untranslatable, he chose to compose the novel in the bilingual style that characterized the stories in *Agua* and also conformed to the methods of translation employed in *Canciones y cuentos*.

Silverio Muñoz has observed an interesting evolution in Arguedas's narrative. In particular, he finds discrepancies in the representations of indigenous culture between the first and second book. The initial realism of *Agua* that responded to *indigenista* theories of Mariátegui is no longer present in *Yawar fiesta*. Instead, Muñoz finds ambiguity in the ideological underpinnings of Arguedas's second book. He attributes this evolution in Arguedas's writings to his increasing commitment to anthropological investigation. Muñoz points out that the division of Latin American society into two entities—one "primitive" and the other modernized—is a product of Western thought. He suggests that "cultural anthropologism" influences Arguedas's representation of Peruvian society in *Yawar fiesta*.[32]

The title of the novel reflects Arguedas's stylistic decision to employ a mixture of languages to represent the cultural synthesis that is the book's underlying theme. As the title suggests, the novel focuses on the preparation for and the celebration of the *turupukllay*, or *yawar fiesta, yawar* meaning "blood." A rudimentary version of the 1941 novel, a story titled "Yawar (Fiesta)," was published in *Revista Americana de Buenos Aires*.[33] Both the preliminary story and the published novel focus on the reality of Puquio, where Arguedas spent much of his youth. He later came to know the area well as an anthropologist in 1952 and again in 1956. The corrida dramatized in the story represents a dramatic contest between the opposing indigenous and Spanish worlds of Peru, resulting in the triumph of the Andean peoples. In this regard, the novel expresses the same conviction found in his essays on folklore: indigenous and mestizo culture should be preserved at all costs.

Muñoz criticizes Arguedas's oversimplified representation of cultural conflict in the novel. He argues that the "turupukllay" [bullfight] dramatized in the story, which purports to celebrate the prestige of Andean culture, in fact reflects the power of the dominant class.[34] *Yawar fiesta* represents Arguedas's first attempt to introduce anthropological knowledge, acquired in the 1930s, into his narrative.

The book is an interesting fusion of ethnography and literature. The same was true for Lydia Cabrera's *Cuentos negros de Cuba*. Both writers carved out an appropriate authorial voice early in their careers that later became crucial to their ethnologic and fiction writings. Whereas Cabrera strategically divested herself of authorial presence, Arguedas fashioned a narrative voice that could mediate between cultures and speak personally and authoritatively about the contextual reality.

In his essays and scientific writings, Arguedas communicates a spirit that integrates the writer with the world being represented. The same is true in *Yawar fiesta*, in which detailed descriptions of Puquio set the contextual stage for the celebration. The novel opens with an insider's celebration of the surroundings: "Ver a nuestro pueblo desde arriba, mirar su torre blanca de cal y canto. [...] Y sentarse un rato en la cumbre para cantar de alegría. Eso no pueden hacer los que viven en los pueblos de la costa."[35] [To see our town from above, to see its tower of white stone. . . . And to sit for a while on the summit, and sing with happiness. Those who live on the coast cannot do that.] The narration, figured from within, offers a personal account of detailed sensory experience. The voice of the indigenous narrator has been transformed into written poetry.

What is perhaps most striking about *Yawar fiesta* is its format: the narration only really begins in the third chapter. The first two chapters are essentially ethnographies of Puquio. The narrative voice that emerges in these two chapters is strikingly similar to the one that guides the reader in the introduction to *Canto kechwa*. *Yawar fiesta* is Arguedas's first literary creation to affirm the confluence of artistic narration and scientific investigation, a hallmark of his writings. Fifteen years separated the two publications, during which Arguedas received formal education as an ethnologist. In both, however, his primary source of authority as an eyewitness and informant remains the same.

In Arguedas's first experiment with the genre of the novel, the narrative voice embodies the central protagonist. In order to effectively translate Quechua reality, Arguedas invented a bicultural "author" to shape the context in which the events are fictionally reconstructed. The narrator, much like an ethnographer, is an insider of the Indian community and takes the reader on a visual and auditory tour of Puquio and its surroundings. It is unclear whether the narrator is white or mestizo, but he is clearly bilingual and has access to and full knowledge of the Andean oral world.

Modifications of the literary language attest to the fact that the narrator is capable of penetrating all levels of society. Arguedas found a linguistic synthesis, or mixture, to be the most appropriate literary mode of expression to evoke the spoken language of mestizo characters. In the 1950 article "La novela y el problema de la expresión literaria en el Perú" (The Novel and the Problem of Literary Expression in Peru), Arguedas reflected on the process whereby he manipulated language and bilingual expression in his fiction. The question he addressed was how to contrive the verbal articulations of Indian characters in written form. The answer was more complex than a simple rendering of Spanish/Quechua bilingualism, for Puquio, like many Peruvian cities, was wonderfully multilingual. Arguedas saw Spanish as the predominant mode of literary expression, and his solution in *Yawar fiesta* was to bypass this multilingualism and to create for his characters a language based on Spanish words incorporated into Quechua that Indians would have learned in their own villages.[36]

The spoken language that Arguedas conveys is artificial and comprises part of the fiction; Spanish terms, pronounced by Indians or mestizos, assume Quechua phonetics. Quechua orality is postulated as a transcription of real speech. For instance, "toro" [bull] is pronounced "turu," and when combined with the Quechua term "pukllay," it means "corrida." Arguedas resisted sacrificing the musical tones of Quechua by contriving a melodic literary language, specific to an Indian collectivity. In this linguistic fiction, contamination occurs two ways: just as Spanish words are "Quechuized," frequently used Quechua terms, like "ayllu" [Indian community], are sprinkled throughout the written Spanish narration.[37]

Arguedas's struggle with language was particularly difficult, because he did not want to commit the same errors as other *indigenista* and region-alist novelists. He had previously condemned these writers for making their Indian protagonists speak in ways that portrayed them as uneducated cari-catures. Ultimately, Arguedas became dissatisfied with the fictionalized orality of *Yawar fiesta*. Although he felt that the hybrid language appropri-ately communicated the articulations of an indigenous collectivity, the so-lution was nevertheless superficial. During a seventeen-year hiatus of liter-ary production between *Yawar fiesta* and *Los ríos profundos*, Arguedas worked to resolve this linguistic dilemma.

Arguedas's return to Puquio, during a much later and very different phase of his intellectual life, prompted him to write a monograph about the setting of his first novel. This article, "Puquio, una cultura en proceso de cambio" (Puquio, a Culture in Process of Change), was published in a 1956 issue of Lima's *Revista del Museo Nacional*, edited by Valcárcel. The study resulted from two visits to Puquio, in 1952 and again in 1956. During the second visit, Arguedas was accompanied by François Bourricaud, a French sociologist, and the folklorist and musicologist Josafat Roel Pineda. A com-parison of the article and the opening chapters of *Yawar fiesta* highlight Arguedas's early attempts to invoke anthropology as a form of mediation. The essay begins in much the same way as *Yawar fiesta*—namely, with a guided tour through the various levels of Puquio's social structure. The underlying theme is change, and the implicit point of reference is Arguedas's childhood experiences. Whereas the novelistic insider's voice is character-ized by a sense of nostalgic reminiscence in the literary rendition, the ar-ticle is written with a more scientific and objective tone. The voice of the first-person narrator in the novel shifts to an anthropological collectivity of investigators in the monograph about Puquio. A simultaneous reading of *Yawar fiesta* and the "Puquio" article reveals the mutual nurturing of Arguedas's literary and ethnographic texts.

Upon returning to the scene of his adolescence, Arguedas found that the quiet agricultural town had been transformed into a busy commercial center. He observed that the modernization of Puquio, a process that gained considerable intensity subsequent to the construction of highways connect-ing the province to coastal cities, profoundly affected the transfer of native oral traditions to newer generations. Arguedas was most struck by the changes in the *naturales*, or Indian inhabitants of the area.

In the ethnography of Puquio, Arguedas invoked the traditional myth of Inkarri, particular to the region, as evidence of this upheaval of tradi-tions. The name of the myth reflects a hybridization of the Quechua word "inka" and the Spanish term "rey" [king]. His transcription of the myth, in both Quechua and Spanish, was the first known published version of the foundational Inkarri story. Arguedas's interviews with members of various generations revealed to him that the myth was destined to disappear with the oldest generation of the population, since youths were entirely ignorant of its existence. The article conveys the urgency that informed Arguedas's work as a collector and preserver of traditional oral lore. His project was twofold: he sought to safeguard the songs and stories he identified with a sacred time in his life, his childhood, the only time when he felt secure and happy; and he endeavored to revitalize these traditions by inserting them into a modern context.

Arguedas chose to include three distinct versions of the Inkarri myth in his monograph of Puquio, each one proceeding from a different informant. Like Cabrera, he perceived orality as a culture of versions and variation. The textualization of these myths entailed their separation from a performative event and the creation of a literary oral context. Arguedas's informants, by no means arbitrarily chosen, were conscious of the redemptive task at hand. They were *naturales*, or natives, distressed that the new generation, *qepa ñeqen*, disowned its cultural heritage. In "Puquio," the ethnographer and his informants are allies in their efforts to ward off the perils of modernization.

A brief analysis that follows the transcribed versions of the Inkarri myth offers some hints about Arguedas's fieldwork practices. He conducted some of the interviews with a tape recorder, asking the natives of Puquio to interpret the significance of the myth that cites Inkarri as God, the creator. Implicit in his questioning is a Western point of reference; Arguedas noted that the informants suppressed and altered their answers, or the responses he anticipated, due to the presence of *mistis*, or members of the dominant class. He concluded that, within a few years, the myth would disappear. But he did not predict the end of the indigenous traditions of Puquio. Arguedas optimistically foresaw the infiltration of mestizo culture into urban settings. Although Arguedas seemed to lament the silencing of generations of oral tradition, he clearly perceived his creation of a written textual corpus as a necessary alternative, a productive step that corresponded with Puquio's rapid process of *mestizaje*.

Arguedas concluded the essay by warning that the displacement of indigenous oral culture could lead to a dangerous kind of skeptical individualism. To counter this tendency, the ethnographer invoked the promised return of Inkarri. In one of his most powerful passages, the voice of the anthropological "we" shifts to that of the collective and poetic "we" of *Yawar fiesta*:

Inkarri vuelve, y no podemos menos que sentir temor ante su posible impotencia para ensamblar individualismos quizá irremediablemente desarrollados. Salvo que detenga al Sol, amarrándolo de nuevo, con cinchos de hierro, sobre la cima del Osqonta, y modifique a los hombres; que todo es posible tratándose de una criatura tan sabia y resistente.[38]

[Inkarri returns, and we feel only fear regarding his possible powerlessness to conjoin individualisms, perhaps hopelessly entrenched. But he may stop the sun, fastening it again, with iron bands, to the summit of Osqonta, and change men. Nothing is impossible for such a wise and strong being as he.]

So ends Arguedas's dramatic account of his return to Puquio. Not only was he guided by his scientific interest in the myth as a cultural artifact, but he clearly identified with the messianic message that the legend proclaimed. He aimed to rescue the fading traditions of past generations and to prove that these were vital to a new mestizo reality.

THE NOVELIST'S LITERARY SILENCE

Overall, the years separating the publications of *Yawar fiesta* in 1941 and *Los ríos profundos* in 1958 are crucial to understanding Arguedas's intellectual development as an anthropologist-writer. While some critics have interpreted this literary silence as a "sterile" period in his career, Murra perceptively notes that it was precisely at this time that Arguedas undertook intensive studies at the Universidad de San Marcos, in Valcárcel's newly created Instituto de Etnología.[39] When Arguedas entered the Instituto, he was an accomplished ethnologist by practice; but his subsequent familiarization with theories of anthropology, fieldwork methodology, and analytical techniques shaped his writing significantly. In 1946, he collaborated with anthropologists from Cornell University, and in 1949 he joined José Matos Mar in an investigation of Tupe. Arguedas later recalled the profound impact his professors, including George Kubler and Luis Valcárcel, had on his work. An important addition to this list is Murra, with whom Arguedas studied later, in 1958, and maintained correspondence until his death. Although Arguedas criticized Valcárcel's approach to *indigenista* studies as narrow-minded, the founder of the Instituto was an instrumental motivator of talented students like Arguedas.[40]

When Valcárcel founded the Instituto, Arguedas was pleased to learn that he could earn his degree, which had been virtually completed since the late 1930s. As a student of ethnology he represented a unique case. How would the young ethnologist reconcile his approach to other cultures, one that depended primarily on personal experience, with the theoretical boundaries required by formal study? Carmen María Pinilla has managed to trace some of the theorists whom Arguedas most likely encountered at San Marcos. Of particular significance were Arguedas's studies with Jorge Muelle, a professor of ethnology and an expert on European culture, particularly the philosophies of Wilhelm Dilthey. Pinilla's insights into Arguedas's interactions with Muelle led her to conclude that Dilthey greatly influenced young ethnologists at San Marcos like Arguedas.[41]

Dilthey's theories must have been quite attractive to the young writer for whom experience was already a primary means of interpretation. The same was true, as we have seen, in Lydia Cabrera's assessment of her role as a participant-observer, sharing what Dilthey terms a "common sphere" with her informants. Arguedas's early essays in *La Prensa* illustrated that his ability to comprehend others relied heavily on his coexistence in their experiential world. According to Dilthey, "Understanding of other people and their expressions is developed on the basis of experience and self-understanding and the constant interaction between them."[42] By re-creating experience, Arguedas's writings assumed a personal and autobiographical tone.

The intellectual projects that prompted him to return to Puquio in the 1950s clearly demonstrate his dual intentions: he sought to acquire ethnographic knowledge and self-knowledge. Dilthey's ideas influenced Arguedas as both a novelist and an ethnographer. The German philosopher taught him that all interpretive writing, including poetry, entails an explanation of life. For Dilthey, the strength of poetry is its direct and unmediated expression of life. Although anthropological reflection does the same, it is far more systematic. The German's notions of interpretation validated Arguedas's unavoidable fusion of personal experience and scientific exegesis, and inspired him to invoke ethnography in his efforts to inscribe and preserve Quechua orality.

During the 1940s, Arguedas continued to collect, translate, and edit Andean folklore and to collaborate with *La Prensa*. Whereas his early articles in *La Prensa* had a tone of personal reminiscence, a more scientific approach appears in his later publications. In 1947, Arguedas joined the Ministry of Public Education as general curator of folklore, and worked with Francisco Izquierdo Ríos, head of the division of folklore and popular art. The two folklorists conducted the first national poll of teachers, which resulted in the publication of *Mitos, leyendas y cuentos peruanos* (Peruvian Myths, Legends, and Stories). In response to deficiencies in previous investigations, the study was based on the premise that folklore provides a useful scientific tool for understanding the evolutionary processes of cultures.

The editors were convinced that their informants, literate teachers in Peru's primary and secondary schools, would be meticulous and objective compilers of myths, stories, and legends. Despite the complex process of mediation and filtering, Arguedas assures the reader of the excerpts' authenticity. Those who responded to the questionnaire were instructed to preserve the original purity of the stories by avoiding elaboration. The project exemplifies Arguedas's consistent efforts to legitimize Andean folklore by inserting it into Western studies. It seems that Arguedas perceived the marriage of folklore and science, rather than the myths and legends themselves, to be the overriding objective of *Mitos, leyendas y cuentos peruanos*.[43]

In 1951, Arguedas traveled to La Paz, Bolivia, where he represented Peru at the Conference of Experts in Indigenous Work. He found the capital city awe-inspiring, and compared La Paz to Cuzco, the spiritual center of the Inca nation. His reactions to the scenery and architecture of La Paz are echoed in his 1947 monograph of Cuzco, and later in Ernesto's ramblings through the city streets in *Los ríos profundos*. For Arguedas, ancient cities possessed profound symbolic importance; they offered productive examples of a melting pot of Western and Amerindian cultures.

Although Arguedas did not produce a literary work after *Yawar fiesta* until 1954, when a short piece entitled *Diamantes y pedernales* (Diamonds and Flint) appeared, he continued to use his expository writings to explore the communication between the cultures of Peru. One technique was to emphasize the beauty and integrity made possible by a melding of cultures. In "El Ollantay: Lo autóctono y lo occidental en el estilo de los dramas coloniales quechuas" (Ollantay: The Autochthonous and the Occidental in the Style of Colonial Quechua Dramas), a 1952 article that has received little critical attention, Arguedas ingenuously tackled the cross-cultural dilemma. The article responded to the publication of translations of *Ollantay* and *Usca Paucar*, two Quechua dramas from the colonial period.

"El Ollantay" opens with an analysis of the shortcomings of Quechua literary studies. Arguedas felt that a translator who was merely a historian or linguist lacked the ability to capture the complex nuances that permeate a poet's expression of his world. He noted that this was especially true of Quechua writings, composed in a language possessing a very limited written literary tradition. Because Quechua linguistic studies were omitted from university curricula, Arguedas pointed out, only historians and archaeologists studied Quechua. This preliminary argument is also a justification for Arguedas's own analysis, which benefited from both science and poetics.

Although Arguedas pronounced his respect for the work of J. M. B. Farfán Ayerbe, the translator of *Ollantay*, he criticized the translation for being too literary. Arguedas recognized that the linguist was well versed in the native languages of the Quechua region, but implied that he lacked personal knowledge of the Quechua mind.

The second part of the article is dedicated to a close reading of some excerpts from *Ollantay*. Arguedas's own translations of the text are printed in juxtaposition with Farfán's. Arguedas distanced himself from linguists like Farfán by insisting on his own status as an insider, emphasizing his "intimate and very personal knowledge" of both the ancient and present-day Peruvian man.[44] Arguedas argued for a distinction between scholarly Quechua poetry and folkloric poetry, suggesting that the latter expresses a conception of the world that is magical and cosmic. He asserted that writers of colonial Quechua literature, in contrast, were influenced by European thinking, though their profound understanding of Quechua enabled them to penetrate the aesthetics of the Andean natural world. Arguedas acknowledged that a cursory reading of the play could lead one to categorize it as pure Quechua literature. After close analysis of the linguistic subtleties of *Ollantay*, however, he concluded that the drama was composed in a highly occidental style. Rather than suppress the Western elements, as Father Lira did in his translations, Arguedas heralded their presence in *Ollantay* as evidence of the great potential for a hybridized literature. Arguedas approached the sphere of Western culture as if he were at once native and foreign to it. He demonstrated the potential for Quechua literature by placing it on a par with European poetry, while simultaneously introducing a new kind of hybridized literary production, which he was privileged to compose.

LOS RÍOS PROFUNDOS: AN ARCHAEOLOGY OF THE ORAL

During the 1950s and 1960s, Arguedas became adept at drawing from science and fiction in his writing. His ethnographies are literary insofar as they are embedded with layers of discourse that contain a plurality of voices, including the voice of the subject. Arguedas's fictions debunk Western literary models by revealing the literariness of anthropology.[45] His greatest narrative achievement in this regard was his celebrated novel, *Los ríos profundos*. The novel took shape over more than fifteen years, while Arguedas was publishing prolifically as an ethnographer. In the years between the publications of *Yawar fiesta* and *Los ríos profundos*, when Arguedas was honing his fieldwork methods, his literary and ethnographic efforts complemented each other completely. In both cases, textual production entailed the author/ethnographer's use of anthropological discourse to gain knowledge of the Andean traditions that constituted an important part of his identity.

Arguedas began to write the novel, which was originally conceived as an adventure tale, as early as 1942 or 1943, just after the publication of *Yawar fiesta*. The project lay dormant for a number of years. Then, in the late 1940s, upon traveling to Huancayo to do a study for the Instituto de Estudios Etnológicos, Arguedas was inspired to once again pick up the novel.

The eloquent style of *Los ríos profundos* re-creates the natural and musical world of the Andes. The historical context of the novel is significantly broader than that of his previous literary creations: we witness the interaction of all of the sierra's social groups—*colonos* (Indian farmers) and *caciques* (local rulers), wandering musicians, priests, *chicheras* (barmaids), soldiers, and mestizos, both poor and middle-class. As in *Agua*, Arguedas employed the figure of the child narrator-protagonist to express the profound communication between the protagonist and his surroundings. Ernesto, now a young boy of fourteen, possesses a remarkable memory. In *Los ríos profundos*, Arguedas adapted the *Bildungsroman* to the Andean case; the young protagonist, a native speaker of Quechua, is thrust into an unfriendly Spanish-speaking world.[46] The novel is foremost an autobiography that narrates in first person Ernesto's adventures and trials. The young protagonist, like the author, lived among Indians in his early childhood and learned Quechua before being schooled in Spanish.

The first phase of Ernesto's ramblings takes place in Cuzco, the ancient center of the Inca civilization. He and his father arrive by train and make their way to the hacienda of the Viejo, Ernesto's wealthy and authoritarian uncle. The young boy quickly runs off to explore the secrets of the city. His excursion is significant for two reasons: Arguedas made a similar journey with his own father at a young age; and in 1947 he composed a detailed account of the city's sights and sounds in his earlier essay entitled "Cusco." The essay is a vital example of the circularity and unity of Arguedas's intellectual work. Its publication coincided with his renewed efforts to compose his second novel. Arguedas's expository description of Cuzco begins in much the same way as Ernesto's meditations on the architectural wonders of the Inca city:

> En sus muros se puede contemplar el arte de construir de todas las edades: la arquitectura ciclópea, la piedra gigantesca dominada por el hombre prehistórico; muros de elementos irregulares ordenados por quienes

conocían el poder de unir en superficies compactas la piedra caótica y primitiva. [...] Los conquistadores cristianos levantaron los arcos y columnas de sus moradas y templos sobre las aceradas murallas indias. Y de este modo, el Cusco se convirtió en un monumento arqueológico e histórico cuyo mágico semblante perturba y conmueve, porque contiene el lenguaje humano de todos los tiempos en su forma más perdurable y universal: la arquitectura.[47]

[In its walls one can contemplate the ancient art of mortarless stone construction on a monumental scale, enormous stones dominated by prehistoric man. Here are walls built by men who mastered the art of assembling primitive, chaotic, and asymmetrical parts into regular and powerful surfaces. . . . The Christian conquerors raised arches and columns for their dwellings and temples on top of the solid Indian walls. Thus, Cuzco was transformed into an archaeological and historic monument whose magical appearance moves and disturbs, because it invokes the timeless, most enduring, and universal human idiom: architecture.]

For Arguedas, architecture, like music, was an ideal metaphor for the simultaneous expression of cultures. Ernesto's encounter with the walls of Cuzco is similarly poetic; the ancient stones inspire him to recall the Quechua songs of his childhood: "Eran más grandes y extrañas de cuanto había imaginado las piedras del muro incaico; bullían bajo el segundo piso encalado que por el lado de la calle angosta, era ciego. Me acordé, entonces, de las canciones quechuas que repiten una frase patética constante: '*yawar mayu*', río de sangre. [...]"[48] [The stones of the Inca wall were larger and stranger than I had imagined; they seemed to be bubbling up beneath the whitewashed second story, which had no windows on the side facing the narrow street. Then I remembered the Quechua songs that continually repeat one pathetic phrase: *yawar mayu,* "bloody river." . . .][49] Just as the *wayno* preserved the oral memory of generations of Andean peoples, the walls of Cuzco contained visible traces of past cultures.

The overlapping of music with architectural and natural beauty is emblematic of Arguedas's writings; and the image of the palimpsest evokes the possibility of an indestructible memory. Culture, in his estimation, is a cumulative process whereby past forms are inscribed in the memory of a community. In his writings, Arguedas attempted to re-create this dynamic process by textualizing distinct, and at times opposing, layers of oral discourse. *Los ríos profundos* is his most accomplished literary creation in this regard; he eloquently textualized the heterogeneous cultures of Peru. The interplay of voices and songs essentially evokes an oral context that allows one to hear songs, poems, and stories of Quechua oral tradition.

The essay "Cusco" and the opening chapter of *Los ríos profundos* take the reader on a similar tour of the layers of history present in the ancient city. In both, the narrator serves as a mediator or guide who selects and brings together the sights and sounds of his surroundings. Each visual image inspires the narrator-protagonist of the novel to recall the natural habitat of the town where he was nurtured. The natural images of his recollection are saturated with sounds and songs, and the excursion takes on a sonorous quality. Throughout the novel, music and natural images are intertwined to evoke the oral tradition of the Andean world.

Angel Rama and Julio Ortega have perceived an interplay of three distinct, yet overlapping, narrators: Ernesto as an adult dominates the narration with a retrospective look at his adolescent years; Ernesto, a young boy of fourteen, is a witness to the events he experiences; and a third, more removed and academic voice intervenes to contribute ethnographic commentary.[50] This final voice is the most striking with regard to the confluence of Arguedas's anthropological and literary works. The constant interplay of narrative voices is indicative of the contradiction Arguedas sensed between the two discourses and the overall disharmony at the core of his nation, an unrest he sought to rectify.

Each of the narrators is bilingual. In contrast to Arguedas's previous works of fiction, the narrator translates almost all of the Quechua-speakers' articulations into Spanish. Only a few Quechua terms or phrases are expressed in the original language, followed by translations in parentheses or footnotes. In the case of interpolated songs, Arguedas has included Spanish translations with the Quechua verses, thereby preserving the original lyrics while making them readable for a Western public. Arguedas's solution to the linguistic dilemma that frustrated him in his earlier writings was his conscious stylistic decision to compose the text in Andeanized Spanish, a fictitious literary language. *Los ríos profundos* is Arguedas's most successful attempt to manipulate diverse discourses to convey the dissonances he perceived at the center of Peruvian society.

Mikhail Bakhtin has emphasized that the novel, in general terms, can be seen as a plurality of "social speech types"—even of languages—and of individual voices that are artistically organized: "[T]his internal stratification present in every language at any given moment of its historical existence is the indispensable prerequisite for the novel as a genre."[51] His notion of "heteroglossia" assumes that these diverse languages and speech types intersect with one another, thereby giving meaning to utterances and their contexts. Bakhtin rightly sees the mixing of languages and discourses as an artistic device. He emphasizes that novelistic hybridization represents an intentional stylistic activity. In *Los ríos profundos*, Arguedas constructs a fictional relationship between voice and writing by creating an effect of Andean orality. He strove to evoke in writing the encounter between Peru's Quechua-speaking and Hispanic worlds. Arguedas invoked utterances in Quechua to express untranslatable details of the sierra, and to prove his conviction that Quechua is uniquely linked to the natural realm.

In *Los ríos profundos* Arguedas conveys oral discourse in writing to portray a boy's coming-of-age in Peru. On the most basic level, the *Bildungsroman* is an ideal literary form to verbalize one's story. Most of the language in the text is figured as speech, and it seems that the narrator is speaking to us directly, rather than writing his recollections. But Arguedas's strategies for representing the oral go beyond a self-reconstruction that appeals to the reader as listener. His principal narrator serves as a focal point where disparate voices of Peru's heterogeneous culture assemble and overlap.

Arguedas employs a stylistic reminiscent of the oral to re-create the sonorous aspects of his version of Peru: voices, stories, and songs permeate each chapter, resulting in a rhythmic literary composition. Songs and traditional musical instruments, rather than visual images, convey the overriding ideology of the book. Almost every chapter ends with a meditation on nature's harmonious coexistence with man. Memory, nature, sound, and Ernesto's native Quechua are linked in a realm that transcends the violent world where the young boy struggles to survive. The proliferation of sonorous imagery in *Los ríos profundos* demonstrates Arguedas's vision that orality and, more specifically, oral cultures' means of preserving and transmitting knowledge could be a viable alternative to Western literate modes of thinking.

The first chapter of *Los ríos profundos* overflows with symbols of *mestizaje*: colonial structures built by indigenous artisans, *waynos*, and other songs with intermingling voices. The reader, cast as a traveler, follows the narrator-protagonist on a guided tour of the ancient streets of Cuzco. This traveler is shaken from silence to take in the sounds resonating from the cathedral's facade: "En el silencio, las torres y el atrio repetían la menor resonancia, igual que las montañas de roca que orillan los lagos helados. La roca devuelve profundamente el grito de los patos o la voz humana. Ese eco es difuso y parece que naciera del propio pecho del viajero, atento, oprimido por el silencio."[52] [In the silence, the towers and the terrace echoed the smallest sound, like the rocky mountains that border the icy lakes. The rocks send back deep echoes of the cry of the ducks or of the human voice. The echo is diffused, and seems to spring from the very breast of the traveler, who is alert to the silence and oppressed by it.].[53] At this point, the reader is urged to listen to the rich overlapping voices of the textuality.

Arguedas demonstrates his conviction that language is primarily sound and, by extension, that writing should be heard. He achieves the most "oral" moments by constructing an intricate fabric of symbols and natural images that resound throughout the text. *Los ríos profundos*, a book that took shape over Arguedas's most prolific years as an ethnologist, can be read as an archaeology of the oral.

The culminating image of the first chapter is that of the songs emanating from the bell of the María Angola. The María Angola is a symbol of syncretism: the legend surrounding it represents a fusion of Christianity and Cuzco's oral tradition. Not surprisingly, the María Angola is also the central and most poetic image of the introduction to the essay "Cusco," entitled "El paisaje y las leyendas de la fundación: El Cusco preincaico" (The Countryside and the Legends of Foundation: Pre-Inca Cuzco). The two passages describing the melodies ringing from the legendary bell of the cathedral of Cuzco are virtually interchangeable. In the essay, Arguedas invokes the mythic voice of the bell and links it to the sounds of nature:

> Y antes del alba, el último toque de la campana legendaria de la catedral latina, la voz de la "María Angola," domina el horizonte del Cusco; llega a los montes lejanos, a las llanuras del valle; se difunde en la ciudad como el agua más clara de los grandes ríos; y ya sea nublada y lóbrega la noche, o clara y resplandeciente de estrellas, el sonido de esta campana inspira al visitante, le comunica todo el poder evocador de la gran ciudad, su mágica e ilimitada profundidad estética. [...][54]

> [And before dawn, the final chime of the Latin cathedral's legendary bell, the voice of "María Angola," dominates Cuzco's horizons. It reaches the distant mountains and fills the valleys; it diffuses in the city like the clear water of powerful rivers. Whether the night is dark and cloudy or clear and resplendent with stars, the sound of the bell inspires the visitor and conveys all of this great city's evocative power, its magical and limitless aesthetic profundity. . . .]

The sound waves disseminating from the tolling bell have an equally powerful impact on Ernesto. He imagines that they surge across the countryside, turning the towers, patios, and walls of the ancient city of Cuzco into gold. The ringing of the bell signals a pause in the narrator's linear retelling of events, and the reader witnesses a crescendo of rich music: "Yo sabía que la voz de la campana llegaba a cinco leguas de distancia. Creí que estallaría en la plaza. Pero surgía lentamente, a intervalos suficientes; y el canto se acrecentaba, atravesaba los elementos; y todo se convertía en esa música cuzqueña, que abría las puertas de la memoria."[55] [I knew the voice of the bell carried a distance of five leagues. I thought the plaza would explode with sound. But the vibrations expanded slowly, at spaced intervals—growing stronger, piercing the elements, transmuting everything into that Cuzco music that opened the doors of memory.][56] Thus, a poetic representation of the oral eclipses and silences the narrative discourse. The description itself is figured to imitate the progressive heightening of the bell's toll.

The María Angola's song prompts Ernesto to recollect the mentors of his childhood, Don Maywa and Don Victo Pusa. Much of the imagery in the novel traces an implicit connection between music, memory, and nature. By incorporating the legend of the María Angola, Arguedas reinvented a piece of Andean lore by inserting it into a new context. Arguedas's remarkable descriptions of Cuzco, in both the essay and the novel, reflect his conception of an alternative to Western modernity made possible by a communion between nature and the Andean peoples. For him, orality transcended the dangers of skeptical individuality by offering both a way of thinking about a collective future and a way to preserve the integrity of past generations.

Arguedas designates sound as a primary organizing element of the narrative by ending the first three chapters in song. The first chapter closes with Ernesto's reflections on the Apurímac, whose name denotes "God who speaks." Arguedas again invokes the motif of the traveler who listens to the voice of the sacred river, one of the "deep rivers" of the title:

> El viajero oriundo de las tierras frías se acerca al río, aturdido, febril, con las venas hinchadas. La voz del río aumenta; no ensordece, exalta. A los niños los cautiva, les infunde presentimientos de mundos desconocidos. [...] La corriente marcha como a paso de caballos, de grandes caballos cerriles. —*¡Apurímac mayu! ¡Apurímac mayu!*–repiten los niños de habla quechua, con ternura y algo de espanto.[57]

> [The traveler from the cold highlands nears the river in a state of confusion, feverish, with swollen veins. The voice of the river grows louder, but doesn't become deafening; instead, it makes one feel excited. It charms children, giving them intimations of unknown worlds. . . . The current rushes down as though keeping time with the hoofbeats of horses, of great wild horses. "Apurímac mayu! Apurímac mayu!" the Quechua-speaking children repeat with tenderness and a touch of fear.][58]

The voice of the powerful river intensifies as the traveler nears its source. Arguedas re-creates the melodic current with rhythmic, poetic language. The description culminates with a sentence replete with alliteration, evoking a repetitive hoofbeat of untamed horses that brings to mind the pounding waters. Arguedas left the final cries of the children untranslated, demonstrating his conviction that certain Quechuisms were irrevocably infused with the material they signified.

William Rowe has argued that in Arguedas's literary writings sound takes on a magical quality, and music furnishes a mode of thinking that represents a utopian alternative to Western reasoning. Although Rowe's argument about Arguedas's invention of a new poetics is well-founded, his conception of orality is idealistic. He exaggerates the evanescent nature of oral culture by asserting that sound possesses an intrinsically magical quality and thereby evokes the "soul" of a signified object.[59] In *Los ríos profundos*, Arguedas indeed constructs an ideological hierarchy that privileges sound and orally transmitted knowledge. He articulated this conceit in his essay "Ollantay," when he affirmed that stories and parables comprised the level closest to pure indigenous literature.[60] Arguedas, however, understood that Quechua oral culture did not exist in a pristine and utopian state. By inscribing Andean voices, he aimed to establish oral culture as an important source of contemporary Peruvian national identity.

One way Arguedas attributes priority to the oral is by deeming certain terms untranslatable. For example, Ernesto envisions the voice of the bell as transcending the ancient city, penetrating the mountain lakes, and transforming the ancient creatures.[61] For Arguedas, spoken Quechua possessed a magical presence and served as a metaphor for purity and truth. In the article "El Ollantay" he explained his theories regarding orality, arguing that a traditional song in Quechua not only preserves the form of the song with greater purity, but its very content is much closer to authentic Quechua songs.[62] In all of his writing, Arguedas struggled to rewrite the oral and to thereby achieve a faithful mimesis of spoken discourse. By creating a rhetorical effect of orality, Arguedas simultaneously used Western literary discourse to dismantle it.

Arguedas intended that readers perceive an intrinsic link between Quechua orality and authentic cultural expression. But assumptions underlying this notion reflect a logocentric bias that favors speech over writing. Herein lies the complexity involved in representing orality in written discourse. Arguedas, like Lydia Cabrera, was inescapably bound to writing, even as he sought to celebrate the dignity of origins and truth found in the realm of speaking. The most significant achievement of each writer was to transform Western literary tradition by illustrating the poetic capacity of non-Western forms of discourse.

An interesting way to look at the musical moments in Arguedas's writings, and particularly those found in *Los ríos profundos*, is to contemplate the ways the author contrived oral discourse and wove it into his narrative. For Arguedas, orality was not an academic study, but a way of being. Critics have at times misrepresented Arguedas's fictions by casting them as poetic returns to a utopian past in which music and legends were the primary modes of tribal knowledge. Arguedas's literary and ethnographic writings are about Peru's present and future. Arguedas was deeply troubled by the social discrimination against Andean peoples in contemporary Peru, and it was this concern that shaped his treatment of oral culture in writing. His ability to fabricate perfect musical moments stemmed from his rigorous practice as a musicologist and his desire to carve out a space in Western discourse for the elements of Andean culture that he feared would disappear.

The episode when Ernesto composes a love letter destined for Salvinia represents a tour de force of orally infused writing. Before putting pen to paper, Ernesto contemplates the recipient of the letter, concluding that he must choose the finest Spanish words for his letter to be granted access to the literate, upper-class world of the adored one. He compares the task of writing to a battle and begins, "Usted es la dueña de mi alma, adorada niña" [You are the mistress of my soul, dear girl], only to drop his pen in desperation after several lines of conventional lyric poetry. Ernesto asks himself how he might write differently to young indigenous girls of his past: "'Si yo pudiera escribirles, mi amor brotaría como un río cristalino; mi carta podría ser como un canto que va por los cielos y llega a su destino.' ¡Escribir! Escribir para ellas era inútil, inservible. '¡Anda; espéralas en los caminos, y canta!'" ["If I could write to them my love would flow like a clear river; my letter could be like a song that goes through the sky to reach its destination." Writing! Writing for them was useless, futile. "Go; wait for them on the roads and sing!"]

The revised version of the letter offers a dramatic counterpoint to the rigid prose of the first letter:

> *"Uyriy chay k'atik'niki siwar k'entita..."*
> "Escucha al picaflor esmeralda que te sigue; te ha de hablar de mí; no seas cruel, escúchale. Lleva fatigadas las pequeñas alas, no podrá volar más, detente ya. Está cerca la piedra blanca donde descansan los viajeros, espera allí y escúchale; oye su llanto; es sólo el mensajero de mi joven corazón, te ha de hablar de mí. Oye, hermosa, tus ojos como estrellas grandes, bella flor, no huyas más, detente! Una orden de los cielos te traigo: ¡te mandan ser mi tierna amante [...]!"[63]

> ["*Uyariy chay k'atik'niki siwar k'entita . . .*"
> "Listen to the emerald hummingbird who follows you; he shall speak to you of me; do not be cruel, hear him. His little wings are tired, he can fly no

farther; pause a moment. The white stone where the travelers rest is nearby; wait there and listen to him; hear his sobs; he is only the messenger of my young heart; he shall speak to you of me. Listen, my lovely one, your eyes are like large stars; beautiful flower, do not flee any more, halt! An order from the heavens I bring you; they command you to be my tender lover . . . !"][64]

Whereas the first letter is the product of a struggle to write in formal Spanish, the revised version is cast as a textualized performance. It summons the reader to hear, not merely read, the voice of the young poet. The episode is symbolic of Arguedas's own writing process. The creative poetics of Quechua voices is celebrated as the most sublime form of literary expression, one that should replace stilted Western forms of romantic poetry. The words of the second letter are expressed informally as a song or performance that is meant to be heard rather than read. The ellipses in the text mimic the pauses that the voice of a singer might make. The songwriter calls out many times for the young girl to listen and to partake in the song. Although the opening exhortation is untranslated, we can assume that it urges the girl to listen to the song of the emerald hummingbird. The episode illustrates the thesis Arguedas frequently formulated in his expository writings: writing infused with Quechua orality surpassed Western poetics as a means of evoking the nuances of Peruvian reality.

In *Los ríos profundos* and the essays and articles that coincided with its creation, the voices of the creative writer and the scientific ethnographer overlap. The sixth chapter of the novel is the most dramatic example of Arguedas's creative stratification of distinct discourses. The title, "Zumbayllu," one of two Quechua chapter titles in the book, denotes a symbol of *mestizo* culture. The term "zumbayllu" [little top], like "yawar fiesta," is a hybrid of Spanish and Quechua: it synthesizes an onomatopoeic Spanish verb, "zumbar" [to hum] with a Quechua onomatopoeia "yllu." The first portion of the chapter explains this linguistic phenomenon. The voice of the narrator-protagonist is replaced by the objective voice of the anthropologist-narrator. Arguedas clearly felt that an etymological explanation would help the reader comprehend the poetic significance of the term. This early part of the chapter repeats almost verbatim an article entitled "Acerca del intenso significado de dos voces quechuas" (Concerning the Profound Meaning of Two Quechua Words) that was published in *La Prensa* more than ten years prior to *Los ríos profundos*.

Excluding minor alterations, the underlying thesis in both the article and the novel is the same.[65] Arguedas analyzed in great detail a concept that subtends all of his writings on Quechua phonetics: the epistemological role played by onomatopoeic terms. He set aside space in the novel to move the reader through a detailed process from the signifier to the signified. Both texts begin in the same way, explaining that the Quechua ending "yllu" is onomatopoeic, representing the music produced by small wings in flight.[66] The pages that follow reflect on examples of the suffix "yllu," hybridized with numerous Quechua terms. The expository portion of the chapter serves as a glossary for untranslated language that surfaces later in the novel. For Arguedas, Quechua onomatopoeia transcended a simple imitation of sounds and embraced an entire system of signification linking a sign to an object. Arguedas believed that onomatopoeic language in Quechua exemplified a particularly unmediated representation of life.[67] The *zumbayllu* symbolizes for Ernesto a cosmic link to the past and a means for escaping the harsh realities of the present. But more significantly, it is the most pervasive example of Arguedas's endeavor to textualize oral discourse.

Curiously, Arguedas attempted a descriptive translation of "zumbayllu," whereas in other instances he regarded certain Quechuisms as untranslatable. By incorporating the explanation of the onomatopoeic properties of "yllu" into the text, and not making it part of a footnote, Arguedas acknowledged a readership unaware of the linguistic properties of Quechua. The trappings of the methods for reading the novel are inscribed within the text itself. The term "zumbayllu" only acquires the magical power to connect sound and sign after it has been explained as doing just that. In this way, the circularity and mutual influencing in so many of Arguedas's ethnographic and literary texts take on new meaning. By including an almost verbatim version of the 1948 article in his novel, Arguedas demonstrated that, for him, anthropological mediation was inherent in the process of creating a narrational context embedded with orality.

After the four-page introductory portion of the chapter, the narrator signals a return to the story line with one of the most oral of literary tropes, an interjection. *¡Zumbayllu!* is not proclaimed by Ernesto, nor is it set apart from the text by quotations; rather, it seems to be a dramatic exclamation made by the narrator himself. As the boys scramble to the school patio repeating the name of the magical spinning toy, Ernesto follows with great curiosity. Intrigued by the name of the enchanted object, he recalls similar words, like *tankayllu* and *pinkuyllus*, the same utterances described by the narrator-ethnographer in the first part of the chapter. The *zumbayllu* transcends boundaries of time and space, possessing a power that links all beings in a collective harmony. A cosmic force emanates from the spinning top in the form of resonating sound. The object is, foremost, sound materialized; it unchains a multitude of oral memories. Before he sees the *zumbayllu*, Ernesto is charmed by its melodious song:

Yo no pude ver el pequeño trompo ni la forma cómo Antero lo encordelaba.
[...] Luego escuché un canto delgado [...] el canto del *zumbayllu* se
propagó con una claridad extraña; parecía tener agudo filo. Todo el aire
debía estar henchido de esa voz delgada; y toda la tierra, ese piso arenoso
del que parecía brotar.
—!*Zumbayllu, zumbayllu!*[68]

[I couldn't see the little top, nor how Antero wound it. . . . Then I heard a
delicate humming sound . . . the song of the *zumbayllu* was diffused with a
strange clarity; it seemed to have a sharp edge. All the air must have been
filled with its delicate voice, and all the earth, that sandy ground from which
it seemed to have sprung.
   Zumbayllu, zumbayllu!][69]

The song of the *zumbayllu*, in contrast to a human voice or a bird's song,
does not disperse with the wind. It pours out with intensity, subsuming its
surroundings like a swarming chorus of *tankayllus*. The repetition of the
top's captivating name is ambiguous; it is unclear whether *¡Zumbayllu,
zumbayllu!* alludes to a re-creation of the music radiating from the spinning motion or to Ernesto's own exclamation. Arguedas effectively communicates the oral properties of the emblematic object by positioning the
reader with Ernesto, allowing both to listen to the top for the first time.
   The *zumbayllu*, an embodiment of the oral in the text, illustrates
Arguedas's conviction that voice is a metaphor for origins and truth. When
Ernesto launches the humming top, he is empowered and transported to a
natural realm where he feels safe from the hostilities of the school patio.
The ability of the *zumbayllu* to transcend evil and to communicate beyond
the barriers of the city reflects Arguedas's belief in the unifying powers of
music. Ernesto uses his magical toy to contact his father and to send covert
messages to Doña Felipa.
   In "Yawar mayu," the tenth chapter, the battle between the soldiers and
the Andean townspeople is played out, in part, as a musical conflict.
Arguedas creatively represents two opposing styles of music in writing,
and the chapter is constructed as a dialogue between contrasting forms of
musical expression. Rather than explicitly describe the songs of the military bands, Arguedas's cacophonous prose re-creates the visual and mechanical aspects of the harsh melodies: "Los clarinetes negros y sus piezas
de metal, tan intrincadas, nos cautivaron; yo miraba funcionar los delgados
brazos de plata que movían los tapones, cómo descubrían y cerraban los
huecos del instrumento, cómo dejaban escapar el aire y los sonidos tan
distintos."[70] [We were intrigued by the black clarinets with their intricate
metal parts; I watched the functioning of the thin silver arms that moved

the stops, how they opened and closed the holes of the instrument, how they let out the air to make such unusual sounds.][71] He offers a purely functional and impersonal representation of Western music. In striking contrast is the intensely moving song of a *kimichu*, a roving Andean musician, who enchants listeners with his penetrating voice and crystalline song.

The central portion of the chapter takes place in Doña Felipa's bar and depicts the performances of the *kimichu* and of a talented musician, Oblitas. Arguedas exalts the Andean songs by juxtaposing them with the harsh tonalities of the marching band. After listening to the heroic yet mournful song of the singer, Ernesto reflects, "Con una música de éstas puede el hombre llorar hasta consumirse, hasta desaparecer, pero podría igualmente luchar contra una legión de cóndores y de leones o contra los monstruos que se dice habitan en el fondo de los lagos de altura y en las faldas llenas de sobras de las montañas."[72] [With music such as this a man could weep until he was completely consumed, until he vanished, or could just as easily do battle with a legion of condors and pumas, or with the monsters that are said to inhabit the depths of the highland lakes and the shadowy mountain slopes.][73] The traditional songs, most often *waynos*, are intricately woven into the text and achieve a central function in the book. They indicate moments of profound artistic reflection, confirming Arguedas's belief in the ideological power of music and orality.

Los ríos profundos attempts to inscribe oral Quechua culture into novelistic discourse by using the philological instruments made available by ethnography and linguistics.[74] Anthropology was an effective mediating element for Arguedas in his quest to defend Andean culture and incorporate it into Western literary discourse. Arguedas's solution to the challenge of representing the linguistic diversity that surrounded him was to create an objective and academic narrative voice, well versed in the subtleties of Quechua, to convey Andean traditions from an ethnographic point of view. His inventive poetics, an amalgamation of music, anthropology, and autobiography, crystallized in this 1958 novel, which claimed Lima's national prize, Fomento a la Cultura Ricardo Palma, in 1959 and was a finalist for the 1963 William Faulkner Prize, awarded in the United States. It has since been translated into several languages and has inspired worldwide critical attention.

PERU AND BEYOND

In the 1960s, Arguedas continued to publish both literary and ethnologic pieces prolifically. Murra, who corresponded with Arguedas faithfully until the author's death, insists on the significance of his prolonged stays in Santiago, Chile, where he conceived the bulk of his artistic work, including *Los ríos profundos*, *Todas las sangres* (Men of All Bloods), *El zorro de arriba y el zorro de abajo* (*The Fox from Up Above and the Fox from Down Below*), as well as some short stories.[75] The two anthropologists collaborated frequently during the final decade of Arguedas's life, editing oral texts, advocating the use of Quechua in radio programs, and attending numerous professional congresses together. Arguedas's self-imposed exile allowed him to recuperate from prolonged psychological illness with the aid of his psychoanalyst, Dr. Lola Hoffmann. In Chile, Arguedas ended his marriage with Celia Bustamante and became romantically involved with Sybila Arredondo. As in Cabrera's case, distance and displacement broadened his conception of context; Arguedas retreated into the comfortable foreignness of an alien world and confidently took up his creative pen.

Arguedas became more aware of literary circles outside of his native country when, in 1958, a UNESCO grant enabled him to travel to Europe for research purposes. He was particularly stirred by the beauty of Paris and wrote a laudatory article that appeared in a Sunday supplement to *El Comercio*. The article is an intriguing complement to *Los ríos profundos*, published in the same year. In "París y la patria" (Paris and the Homeland), Arguedas fashioned himself as a bicultural subject and extolled the positive aspects of Western culture. He claimed that upon setting foot in the capital of the Western world, he felt so comfortable that he yearned to speak his native Quechua with French passersby. Arguedas attempted to portray examples of "Europeanization" in a positive light, arguing that colonized nations had the good fortune of benefiting from Western culture introduced by a European elite.[76] Arguedas's exposure to countries outside of Peru and his growing knowledge of his designated reader shaped his discourse significantly. After the enthusiastic reception of *Los ríos profundos*, Arguedas began to perceive himself as the inventor of a new type of art. His description of Paris was a small part of an overall campaign to create space for a kind of *neoindigenista* writing that would transcend national boundaries and unite the literatures of the Americas.

Perhaps Arguedas's most striking article in this regard was his "Reflexiones peruanas sobre un narrador mexicano" (Peruvian Reflections concerning a Mexican Writer), published in *El Comercio* in 1964. The article was one of his few critical meditations on literature composed outside of the Andes. Arguedas's travels in Mexico had a profound impact on his plans to effect change in his native country. Arguedas was impressed by the strong connection between the Mexican state and culture. He saw the possibility of using state power to promote a kind of political culture that might mitigate conflict between the Quechua-speaking and Spanish-speaking worlds.[77] Arguedas's enthusiasm for Juan Rulfo's prose is not surprising, since Rulfo, who grew up in Jalisco, was also deeply influenced by his rural surroundings. Arguedas marveled at Rulfo's ability to imbue his narrative with sonorous traces of Mexican rural life.

After reading *El llano en llamas* (*The Burning Plain and Other Stories*) and *Pedro Páramo*, Arguedas concluded that the Mexican mestizo and the Andean mestizo were remarkably distinct: the former transformed into a new being, with new customs and language, while the latter endured a much longer period of colonial servitude. Arguedas read Rulfo's work for both its literary and its ethnologic value, and recommended it to Peruvians, who would find Mexico to be a world distinct from Peru, but similar in its fusion of Spanish and ancient American cultures.[78] Arguedas envisioned *neoindigenista* writings as emanating from a congress of cultures. He asserted that this literature, as demonstrated by the accomplishments of Rulfo, should serve as a model for European writers, thereby reversing the flow of cultural influence.

Arguedas's most rigorous folkloric investigation directly following *Los ríos profundos* was his translation of a compilation of Quechua stories collected in Lucanamarca, a village in the central sierra region of Peru. The study culminated in a lengthy article, entitled "Cuentos religioso-mágicos quechuas de Lucanamarca" (Religious-Magical Quechua Stories from Lucanamarca), which appeared in the 1960–61 issue of *Folklore Americano*. The article contains the Quechua texts and Spanish translations of seven stories Arguedas taped in the field, and the introduction offers a detailed account of his primary informant's background. Don Luis Gilberto Pérez, a member of a small landowning family, came to be one of Lima's most popular interpreters of Indian *waynos* and achieved fame in the city's *coliseos*, venues for the performance of stylized Andean songs and dances.

Arguedas wrote that Don Luis, despite not being Indian, spoke Quechua and sang his town's repertoire of songs with purity and clarity.[79] Don Luis was similar to the mestizo heroes celebrated in Arguedas's novels. Like Rendón Willka of *Todas las sangres*, he was a "cholo bueno" [good mestizo] and symbolized the transition from Indian to mestizo culture experienced by many inhabitants of the sierra who left the mountains in search of better lives in Lima. This mestizo type, who maintains a foot in each world, is characteristically ambivalent; he cannot completely readapt to the ways of the village, and yet his fundamental values are permanently rooted in rural life.

Arguedas's principal strategy in the study of Lucanamarca was to portray himself as a credible mediator and a conveyer of oral truths. He made a distinction between his role as a fiction writer and his role as an ethnologist, affirming that the reader of his fiction would encounter a style quite distinct from the Quechua narrations published in his translations. As in the early translations, such as *Canto kechwa*, Arguedas insisted that the nonliterary qualities of the translations were proof of their authenticity. A translator of folkloric material must take great care to remain faithful to details, form, and content, more so than with written literature.[80] His conviction reflects a somewhat ambiguous attempt to reconcile the use of anthropological knowledge to create artistic works. In the articles that coincided with Arguedas's university studies, published during the 1940s and 1950s, he struggled to divest his writings of creative intervention and to cast folklore in a purely academic light. After the publication of *Los ríos profundos*, however, Arguedas became increasingly aware of the literary conventions wrapped up in anthropological mediation.

Anthropology's complicity with art offered Arguedas the possibility of expressing knowledge about Peru's nonhegemonic cultures in a way that was legitimate with regard to Western ideology. In a letter written to Alejandro Ortiz Rescaniere, Arguedas recalled convincing his protégé of the relationship between anthropology and art, commenting that one could not be an ethnologist without possessing an aptitude for feeling and a knowledge of the arts.[81] The two anthropologists corresponded regularly during the 1960s when Ortiz was receiving formal theoretical training in Paris under Claude Lévi-Strauss. In 1966, Arguedas wrote a letter to Lévi-Strauss informing him that he was entrusting Ortiz with a corpus of myths and stories so that the young anthropologist could undertake a much-needed compilation of the materials.

Ortiz worked intensely with Arguedas to collect folkloric material; both realized that Quechua culture was in danger of annihilation. Ortiz's investigations were instrumental in furthering knowledge of the Inkarri myth. In 1963, he met a valuable informant in Vicos, Juan Caleto, who offered him a version of the story distinct from the two previously collected by Arguedas. Two years later, Arguedas and Ortiz delivered a lecture at a conference organized by the Instituto de Altos Estudios de América Latina in Paris in which they elaborated on the Vicos version. For Arguedas, Ortiz represented a type of anthropologist that Peru lacked, one who relied on a firm theoretical background and could potentially carry on Arguedas's folkloric labors. Ortiz fulfilled Arguedas's dying wish that he carry on his projects to revitalize Andean folklore: in 1973, Ortiz published *De Adaneva a Inkarrí (una visión indígena del Perú)* (The Return of the Inca, An Indigenous Vision of Peru) and dedicated the text to the memory of his mentor.

POET AND SINGER OF TALES

After his success with *Los ríos profundos*, Arguedas continued to experiment with a poetic synthesis of scientific investigation and literary creation. His most sublime piece of this type of writing was a short story
called "La agonía de Rasu-Ñiti" (The Death of Rasu-Ñiti) that appeared in
1962 and has subsequently received little critical attention. Like *Los ríos
profundos*, this folkloric tale considers questions of cultural and personal
identity that intrigued Arguedas as an ethnographer and fiction writer. The
story takes place in a small Indian settlement and focuses on Pedro
Huancayre, the legendary dancer of Puquio also known as Rasu-Ñiti. Upon
completing it, Arguedas wrote to Murra that he was pleased with this tale.
It had matured slowly over the course of eight years, though it took him
only two days to write.[82]

The fragmented narrational viewpoints of *Los ríos profundos* return in
"Rasu-Ñiti"; an impersonal third-person narrator informs the reader of the
significance of the myth while a first-person narrator witnesses the dramatic dying performance of Rasu-Ñiti. The story opens with a detailed
description of the eminent dancer, his family, and their abode. The last
dance of Rasu-Ñiti is agonizing. Accompanied by a harpist and a violin-
ist, he channels spiritual power from the mountain spirit Wamani. The story
lends itself to multiple readings: for the Western reader, it is a magical
story that reveals secrets of a dynamic oral culture; for the Indian or
mestizo reader literate in Spanish, it conveys a familiar and verisimilar
world.[83]

By the end of the story, the impersonal narrator is replaced by one who
speaks directly for the Indian or mestizo community of the small town and
who, like them, marvels at the cosmic significance of the events. "Rasu-
Ñiti" is unique among Arguedas's experiments with ethnographic poetics
because, rather than drawing from Andean folklore, the tale mimics popular Quechua lore. The story represents a creative solution to the predicament that Arguedas faced in his efforts to translate oral tradition into writing. Like Lydia Cabrera in *Ayapá: Cuentos de Jicotea*, Arguedas reinvented,
in literary form, the art of oral storytelling. He assumed the role of bard and
playfully formulated a literary language that evoked the dynamic style of
the storytellers he witnessed as a child and studied as an ethnographer. To
conjure up the oral context in which a story like this would have been
repeatedly performed, the text is embedded with sounds and musical instruments. In Rasu-Ñiti's climactic final performance, the sounds of the
dance resonate in the narrator's ears:

Yo vi al gran padre "Untu," trajeado de negro y rojo, cubierto de espejos, danzar sobre una soga movediza en el cielo, tocando sus tijeras. El canto del acero se oía más fuerte que la voz del violín y del arpa que tocaban a mi lado, junto a mí. [...] La voz de sus tijeras nos rendía, iba del cielo al mundo, a los ojos y al latido de los millares de indios y mestizos que lo veíamos avanzar desde el inmenso eucalipto a la torre.[84]

[I saw the great father "Untu," clothed in black and red, covered with mirrors, dancing on the unsteady rope in the sky, playing his scissors. The song of the steel was louder than that of the violin and harp, though they were played right by my side. . . . The voice of his scissors flowed from the heavens to the earth, cutting through the pulsating crowd of Indians and mestizos. With our own eyes we saw him advance from the immense eucalyptus to the tower.]

The performance is a collective experience in which the reader is invited to participate and to witness the secret forces that determine the steps of the dancer who inhabits an immortal world. Rasu-Ñiti's final dance is part of an infinite cycle of dancers and musicians who are woven into a fabric of traditions of a sacred world that is immune to the forces of modernity. "Rasu-Ñiti" condensed Arguedas's vision of the perpetual regeneration of Andean oral tradition into an enchanting tale.

A strikingly similar gesture of creation resulted in a text called "Pongoz mosqoynin" (El sueño del pongo, The Dream of the Indian Servant), which appeared in 1965, a year after the publication of his novel *Todas las sangres*. Arguedas claimed to have heard the story in Lima from an Indian from the province of Quispicanchis. He committed the story to memory. Arguedas was inspired to transcribe and translate his version of the story, which he felt to be a lasting example of the richness of Andean culture and a symbol of the vitality of Quechua as a literary language.

The story is paradigmatic of the dialectic relationship of poetry and science that subtends all of Arguedas's writings. In "El sueño del pongo," Arguedas's mediation entails the transcription, creative renovation, and translation of a story he heard in Quechua. He explicitly resisted categorizing the publication as folklore and suggested that a study of its sources was beyond the scope of the text. Rather, he emphasized the literary potential of the story as well as its sociological and linguistic significance. Arguedas argued for the possibility of written narrative in Quechua. In both poetry and narrative, he claimed, present-day Quechua, and not just the ancient and scholarly form, should be used.[85] Arguedas sought to revise the *indigenista* tendency to cast Andean traditions and Quechua as remnants of an archaic culture. Poetically, an oral version of "El sueño del pongo" outlived Arguedas: a recording of the author reading the story circulated after his death.

While Arguedas was creatively fictionalizing elements of the Quechua storytelling tradition he loved, he also tried his hand as a poet in his native language. After decades of praising Quechua as the most poetic of languages, Arguedas put his theories into practice. His first poetic endeavor was a *haylli-taki*, or hymn, entitled "Tupac Amaru kamaq taytanchisman. A nuestro padre creador Tupac Amaru" (To Our Father and Creator Tupac Amaru), which was published in a bilingual version in 1962. Although the experiment reflects Arguedas's efforts to forge a new kind of modern Quechua literature, it is crucial to recognize that all of his published poems were accompanied by Spanish translations. Arguedas's readership broadened somewhat to include monolingual speakers of Quechua, but otherwise remained virtually the same audience that had read his fiction writings.

As the introductory remarks preceding the poem indicate, Arguedas remained faithful to his assertion that modern Quechua should be incorporated as an official literary language.[86] He warned readers that the poem was originally composed in *chanka*, the Quechua dialect that was his mother tongue, and later translated into Spanish. Arguedas used the introductory notes of the poem as a forum for his claim that Quechua was one of the most powerful and spiritual of languages for literary expression. He proclaimed present-day Quechua to be "millennial," a language in which one could write as beautifully as any language possessing centuries of literary tradition.[87] "Tupac Amaru" conveyed Arguedas's desire to radicalize *indigenista* writings by fusing an ancient past with a millennial vision of Peruvian modernity.

"Tupac Amaru" is one of the seven poems by Arguedas that have recently been compiled into a volume called *Katatay: Temblar* (Katatay: "To Tremble" and Other Poems). In the poem that inaugurates the collection, a chorus of Indian voices exalts Tupac Amaru and evokes the community's solidarity with the spiritual powers of nature. The lyric verses chronicle the violent and corrupting forces of modernity and solicit the Andean leader's eternal guidance. "Tupac Amaru" was the poetic expression of the anguish and urgency that characterized Arguedas's ethnographic and folkloric work during the final decade of his life. Faced with the possible extinction of a culture he cherished, he offered an optimistic outlook on the future of the resilient race.

Even in his most scientific undertakings, Arguedas did not divest his writings of the poetic imagery he associated with Quechua culture. An unparalleled example of this fusion of document and creative elaboration is his 1962 doctoral thesis "Las comunidades de España y del Perú" (The Communities of Spain and Peru), which represented the culmination of Arguedas's 1958 fieldwork in Spain. At first glance, the comparative study of agrarian regions in Spain and Peru seems odd for an *indigenista* whose poetry called out for the triumph of the Indian race over the evil members of the colonizing class. Why would an ethnographer seek to illuminate the social realities of a country that had inflicted so much pain on his people? The answer partially lies in the fact that Arguedas's innovative approach to *indigenismo* recognized the worth of a mestizo culture that subscribed to the teachings of Western culture. Furthermore, in the Spanish communities of La Muga de Sayago and Bermillo de Sayago, located in the region of Zamora, Arguedas relived his childhood experiences as he coexisted with some of Spain's poorest farmers, whose lives had gone unchanged for decades.

After completing his thesis, Arguedas graduated from the doctoral program at the Universidad de San Marcos with a degree in ethnology. The preface to the doctoral study reveals his awareness that the anthropological writing in the text is touched by novelistic discourse.[88] As Murra has pointed out, Arguedas's creative sensibility enriched his ethnographies, endowing them with poetic descriptions of his informants and their natural surroundings.[89] The act of textualizing experience and creating a cultural fiction is remarkably similar in Arguedas's thesis and in some of his best artistic writing. Some of the most poignant passages, describing the splendid topography of Sayago, could easily be found in the pages of *Los ríos profundos*.

Like his investigations of Peruvian communities, Arguedas's comparative study was motivated by the belief that a comprehensive understanding of ancient forms of communal organization could illuminate modern practices. In *Las comunidades*, which incorporates maps, data, photographs, and transcriptions of songs, he concluded that the towns of Sayago offer a general picture of a culture that is undeniably similar to the socioeconomic structure of semicolonial Andean Peru, particularly the communities of Puquio. In his estimation, the most striking difference is that the Spanish towns lack the endogenous forces, like traditional song and dance, that strengthen the communal ethos of Peru's Andean peoples. To his dismay, Arguedas found the cultural practices of La Muga and Bermillo to be stagnant; their traditions of dance and song never evolved or became transformed like those in Peru's sierra. Rather, they were systematically suppressed by state officials and cast as forms of cultural propaganda. Although Arguedas did not explicitly link this fate with that of Peru, the overall comparison suggests that his rhetoric was shaped by a desire to ward off the annihilation of Andean culture. By asserting a kind of solidarity between the poor and oppressed communities of the two nations, Arguedas astutely condemned the oppressive forces of modernity impinging on Andean communities without alienating his Western readership.

After completing his classes at San Marcos in 1962, Arguedas wrote to Hoffmann that he intended to abandon his ethnologic studies and dedicate all of his energies to his third novel. *Todas las sangres*, an ambitious novel published in 1963, is a fictional account of the struggle between Peru's social classes. Arguedas departed from a dualist approach to *indigenista* writings and created a book populated by characters representing various opposing ideological positions. Indians, whites, and mestizos, both wealthy and impoverished, city folk and rural dwellers, industrialists and agriculturists are just some of the social groups that inhabit the novel. He also broke with the stylistic device of narrating from the point of view of a young protagonist. Rather, in *Todas las sangres*, the plot consists primarily of multiple dialogues that intersect to create a sense of social mobility. The novel was Arguedas's most earnest attempt to give faithful testimony about the social reality of Peru.

Arguedas's fictional depiction of the internal struggles of Peruvian society proved to be so compelling that a group of intellectuals called for a formal assembly to debate its historic validity. On June 23, 1965, Arguedas joined sociologists, literary critics, and economists at Lima's Instituto de Estudios Peruanos for a round table discussion.[90] Arguedas was upset to learn that the intellectuals overwhelmingly agreed that his novel misrepresented the social realities of Peru. Jorge Bravo Bresani criticized the book's portrayal of Indians as too purist and idealistic. During the meeting, Arguedas reacted to the scathing remarks with disbelief: "Si no es testimonio, entonces yo he vivido por gusto, he vivido en vano, o no he vivido."[91] [If it is not testimony, then I have lived pointlessly, I have lived in vain, or I have not lived.] Arguedas was understandably devastated by his colleagues' criticisms. For him, good literature, like ethnography, meant the scrupulous expression of realistic detail. Social reality, in his eyes, was wrapped up with personal experience.

Overall, Bravo Bresani, Aníbal Quijano, Henri Favre, and others were correct in their assessment of the book's shortcomings as a scientific document.[92] The novel artificially compartmentalizes Peruvian society and offers a distorted version of reality. But *Todas las sangres*—indeed, any novel or ethnography—is by nature a cultural fiction. Vargas Llosa has rightly argued that the novel's lack of social validity did not cause its downfall; rather, it failed because it assumed that what is true in literature can be measured in terms of objective reality.[93] This controversy anticipates some

of the issues involved in taking life stories portrayed in testimonial literature at face value.

During the final years of his life, Arguedas broke with official cultural
groups, renouncing his idea that state resources could revitalize Andean
traditions and achieve harmony with modernized Peruvian culture.[94] Instead, Arguedas dedicated his investigative efforts to a personal endeavor,
the systematic compilation of oral literature, a project he undertook with
great urgency. In his opinion, oral lore was more vulnerable to the forces of
modernization than any other form of traditional expression. Arguedas's
final creative and scientific endeavor as ethnologist/translator/novelist focused on *Dioses y hombres de Huarochirí* (Gods and Men of Huarochiri),
a popular Quechua text offering insights into the mythology of ancient
Peru. Father Francisco de Avila originally transcribed the legend in the
early seventeenth century. For years, Murra had insisted that Arguedas attempt a Spanish translation of Avila's Quechua text; but Arguedas, fearing
that the task was beyond his capabilities, had resisted. Finally, in 1966, he
agreed to edit and translate the text in conjunction with a program called
"La colección de fuentes e investigaciones para la historia del Perú" (The
Collection of Sources and Investigations for the History of Peru). The program to vindicate the sources of Peruvian traditions, directed by Luis
Valcárcel and Carlos Araníbar, was governed by a tenet that echoed
Arguedas's ethnological goals: "The purpose of all history . . . is the understanding of the present."[95]
    Arguedas's career as an ethnographer was primarily concerned with
the revitalization of contemporary Andean traditions within a Western context. In *Dioses y hombres*, however, he dealt with native traditions still
steeped in ancient religious practices. Arguedas concluded that the Quechua
manuscript was most likely composed by various informants from the province of Huarochirí. Arguedas was captivated by material aspects of the oral
world—gods, men, animals, abysses—that evoked memories of Quechua
stories he had heard in his childhood.[96]
    Arguedas collaborated with French Peruvianist Pierre Duviols, who
contributed an essay on the life and works of Father Avila to *Dioses y
hombres*. In his introduction to the translation, Arguedas celebrated the
oral properties embedded in the textuality. In many ways, the manuscript
elicits a reading that Arguedas envisioned for his own literary creations:
the reader should hear a voice devoid of literary concerns and intentions,

that of a native or various natives. The ethnologist and the historian should be able to *witness* the action, *feel* the tremblings of those who believed in the gods.[97] Arguedas's attempt to textualize, in Spanish, pre-Hispanic oral accounts of Quechua tradition is doubly significant if one takes into account his final foray as a novelist. The mythical foxes of the title of his posthumous publication, *El zorro de arriba y el zorro de abajo*, were extracted directly from the fifth chapter of *Dioses y hombres*, "Como antiguamente pareció Pariacaca en un cerro llamado Condorcato y lo que sucedió" (How, in Ancient Times, Pariacaca Appeared on a Hill Called Condorcato and What Happened).

Arguedas ended his life in the midst of a project aimed at exemplifying the unity of Quechua oral tradition and modern literary tradition. The fragmentary novel, Arguedas's most radical attempt to subvert conventional literary traditions, consisted of excerpts from the diaries of the suicidal author interspersed with narrative discourse ridden with colloquial jargon. Reelaboration of the Quechua legend was only tangential to the overall depiction of the confused and infernal world of *El zorro*. The reader witnesses the emotional deterioration of the disillusioned writer. In his final literary confession, "¿Último diario?" (Final Diary?), composed one month before he shot himself, Arguedas wrote of his intention to convey the brutal realities of the novel through the eyes of the pre-Hispanic legendary foxes. He was unable, however, to bring this idea to fruition; the foxes only intervene superficially on two occasions in the entire novel.

The fragmentation and incompleteness of *El zorro* represent the irreconcilable conflict of dissonant voices that plagued Peru and haunted Arguedas. Arguedas used anthropological discourse to gain insight into a part of himself that endowed him with the spirit to express his Quechua past in poetry and literature. Vargas Llosa has argued that Arguedas was unable to accept the imminent extinction of a Quechua culture that had nurtured him during his most cherished years. His writings represented an exhaustive effort to revive Peruvian archaic culture in the form of a "literary utopia," an unattainable goal that preoccupied Arguedas throughout his life.[98] Ultimately, Arguedas realized that the reinvention of Andean archaic traditions entailed the construction of cultural fictions, thereby undermining his attempts to control identity—that of others as well as his own.

ARGUEDAS: AN ANDEAN *HABLADOR*

Vargas Llosa's comprehensive study of his compatriot's life and works, *La utopía arcaica: José María Arguedas y las ficciones del Indigenismo*

(*Archaic Utopia: José María Arguedas and the Fictions of Indigenism*), sheds light on Arguedas's profound solidarity with the archaic facets of Andean culture. Vargas Llosa's critical study is a scholarly answer to several of the compelling issues raised in his novel *El hablador* (*The Storyteller*), published nearly a decade before. As González Echevarría notes, Vargas Llosa's novel delves into the underlying issues of anthropological discourse and prompts us to ask whether one can truly write about the Other without doing irreparable damage to the Other's culture. Vargas Llosa's novel aspires to be a kind of ethnography of anthropology.[99] It addresses the idea that Western intellectuals share a desire to penetrate and interpret "primitive" cultures.

The opening pages of *El hablador* depict the streets of Florence and trace the narrator's wanderings among some striking icons of Western culture. A photograph in a gallery provokes a chain of memories that incite his obsessive quest to comprehend the mysterious figure of the "hablador," or "storyteller." The narrator's recollections hark back to his days when, at the Universidad de San Marcos, he first came into contact with Saúl Zaratas, nicknamed "Mascarita" because of the dark birthmark masking his face and permanently marking him with otherness. He remembers that Mascarita ultimately became disenchanted with his anthropological studies when he realized that the work of ethnologists was akin to that of rubber workers and timber merchants, who gradually contributed to the extermination of the Indian cultures of the Amazon.

Mascarita slowly departed from university life and sought refuge among the Indian communities he respected and loved. He gained profound knowledge of the Indians' practices and traditions by coexisting with them. The narrator's approach to anthropology was dramatically different: he practiced the methodical and objective investigation of indigenous peoples and saw socialism as the key to the coexistence of modern Peru and archaic Peru. He concludes, however, that perhaps the two approaches to Peru's primitive cultures were equally idealistic.[100] The narrator, a novelist who shares concerns about cultural identity with Vargas Llosa and Arguedas, undertakes the project of writing a fictional account about the Machiguengas, thirty years after his first encounters with Saúl Zaratas.

El hablador offers two extreme paradigms for gaining knowledge of the Other. Mascarita, a former student of ethnology, underwent a dramatic religious and cultural conversion, which the story suggests is analogous to Gregor Samsa's metamorphosis. He was transformed into the insider par excellence, the enigmatic Machiguenga storyteller. Chapters that evoke the magical oral narrations of the "hablador" alternate with those recounting the narrator-writer's recollections. They are written in a style that mimics the oral retelling of stories and legends among a collectivity; among other things, it evokes fantastic adventures and a mythic past. The narrator re-writes in Spanish the transcriptions of Machiguenga oral culture, borrowing discursive techniques from professional ethnography and literature. In these chapters, the voice of the "fuente viva" is doubly removed: the fictionalized narrator-writer creates an illusion of presentness and authenticity associated with oral discourse.

Jorge Marcone suggests that, if we understand the rendering of "authentic" oral discourse as a rhetorical illusion, *El hablador* can be read as a fictional ethnography that possesses ethnological value. The novel proposes that the fictional re-creation of orality, by means of assigning a discursive structure and communicative setting, fulfills a complementary ethnographic function.[101] Marcone interprets Vargas Llosa's novel as an ethnography that is nostalgic for an idealized past in which cultural knowledge was conveyed by voice.

Vargas Llosa's novel sheds light on Arguedas's tendency to position himself simultaneously as an outsider and an insider. Arguably, Arguedas perceived himself as an "hablador" and capitalized on these talents, as much as he sympathized with the plight of the narrator-writer. From his writing desk in Florence, the primary narrator of *El hablador* recalls countless frustrated attempts to write the tale of the storytellers. He is faced with the difficult task of inventing, in scholarly Spanish, a literary form that would credibly reflect the storytelling style of a primitive man.[102] *El hablador* questions the capacity of official discourse to represent "primitive" culture, and calls for a distinction between fiction and professional ethnography.

The narrator in Vargas Llosa's novel creates an account of the writing process and the plight of the modern writer, rather than an interpretation of Machiguenga culture. *El hablador* dramatizes the paradox that led Arguedas to take his own life: Can an insider convey his or her culture when discourse presupposes the necessity of an outside? Arguedas's answer to this predicament was to create the illusion of inhabiting Peru's dominant culture and appropriating its official language, while simultaneously identifying spiritually with what he perceived as his native culture. Ultimately, neither personal experience nor scientific investigation can be construed as innocent means of interpretation. Arguedas's writings demonstrate that fiction pervades any attempt to construe the Other's voice in writing, and scientific and literary disciplines always come together in the interpretation of other cultures.

4

Barnet and Burgos as Ghostwriters: Fictionalization of the Oral in *testimonio*

Pero lo fundamental del lenguaje en la novela-testimonio es que se apoye en la lengua hablada. Sólo así posee vida. Pero una lengua hablada decantada como ya hemos dicho. Yo jamás escribiría ningún libro reproduciendo fidedignamente lo que la grabadora me dicte. De la grabadora tomaría el tono del lenguaje y la anécdota; lo demás el estilo y los matices, serían siempre mi contribución.

—Miguel Barnet, *La fuente viva*

[But the fundamental aspect of language in the testimonial novel is that it is based on spoken language. Only in this way is it alive. But, as we have stated, this spoken language is "decanted." I would never write a book by reproducing exactly what is on the audiotape. I take the tone of the language and the anecdotes from the tape; the style and the nuances are always my own contribution.]

IN A 1970 ESSAY ENTITLED "LA NOVELA TESTIMIONIO: SOCIO-LITERATURA," THE CUBAN ethnologist and writer Miguel Barnet shed light on the methodology and creative process that culminated in *Biografía de un cimarrón* (*The Autobiography of a Runaway Slave*). This book was initially presented as an ethnographic study, but it enjoyed international success as a work of literature. Shortly after the book's publication in 1966, critics of Casa de las Américas canonized *testimonio* as an authentically Spanish American form of nonfiction narrative that faithfully documented the region's reality and possessed an undeniable literary quality.

Barnet was among the first to define the rules and mechanics of testimonial literature. The revolutionary discourse of his essay, written the same year he accepted the Casa de las Américas award for *testimonio*, pronounced the death of fiction; it attributed the crisis to the elitist tendencies of the bourgeois novel. In the wake of European aristocratic forms of literary expression, he proclaimed the genesis of a new Spanish American literature, a narrative based on the sensibilities of the people whose experiences left a profound mark on Cuba's national history and psychology.

This essay/manifesto was later published as part of a collection of Barnet's essays called *La fuente viva* (The Living Source). The title of the collection underscores a central theme in all of Barnet's, Cabrera's, and Arguedas's writings, both literary and scientific: the spoken word, as transcribed from the *fuente viva*, captures the essence of a culture. Barnet proposed to revolutionize literary discourse by giving voice to the powerless and the oppressed, whose values had been systematically undermined by a system based on mass production of material goods.[1] In this context, *testimonio* should be understood as a complex form of cross-cultural communication, fraught with tension arising from the unequal political positions of the coproducers of the text. A crucial part of testimonial writing is the invention of a narrator-informant who represents collective experience. Testimonial narratives gain their authority by creating the effect of an eyewitness retelling his or her life story.

In Barnet's view, oral structures and nuances are indispensable for the expression of a collective reality. *La fuente viva* contributed to an ongoing process of self-canonization: Barnet explicitly legitimized his work's authenticity by stating its mission to preserve the purity of the Other's spoken discourse. He, like Cabrera and Arguedas, explored the discursive possibilities of anthropology in his efforts to contrive the effect of orality in writing. Barnet, however, surpassed the others by taking the aesthetics of orality to their extreme in his fiction.

Like his compatriot Lydia Cabrera, Barnet spent his formative years away from his native country, attending school in the United States. As a teenager, he dreamed of becoming an opera singer, but found his muse in poetry by the time he was twenty. He, like many youths of his generation, became aware of Cuban culture by reading publications like *Lunes de Revolución* and *Hoy*, in which he published some of his earliest poems. In the 1950s Barnet first came into contact with professors who would eventually guide his anthropological studies. In those same years he attended religious ceremonies of the Lucumí tradition and the cult of Palo Monte and, for the first time, he felt the "vibration" of poetry. Barnet's captivation with this other world coincided with his growing consciousness of Cuba's history and national culture. His first encounters with Afro-Cuban traditions were as an outsider.[2]

The anthropologist Argeliers León became an important mentor for Barnet. Barnet's first experience with Afro-Cuban culture was marked by a striking literary propriety. He, like the aimless narrator-protagonist of the opening scenes of Alejo Carpentier's *Los pasos perdidos* (*The Lost Steps*), was drawn to an exhibit of Cuban musical instruments, many of which were African in origin. Barnet and León first met at the exhibit, and Barnet later attended a seminar on folklore organized by León at the National Theater.

In 1960, Barnet began working as secretary to León, who was then director of the music department of the National Library of Cuba. León introduced Barnet to the Institute of Ethnology and Folklore, which was created in 1961 and was affiliated with the Academy of Sciences. Barnet attributed his formation as an ethnographer to his seven years of study at the Academy of Sciences, where he enrolled in classes on ethnology and social anthropology. He also became familiar with Fernando Ortiz's work in the early 1960s, and often visited Ortiz in his home. He recalled that Ortiz never ceased to criticize the antiquated readings assigned in university courses, and gave Barnet works by Brazilian and North American anthropologists to supplement his studies.

Like Cabrera and most Cuban writers, Barnet was a member of Havana's bourgeoisie. Arguedas, in contrast, was initially a member of an uprooted indigenous culture and later became a privileged intellectual. A native of Havana, Barnet was largely unfamiliar with Cuba's rural culture during the early decades of his life. This changed with the onset of the revolution, when he first became aware of the heterogeneity of Cuba's population. Ortiz urged him to explore the underground world of Afro-Cuban religions that was generally concealed from the Catholic urban bourgeoisie. Barnet's poetry, published during the early years of the revolutionary government, traces the creation of his literary persona, reflecting his growing awareness of the diverse nature of Cuba's culture and syncretic religions. Barnet first realized orality's affinity with poetic expression in his early collections.

His first book of poetry, *La piedra fina y el pavorreal* (The Gem and the Peacock), was published in 1963 but had been a work in progress since 1959. Barnet dedicated the collection to Tonde, a Palmira *santero*, in memory of his first visit to a Lucumí temple.[3] The collection begins with "Poema 1," an ode to the urban landscape of Havana. In sharp contrast, several of the subsequent poems are infused with natural imagery drawn from the spiritual forces of the *monte*. The poem "Trinidad" reflects Barnet's early attempts to contrive an oral performance in writing. He evokes a ceremony that takes place in the house of a *santero*, where an old man's tales of Oyá and Osain captivate listeners. The poem reveals Barnet's conviction that storytelling constitutes a privileged mode of producing authentic meaning, and suggests that spoken performance is linked to memory, tradition, and communal knowledge. The final verse of "Trinidad" tells the reader that the poet strives to emulate the singer of tales.

"Trinidad" and other poems composed in the 1960s reflect Barnet's growing affinity for the occult mysteries of Cuba's rustic culture. From the beginning of his career as a writer, Barnet realized poetry's affiliation with the oral. Poetry provided him with a seemingly authentic way to approach a culture in which meaning was predominantly contingent on oral communication. As an accomplished ethnographer, Barnet later drew from these early writerly moments to create an ethnographic poetics to mediate between oral narratives and writing.

The varied subject matter of *La piedra fina*, a mélange of autobiographical, urban, and rural themes, was most likely deemed appropriate by a revolutionary government that was interested in promoting cultural diversity. In the mid-1960s, however, Barnet and a generation of poets known as El Puente (The Bridge) came under government suspicion for neglecting political themes in their writings. Several of the group's intellectuals were detained in camps known as Unidades Militares de Ayuda a la Producción (Military Units to Aid Production), and cut off from cultural life. These concentration camps, run by the Cuban army, were intended for homosexuals and other "antisocial" elements. Barnet distanced himself from El Puente during these years and did not publish another collection of poetry until 1967. During the same period, he actively pursued his studies of ethnology and began the project that culminated in *Biografía de un cimarrón*.

BIOGRAFÍA DE UN CIMARRÓN: MASQUERADES AS ETHNOGRAPHY

In 1963, Barnet was struck by a newspaper article about Cuban citizens who had lived for more than a century. He had interviewed several elderly people as a member of Juan Pérez de la Riva's study of Cuban slave quarters. The investigation, undertaken by a team of intellectuals including Manuel Moreno Fraginals, Isaac Barreal, and María Teresa Linares, culminated in the 1975 publication of *El barracón: Esclavitud y capitalismo en Cuba* (Slave Quarters: Capitalism and Slavery in Cuba). Barnet was thus already familiar with the techniques of ethnographic field interviews when two of the elderly subjects mentioned in the newspaper article caught his attention: a woman who was an ex-slave as well as a *santera*; and Esteban Montejo, who claimed that he had been a runaway slave in the wilderness of Las Villas.

Curiously, Barnet disregarded the woman, despite the fact that she would have been an ideal informant about Afro-Cuban religions. Instead, he seized upon the story of Montejo because the man claimed to be a runaway slave, a phenomenon about which very little was known. Barnet's decision to interview black informants reflected his awareness of the revolution's commitment to the nation's black inhabitants. His elaboration of Montejo's biography can be seen as a form of political propaganda. The fact that Montejo is presented as a *cimarrón*, or runaway slave, rather than as a slave or a soldier, articulates his identity as a revolutionary.

Ultimately, critics celebrated *Biografía* as an important contribution to Cuban letters. Like other enduring literary products of the revolutionary era, the book offered a revision of Cuba's political history. By focusing on the importance of blacks for revolutionary national culture, Barnet subtly critiqued both prerevolutionary society and capitalist regimes plagued by racial discrimination. At a time when Cuba's sociopolitical system was changing dramatically, he perceived a need to rediscover the nation's history through the experiences of nonwhites. Anthropology provided a legitimate way to critique contemporary society and demystify the important role played by blacks in Cuba's history. Like Cabrera and Arguedas, Barnet's intellectual pursuits were based largely on the ethnographic conceit of salvaging authentic culture and instituting national diversity.

The first edition of *Biografía* appeared in Cuba in 1966 with a modest purple cover inscribed with the title, Barnet's name, the words "Academia de Ciencias," and the date of publication. According to Barnet, the simple presentation gave the book a scientific appearance. The Institute of Ethnology and Folklore, an organization that descended from Fernando Ortiz's Society of Afro-Cuban Studies, published the book as an ethnographic account intended to complement *El barracón*. *Biografía* aligned itself with ethnology in order to secure its authenticity as a primary account. The trappings of scientific discourse—an unassuming cover, a photograph of the subject, an explanatory prologue written by the ethnographer and composed in the voice of an authoritative "we," editorial notes, and a glossary of terms—emphasized the verifiable nature of Montejo's story. These extratextual artifacts are an important part of the textuality, because they evoke the underlying methodology and reveal fissures in a text that allegedly re-creates spontaneous oral discourse.[4]

Writers of testimonial literature share with anthropologists a commitment to producing realist texts. Kay B. Warren has observed the transparency of the genre:

> Realist modes of representation create the illusion of an unmediated window on the world to allow the vicarious experience of social realities outside the reader's own life experience. *Testimonios* gain their narrative power

through the metaphor of witnessing. They offer eyewitness experiences of injustice and violence in cinematographic detail, and thereby create the effect of witnesses presenting evidence to the court of public opinion.[5]

This "unmediated window" is produced textually by scripting a coherent life story, one that seemingly re-creates the voice of a non-Western subject. In testimonial literature, the first-person narrative of the eyewitness-protagonist replaces the ethnographic conceit of "having been there" as a source of authority. The testimonial subject negotiates the retelling of his or her memories with the coproducer of the text.

At first blush, the text of *Biografía* reads as a seamless first-person narration of a life story. Presented as unmediated speech, Montejo's tall tales convey a sense of presentness and authenticity. However, as Antonio Vera León points out, this illusion of immediacy contradicts the biographical intentions expressed in the title. His analysis reveals that the transcriber cannot completely erase his or her political goals from the text. Indeed, the transcriber's discursive strategies determine the ways in which readers understand and interpret the testimonial subject's discourse. Ultimately, writing emerges as a political practice, and *testimonio* can be read as the manifestation of political and discursive tension.[6]

As Jorge Marcone observes, testimonial narrative can, for all practical purposes, be read as a citation. The illusion of immediacy arises from rhetorical strategies that draw upon anthropological discourse. Marcone believes that in all ethnography, whether literary or academic, transparency is a discursive utopia that characterizes representations of the Other.[7] Prologues and headings that give structure to the narrative expose the author's explicit involvement in the retelling of the subject's story. The writer inevitably becomes entangled in the process of oral remembrance that he promises not to contaminate. By invoking ethnographic discursive modes, Barnet attempted to remain faithful to the authenticity he deemed implicit in oral communication.

Barnet's use of rhetorical strategies borrowed from scientific discourse changed dramatically over time. The prologue of the Spanish edition, which is quite different from that of the English translation, is similar to the descriptions of fieldwork practices found in Lydia Cabrera's anthropological writings, like *El monte*. Barnet used the prologue to establish his authority as an ethnographer, and thereby predetermine the kind of text the reader should anticipate. He conducted interviews with Montejo over the course of several months, first taking notes on file cards and later transporting a Tesla tape recorder, weighing over twenty pounds, to the Veterans' Home where Montejo resided. Barnet maintained that the machine could capture subtleties of the spoken language that the human ear might miss. This faith in the purity of the recorded voice reflects the conceit that the anthropologist can gain control of the Other's language by capturing it on tape. Barnet's description of the tape recorder's ability to capture orality constitutes an important part of the prologue's rhetoric of authority, aimed at convincing the reader of the text's veracity. It also signals his faith in the authenticity and authority conveyed by spoken language.

Barnet's ability to contrive spoken discourse in writing was his primary means of creating a pervasive sense of linguistic reality. He largely based his authority on the assumption that he could speak from within his subject. Elzbieta Sklodowska asserts that Barnet's efforts to textualize the experiences of Cuba's non-Western cultures follow a model of ethnographic realism.[8] Sklodowska's observation cites recent shifts in anthropology from grand cultural theories and an emphasis on the methods of fieldwork to a more introspective and critical look at ethnographic practices. In fact, her interpretation of Barnet's rhetorical strategies reflects a reading that engages the emerging notions of this movement toward an interpretive anthropology.[9] Interpretive anthropology aims to reveal the fissures beneath seemingly holistic accounts of pristine cultures in anthropological models developed during the first half of the twentieth century. Sklodowska invokes some of these practices to critique the methods with which Barnet and Elisabeth Burgos, each writing from an authoritative position, sought to represent coherent stories of their subject's reality.

Like most writers of realist texts, Barnet was self-critical only to the extent that introspection served to enhance the text's legitimacy. Barnet's noticeable absence from the body of the text highlights his efforts to establish complete authority over the textualization of Montejo's account. By manipulating language, Barnet created a sense of "being there" in order to transcend the temporal and spatial gap between the scientific "we" of the observer and the speaking "they" of the living subject. After asserting his authority early on in the prologue, Barnet essentially disappears and writes from Montejo's point of view, thereby sidestepping the dilemma of representing conflicting voices. The reader ostensibly "hears" the reproduction of Montejo's stories and anecdotes.

In the prologue of *Biografía*, Barnet claimed that he was initially motivated by a desire to study African religious practices that had been assimilated into Cuban Catholic tradition. The predetermined focus of the investigation shaped the kind of information he elicited from his source. Although Barnet recognized that his conversations with Montejo strayed from the intended topic, he affirmed that the interviews respected conventional norms of ethnologic research. The concluding remarks of the prologue reveal Barnet's political motivation: a lengthy description of Montejo's character portrays the ex-slave as an exemplary member of Cuba's revolutionary society. Most significantly, Barnet offered a disclaimer in which he defended the scientific grounding of the book. He recognized that the process of giving an informant voice was part of making literature. Nevertheless, he assured his reader that he did not intend to create a literary document or a novel.[10] This self-conscious attempt to bypass literary norms makes *Biografía*, and *testimonio* in general, such striking examples of the tendency of Spanish American narrative to strive for authenticity by engaging the discursive practices of nonliterary discourses.[11]

According to the prologue of *Biografía*, Barnet consulted official histories and other written texts to supplement Montejo's narrative. He constructed an accurate historical context for Montejo's tale by referring to archives in Cienfuegos and Remedios, histories of Cuba, and the complete works of Fernando Ortiz and Ramiro Guerra. It was not until years after the publication of *Biografía* that Barnet acknowledged that he had closely followed the Mexican anthropologist Ricardo Pozas's *Juan Pérez Jolote: Biografía de un tzotzil* (1952) as a model. Apparently, Pozas arrived in Cuba when Barnet's interviews with Montejo were already underway, but Barnet had not yet determined the best way to compile his copious notes and transcriptions. Barnet enrolled in a course in fieldwork methodology offered by Pozas at the Academy of Sciences. The two became friends, and Pozas accompanied Barnet when he interviewed Montejo at the Veterans' Home. He was captivated by the ex-slave's poetic voice, and urged Barnet to follow through with his plan to produce a book. Pozas agreed that Barnet should disregard the idea of a text that would complement *El barracón*, and instead supported his notion to create an ethnographic piece in the same style as *Juan Pérez Jolote*.

Curiously, in a 1996 interview in which Barnet divulged his use of Pozas's text as a model, he referred to it with the subtitle "an ethnographic account," when the book's true title reads "biography of a *tzotzil*." Like Barnet's *Biografía*, Pozas's book opens with a prologue and contains editorial notes that provide historical background and translations of indigenous words. Pozas's prologue lacks a clear description of the methodology behind the book's composition. It states that the biography should be regarded as a brief monograph of the Chamula culture.

The literary quality of Pozas's book is undeniable, and the uniqueness of the protagonist's story leads one to question its accuracy as a synecdochic representation of the Chamula experience. *Juan Pérez Jolote* and *Biografía* open in strikingly similar ways: following the model of the picaresque novel, each subject attempts to trace his dubious genealogy, thereby establishing his marginality. Emphasis on the process of naming attributes mythic qualities to the protagonists. As in the chansons de geste, Pérez Jolote and Montejo are heroic figures that recount their epic adventures.

Both subjects are conscious of legitimizing their experiences by discussing topics that their interlocutors might deem important. Pérez Jolote's life story is organized into a seamless series of events that appears to recreate the protagonist's memory; the book contains no chapter divisions, and it creates an illusion of coherence and wholeness. Pozas, like Barnet, opted to retell the subject's story in chronological order to give a sense of continuity to what must have been an unruly textual process. In both books, the protagonist's life story is marked by important moments of official history. Does the isolation of these moments reflect ways in which Pérez Jolote and Montejo configure their memories, or are these allusions instead manipulations aimed at imposing a realistic context to lend authenticity to an individual's narrative?

Juan Pérez Jolote fled his community at an early age to fight in the Mexican Revolution. When he finally returned to Chamula in 1930, he had forgotten his native language and his family barely recognized him. Pérez Jolote undergoes a poetic conversion that transforms him into an outsider within his own community: he exchanges his rags for traditional garments, but never becomes truly integrated into the society. He assumes an outsider's perspective vis-à-vis the natives of Chamula for the remainder of the text. Because he is an outsider, his observations of indigenous traditions and rituals are not very different from those of an ethnographer working in the field. Similarly, Montejo is outside of the cultures he observes in his wanderings. In both texts, the writer-anthropologists portray firsthand accounts that are substantiated by experience, but in neither does the subject truly speak from inside the culture he describes.

The most remarkable difference between the two texts is their treatment of orality. The first-person narrative format of *Juan Pérez Jolote* leads one to believe that it is a spoken confession. The language, however, more closely resembles the protagonists' voices in regionalist novels than the "decanted" oral discourse of Barnet's *testimonios*. Pozas's strategies for expressing spoken language in writing are similar to those found in Arguedas's early collections of stories; both writers chose to leave certain terms untranslated as a means of authenticating their texts. Pérez Jolote's life story is interrupted by long digressions that intend to explain cultural phenomena. The desire to incorporate the "original" language in these passages often obscures meaning. The resulting text combines confessional dialogue and clinical observation.

Biografía more successfully achieves fluidity and coherence as an unbroken narrative. Barnet struggled to differentiate his voice and Montejo's by evoking, in writing, the dynamics of Montejo's spoken discourse. In *Biografía*, an insistence on the primacy of orality underscores the desire for authenticity and truth. The format and overall intention of *Juan Pérez Jolote* clearly shaped Barnet's thinking; but *Biografía* surpassed its predecessor in complexity, as a text that proposed to reconstruct a simulacrum of spoken monologue.

Barnet's introduction to *The Autobiography of a Runaway Slave*, the title of the 1968 English edition, differs from the Spanish version; it lacks an explicit defense of the scientific grounding of Esteban's accounts. By casting Montejo's "biografía" as autobiography, Barnet explicitly distances himself from the text as a product. The new title suggests that Montejo "wrote" the account, and masks the process of negotiation that actually took place. An illusion of intimacy draws in the reader, thereby diminishing the gap between reader and subject. In the book's preface, Barnet focuses on the need to fill certain blanks in Cuba's polemical history by tapping a source that no "orthodox, schematically-minded" historian would bother to reference.

Montejo, the ethnographer's faithful informant in the Spanish prologue, transforms into the hero of an epic adventure in the English version. A transcription of oral testimony serves Barnet's needs as an ethnographer in the Spanish version as much as his desire to recount the feats of a man, a national hero of sorts, who has experienced more than a century of Cuba's history. Barnet disregards his proclaimed interest in African religions and explains in the English introduction that he is primarily interested in Montejo's experiences as a slave, his life as a runaway, and his role in Cuba's War of Independence.

Montejo's story takes on literary dimensions when Barnet refers to its poetic and surrealist appeal. Whereas the Spanish version resists fiction, *The Autobiography of a Runaway Slave* offers a revision of historical discourse: "Not that this book is primarily a work of history—history merely enters it as the medium in which the man's life is lived." Barnet suggests that living history surpasses conventional accounts of history. He provides the English-speaking reader with a brief overview of the major historical moments encompassed in Montejo's life and conspicuously omits any mention of the ex-slave's relationship with the Cuban revolution. Barnet ends the introduction by re-creating what could be construed as a single storytelling event; he evokes the image of an aged Montejo, seated in a leather chair, concluding his epic life story: "'And I'm not going into the trenches,' he explains, 'or using any of those modern weapons. A machete will do for me.'"[12]

The presentation of *Biografía* as ethnographic discourse attempts to mask the text's literary propriety. By borrowing methods from his training as an ethnographer, Barnet embellished the nonliterary qualities of Montejo's oral history to legitimize the ex-slave's account, a story that in his opinion defied verification and even verged on fantasy. Paradoxically, however, the transparency of these metadiscursive strategies actually has the opposite effect; it enhances the literary quality of the text.[13] Barnet, like Cabrera and Arguedas, belonged to no field exclusively. As a result, his texts can pose as varieties of discourses. Although Barnet may not have been conscious of the experimental nature of the book when he first wrote it, *Biografía* anticipated an aesthetic cultural movement that affected the social sciences and the humanities.

BIOGRAFÍA DE UN CIMARRÓN DISCARDS ITS ETHNOGRAPHIC MASK

Since its publication, Barnet, the "editor," has never ceased to control Montejo's narrative. Although the text claims to be a faithful account of one subject's version of Cuban history, any attempt at the voice of the Other is inherently problematic, because it is inevitably marked by issues of power. Despite the fact that *Biografía* is presented as a monograph, and as an autobiography in the English version, it nevertheless reflects a desire to define a marginal subject from an outside perspective. Sklodowska has argued convincingly that elitist Western ideology is built into the hybridization of discourses found in *testimonios* like Barnet's. Testimonial literature, by nature, cannot represent genuine and spontaneous authorship on behalf of the subject-community. Rather, it is a form of elitist discourse, committed to the cause of democratization, that is capable of accommodating the voice of the subaltern Other.[14] For Barnet, the anthropological monograph provided a discursive form that was ideologically sound by Western standards and could faithfully represent the voice of a member of a disenfranchised class.

As Sklodowska has suggested, we should read *testimonio* "as a peculiar mixture of experience, creation, manipulation, and invention, more akin, perhaps[,] to a novel than to a scientific document." It is a genre that crosses disciplines and belongs wholly to none. If we read *Biografía* through a scientific lens, as Barnet may have initially intended, the redundancies, erasures, fabrications, and exaggerations are unsettling. However, by taking into consideration other paradigms of reading—literary criticism, oral memory, and social sciences—these fissures can be appreciated as rich features of a unique form of cultural production.[15] They are discursive strategies invoked by the author to create a kind of writing that is akin to the rhetorical expression of speech.

Barnet's readings of *Biografía* that followed its publication eroded the scientific facade that initially purported to legitimize it. His 1970 article entitled "La novela testimonio: Socio-literatura," published at a time when he was becoming conscious of the book's impact on an evolving intellectual and political environment, can be read as a second prologue to *Biografía*. Whereas Barnet initially portrayed his role in the text's composition within the accepted norms of ethnographic research, the 1970 article introduced the notion of the "sacred mission" of the *gestor*, or framer and "manager" of the testimonial novel.[16]

Neither author nor editor in the conventional sense, the *gestor* positions himself or herself as one who compiles, orders, and harmonizes the oral expression of the testimonial subject. The *gestor* represents an important shift in authorial position: to appropriate and faithfully inscribe the informant's discourse, the writer must vanish from the text. Lucille Kerr observes this authorial effort to disguise involvement in the text's creation:

> The responsibilities of the author of a testimonial novel may thus appear at once to be both limited and excessive. They are the responsibilities of a figure who seems to have relinquished his or her role as authentic originator but also to have retained (or reassumed) considerable authority and responsibility characteristic of a more conventional author.[17]

Biografía is a good example of testimonial narrative that attempts to mask the inherent contradictions of its own production. The book's introduction, translations, titles, and overall structure reveal the writer's personal agenda and commitment to Western forms of rhetorical expression.

According to Barnet, the creator of a "novela-testimonio" must shed his individuality in order to assume that of the informant and his collectivity. Behind this act of disempowerment, which involves what Barnet terms "ego-suppression," or "ego-discretion," however, lies an ideological structure that implies control and inequality.[18] In a strikingly autobiographical portion of Barnet's 1970 article, he revealed the essence of his relationship with Montejo. For Barnet, solidarity implied a marvelous transformation, or an unfolding, of the ethnographer into his informant. The ethnographer ceases to live his own life to live that of his subject. A "depersonalization" occurs, whereby the writer can only think, speak, and feel what the informant transmits. Therein, argues Barnet, lies the poetry, the mystery, and the writer's access to the collective consciousness.[19]

Barnet, like Lydia Cabrera, fulfilled his desire for authenticity by achieving solidarity with informants. Because Arguedas was aware of the issues involved in cultural representation, he bypassed the dilemma of inscribing another's voice by creating the illusion of writing from within his own otherness. *Biografía*'s textualization of informant-ethnographer symbiosis creates a poetic fusion of voices. By undergoing a conversion to enable him to write about Afro-Cuban experience, Barnet became a sort of Other in relation to his own word. He was essentially his own ghostwriter, and created a unique oral poetics to convey the illusion of a coherent, chronological monologue.

Montejo dictated what his memory told him, and Barnet transposed these recollections into a "decanted" written language. "Decantation" is a complex, paradoxical process. On one hand, it allows the testimonial subject to speak in the writing such that the oral text serves as the origin or authentic form of discourse. At the same time, however, Barnet suggests the need to interfere and alter what Montejo says by contributing his own writing style and nuances, and by eliminating the impurities of speech. The resulting text represents a fictionalization of Montejo's oral narrative.

Antonio Vera León has proposed an interesting link between the term "decantation" and the Cuban sugar industry. He draws a compelling analogy between refining sugar and polishing spoken language. Taking into account the Cuban state's dependence on the sugar industry, Barnet's use of the metaphor situates his conception of *testimonio* in tension with—and at times in alliance with—the sugar discourses associated with power. In this context, Montejo represents the marginalized condition of Cuban citizens resulting from modernization that accompanied growth of the sugar industry. According to Vera León, Barnet ultimately violates oral culture by extracting it from its context and imposing norms of written culture, thereby reaffirming "the monoculture of writing."[20]

Montejo was aware of the social and political implications of Barnet's project. He, too, stood to gain from the public dissemination of his chronicle. Although Montejo was somewhat hesitant to speak at first, he was quickly won over by Barnet's gifts of tobacco, candies, and liquor. According to the prologue of *Biografía*, Montejo's digressions often determined the thematic course of his discussions with Barnet. He was careful to make sure that Barnet recorded the details of his story. Their dialogues, ultimately represented in the text as Montejo's monologue, are the fruit of an ongoing process of negotiation in which both were vying for knowledge. Roberto González Echevarría argues that the most remarkable illusion of the text is Montejo's triumph in this back-and-forth power struggle: "Montejo is the voice of authority, the dictator; Barnet is merely the scribe (the 'editor,' as the English version of the book reads)."[21] By insisting on the primacy of spoken language and asserting its indisputable veracity, Barnet could not avoid undermining his own authority as *gestor*.

"APPROXIMATING MIGUEL BARNET": BARNET AS *CIMARRÓN*

Barnet's multiple reinterpretations of *Biografía* illustrate his efforts to sever his voice from Montejo's and to regain authorial control over the universally acclaimed book. A striking example is the transcription of a taped interview with Barnet, published in the form of an article entitled "Para llegar a Esteban Montejo: Los caminos del cimarrón" (Approximating Esteban Montejo: The Journeys of the *cimarrón*), which appeared in a 1996 issue of the Havana magazine *Contracorriente*. The article has an auspicious opening paragraph, in which Barnet struggles with the difficult task of telling the story of Montejo without seeming "vain." He concludes that, in order to do so, he must distance himself and transform himself into one of the characters in his novels. Imagine Barnet, seated in a leather armchair, as Montejo was, and speaking into the microphone of a Tesla recorder. What better form to express reflections on the creative process behind his masterwork than a transcribed version of his own recorded voice?

The allusion to vanity makes explicit the tense struggle of voices dramatized throughout *Biografía*. Given the autobiographical nature of the article, perhaps a better title would be "Approximating Miguel Barnet." Contrary to his initial attempts to erase himself from the pages of *Biografía*, Barnet speaks freely in the interview about the impact the acclaimed book had on his career. The piece, which promises to inform the reader of the creative process behind Barnet's first testimonial novel, is instead an anecdotal account, sprinkled with colloquialisms, of Barnet's experiences over the course of almost forty years. Barnet confesses that, with three decades separating him from the book's first publication, he can speak more freely about the process behind its creation and the impact it had on his life. He admits that portions of the book's prologue were more academic than his current treatment of the material. Nevertheless, he continued thinking about Montejo in the same way. Whereas in the 1970 article "La novela testimonio: Socio-literatura" Barnet insisted that the *gestor* of a testimonial novel strip himself of his individuality, the 1996 article demonstrates a remarkably different attitude: the gesture of entering Montejo's world was as much Barnet's own quest for self-knowledge and identity as it was an investigation of the Other's culture.

The solidarity Barnet felt with Montejo was based on more than a professional relationship of ethnographer and informant they cultivated over time. In the end, Barnet confessed, Montejo's defense mechanisms and his own were not very different. "Por razones distintas, cada uno de nosotros era un solitario y, por qué no, un cimarrón. Y eso nos identificó a la larga."[22] [For different reasons, each one of us was a loner and, why not, a *cimarrón*. And that was what connected us, in the long run.] Barnet's reflections, which commemorate the book's thirtieth anniversary, ultimately convey the notion that both he and Montejo were immortalized by *Biografía*: "Ojalá Esteban Montejo nos rocíe con un gajo de albahaca y nos dé fuerzas para llegar, como él ha llegado, a los 135 años de vida."[23] [Let's hope that Esteban Montejo consecrates us with a stem of basil and gives us the strength to reach, as he has reached, the age of 135 years.]

The *Contracorriente* interview offers significant details regarding the book's composition. Although *Biografía* is subdivided into four distinct chapters, it resembles a seamless narrative and can be read as a single storytelling event. The article indicates, however, that the interviews took place over the course of more than a year in a variety of contexts. Barnet tells a revealing anecdote regarding Montejo's "performance" as an informant. Despite the fact that Montejo was resistant to the use of a tape recorder, Barnet brought the machine to the barber shop of the Veterans' Home and played it so that the other veterans could hear Montejo's voice. The audience was so enthused that Esteban basked in the attention. In their subsequent encounters, Montejo urged Barnet to bring the Tesla recorder to the shop so that his friends could listen to and take part in his stories.

Montejo may have emphasized his penchant for solitude, but he was actually quite a performer. In fact, many of his "interviews" with Barnet were actually conducted before an audience, amid the laughter and commentary of the old men who congregated in the barber shop, a place where everyone exchanged gossip and love stories.[24] In writing, Barnet reduced the audience to a single interlocutor in order to preserve the pretense of ethnographic method. However, it is likely that Montejo's clever remarks and tall tales responded to some degree to the prodding of fellow veterans. Perhaps some of their gossip and anecdotes are found in the voice of Montejo.

The 1996 interview reveals the extent to which Barnet was a catalyst to Montejo's memory. It becomes clear that the editor was predominantly responsible for constructing a historical context that shaped the informant's discourse. In fact, when the ex-slave's story did not coincide with expectations of historicity, Barnet intervened to make sure Montejo filled in the blanks appropriately. One of the most literary moments in the book resulted from an intervention of this kind. After completing a draft of

Biografía, Barnet circulated the manuscript among his colleagues, including Argeliers León and Calixta Guiteras. After reading an initial version, Antonio Núñez Jiménez, president of the Academy of Sciences, asked Barnet why Montejo had never lived in a cave during his sixteen years as a runaway slave. Barnet posed this question during his next visit to the Veterans' Home, and, to his surprise, Montejo responded nonchalantly that he had indeed spent more than a year in the caves of Guamuhaya in Trinidad. The cave sequence was later inserted into the chapter "La vida en el monte" (Life in el monte), and prefaced by an editorial note in which Barnet cited at length Núñez Jiménez's findings with regard to caves as havens for fugitive slaves. Barnet and Montejo both gained from the addition to the text: the former confirmed the findings of his superior and the latter satisfied the questionings of his interviewer.

Barnet was captivated by Montejo's fabulous stories and inventive imagination. The ex-slave repeatedly insisted on the veracity of incredible anecdotes and memories. Nevertheless, Barnet marveled at spoken language's capacity to convey an authentic account of history. In his narrative, Montejo repeatedly cast himself as an ethnographer of sorts who could distinguish fact from fiction. His rhetoric stemmed from an anxiety to convince his audience not only that he had truly "been there," but that had we been there we would have similar findings.[25] Montejo's narrative suggests that he was aware of what an outsider might consider fantastical. For example, on several occasions he confutes Congo beliefs just as an outsider might deem his own tales fallible:

> Después de la esclavitud yo le hice el cuento a un congo; el cuento de que yo había vivido con los murciélagos y el embustero, ellos a veces eran más jodedores de lo que uno se creía, me dijo: "Usté criollo no sabe ná. En mi tierra ese que usté llama murciélago son tan grande como un palomo rabiche." Yo sabía que eso era cuento. Con esas historias ellos engañaron a medio mundo. Pero lo oí y me divertí por dentro.[26]

> [After Abolition I told a Congolese the story of how I lived with the bats, and the liar—the Congolese were even worse than you could imagine—said, "A Creole like you doesn't know a thing. In my country what you call a bat is as big as a pigeon." I knew this was untrue. They fooled half the world with their tales. But I just listened and was inwardly amused.][27]

Montejo's rhetoric conveys a fundamental distinction between hearing and seeing: the spoken word can betray the truth, whereas eyewitness experience is absolutely certifiable. Paradoxically, however, the authenticity of his own anecdotes relies wholly on the spoken word. For this reason, he manipulated language to neutralize any uncertainty about the veracity of his own stories and emphatically presented himself as an absolute authority. This strategy is apparent when Montejo alludes to seemingly exotic phenomena, as in the story of the *diablillo*:

> Yo le hice el cuento del diablillo una vez a un joven y me dijo que eso era mentira. Pero aunque parezca mentira, es cierto. Un hombre puede criar un diablillo. Sí, señor, un diablillo. Un congo viejo del ingenio Timbirito fue quien me enseñó a hacerlo. [...] Había que oírlo en los cuentos. Lo había visto todo; lo de aquí abajo y lo de arriba también. En verdad que era un poco cascarrabias, pero yo lo entendía. Nunca le dije: "Usted no sabe lo que hable." Ni me reí de él.[28]

> [I once told a young man about the little devil, and he said I was lying. Well, it may sound like a lie, but it's the plain truth. A man can make his own little devil, yes sir, he can. An old Congolese from the Timbirito plantation showed me how to do it. . . . You should have heard his stories. He had seen it all, everything down here below and up above too. He was a bit cantankerous, really, but I got on all right with him. I never said, "You don't know what you're talking about" or laughed at him.][29]

The two passages are indicative of the tension between fact and fiction that subtends *Biografía*. Moralizing stories are distinguished from those that promise to entertain. The cited passages reveal that Montejo, who claimed to know when to laugh and when to take a story at face value, portrayed himself as a faithful arbitrator between didactic truths and pleasurable tales.

The 1996 interview published in *Contracorriente* reveals that Barnet, like Montejo, believed that fact and fiction were mutually exclusive. Although Barnet never denied manipulating syntax and nuances to enhance the linguistic verisimilitude of Montejo's narrative, thirty years after the book's publication we learn that he, like Montejo, saw that excess fabrication could jeopardize the text's legitimacy. Ultimately, he extracted unverifiable material from Montejo's tale to create an effect of realism.

The distinction between fact and fiction that the book upholds can best be understood as a rhetorical strategy to enhance the realism of the narrative. However, as James Clifford argues convincingly, the poetic and the political are inseparable, and cultural representations like *testimonio* are best perceived as the interface between multiple disciplines, both scientific and literary. He writes, "[T]he constructed, artificial nature of cultural accounts . . . undermines overly transparent modes of authority, and it draws attention to the historical predicament of ethnography, the fact that it is always caught up in the invention, not the representation, of cultures."[30]

Although Barnet explicitly defends the notion that ethnology and literature are separate enterprises, the text betrays this perception. Attempts at conveying an illusion of ethnographic realism expose the literariness of *Biografía*.

In his efforts to render cross-cultural experience in writing, Barnet was tempted by certain narrative devices. Years after the book's publication, he justified his manipulation of the text by adopting a flexible approach to the author function. A close reading of *Biografía* demonstrates that Barnet's justifications are embedded in Montejo's rhetoric and storytelling techniques. Barnet took advantage of the fluidity and flexibility of oral discourse to convey a realistic simulacrum of speech. Some critics who have fallen prey to the illusions of realism prevalent in books like *Biografía* subscribe to a dichotomy of fact versus fiction that mistakenly associates literariness with fictionality. The propensity to insist on a distinction between realism and fantasy stems from a discomfort with constructing ostensibly realistic texts out of experiences that are largely contingent on an individual's personal account.

When Barnet first circulated the manuscript of *Biografía* among his colleagues in the mid-1960s, he was likely unaware of its novelty. The prologue introduces the text as a factual ethnography akin to accounts of Afro-Cuban culture put forward by Barnet's mentors like Argeliers León, Juan Pérez de la Riva, and Fernando Ortiz. Only after its publication in 1966 did Barnet begin to theorize about his book's potential as a literary work. An anthropological monograph was recast as an important contribution to the postmodern era. Barnet redefined the text's scientific apparatus—its prologue, editorial notes and glossary—as manifestations of postmodern discursive practices. He defines the book as a critical edition.

What initially must have been a source of uncertainty for Barnet—the text's defiance of norms of classification—became the most celebrated aspect of *Biografía*. His reflections in the 1996 interview stem from a growing awareness of the postmodern era's destabilization of categories of discourse. Barnet portrays himself as a Montejo-like revolutionary, a founder of a new form of written expression, encompassing history, philosophy, sociology, and poetry. Whereas Barnet at first downplayed his poetic sensibility, in the interview he heralds his ability to fuse ethnology with poetics as an ingenuous means of surpassing hackneyed literary conventions by conceiving textuality as a pastiche of genres: "Yo partí de la etnología, de conceptos y presupuestos etnológicos y sociológicos, pero traté de que ese roce con la literatura no perdiera, o mejor, que en ese roce con la literatura pura no se perdieran energías y que la obra con sus personajes y sus paisajes, se viera cargada de sustancias nutricias."[31] [I departed from ethnology, from ethnological and sociological concepts and premises; but I tried to preserve that contact with literature, so that energy wasn't lost in that brush with pure literature, and that the work, with its characters and scenery, would seem loaded with nutritious substances.] The "energy" and "nutritious substances" to which Barnet refers reveal ethnology's complicity with orality.

Implicit in Barnet's statement is a perception that ethnographic writing excludes literary forms. Recently, however, anthropologists have considered the literary qualities of anthropological writing and reread past ethnographies by applying notions of textuality and discursiveness.[32] Barnet's reevaluation of *Biografía* actually coincided with contemporary trends in anthropology that champion the writerly nature of experimental ethnographies. He, like Cabrera and Arguedas, formulated an ethnographic poetics to render oral narrative in writing. As in his first collections of poetry, Barnet developed a literary voice in his testimonial novels by expressing an orally derived poetics. This discursive strategy for contriving voice in writing culminated in *Biografía*, in which Barnet consciously reproduced the syntax and vocabulary of Montejo's spoken discourse in his efforts to create a realistic effect of orality.

ORAL POETICS AND THE WRITTEN VOICE

Barnet shared with Cabrera and Arguedas the notion that one must negotiate an impasse between literate and oral cultures in order to successfully represent the Other's reality. His insistence on the primacy of speech underscores the need for the *gestor* to textualize orality by reconfiguring spoken language. Barnet described oral culture as philosophical, with a metaphysical and mythical foundation. Whereas Esteban belonged to this culture, Barnet characterized himself as an intellectual, a man with a distinct cultural formation.[33] Such an assumption of ideological difference proved necessary for Barnet to construct a fictionalization of Montejo's life story. The tension underlying the literariness of *Biografía* stems from Barnet's own ambiguous perceptions regarding the ability of oral discourse to faithfully represent verifiable truth.

Barnet insisted on the purity and spontaneity of speech; in his opinion, the tonalities and nuances of voice best capture the "essence" of a culture. But the text of *Biografía* represents a linguistic compromise. Barnet felt that a direct transcription of his interviews with Montejo would have portrayed an overly simplistic caricature rather than an authentic and speaking subject. He differs from Cabrera in this regard. In "La novela testimonio: Socio-literatura," Barnet attributed the linguistic realism of *Biografía* to a technique by which he "decanted" written language from the anecdotes and tones of Montejo's speech.

Barnet openly criticized Carlos Fuentes and other Spanish American writers for falsifying orality in writing by mimicking too closely the phonetics of spoken discourse. These writers, he argued, separated language from life, transforming their characters into puppets.[34] Barnet was obviously aware of the complexities involved in transposing another individual's speech into written form by creating a simulacrum of monologue. The artifice that permits us to hear the Other's voice in *testimonio* originates in official and literate discourse. A vindication of orality was an important trait of postboom experimental writing that sought to capture Other voices.

Michel de Certeau adopts the concept of enunciation to describe how speaking effects an appropriation of language and necessitates a contract with the Other. Upon considering how voice enters texts, he focuses on one variant called the "'science of fables,'" which he sees as touching on "all the learned or elitist hermeneutics of speech . . . as they have been elaborated over the past two centuries by ethnology . . . seeking to introduce the 'voice of the people' into the authorized language." Certeau categorizes such hegemonic discourses—ethnology, pedagogy and psychiatry, for example—as "heterologies":

> These different "heterologies" (sciences of the different) have the common characteristic of attempting to *write the voice*. The voice reaching us from a great distance must find a place in the text. Thus primitive orality has to be written in the ethnological discourse. . . . What is audible, but far away, will thus be transformed into texts in conformity with the Western desire to read its products.

Certeau concludes that all "heterological" literature proceeds from a fracture between contextual presence and the writing system. It not only alters voice, but also remains altered by orality.[35]

The gesture of reenacting Montejo's speech was fraught with the hazards of distortion implicit in the practice of redemptive ethnography. How can another's spoken language be conveyed in writing without sacrificing the originality and immediacy of the Other's voice? Montejo's seamless narrative and his performative storytelling are a fiction masquerading as objective discourse. The text, as a mimesis of speech, erases the contextual constructs of its making; gaps in time and factual discrepancies are suppressed. Barnet attempted to create a sense of spontaneity by using the first-person voice of Montejo.

The introduction to *Autobiography of a Runaway Slave* is even more revealing: "I wanted the story to *sound* spontaneous and *as if* it came from the heart, and so I inserted words and expressions characteristic of Esteban wherever they seemed appropriate."[36] The written voice that emerges from the pages of the text purports to be a metaphor for self-presence and authenticity, a phonocentric conceit that subtends much of Spanish American narrative. But the propensity to privilege orality puts into question the very process of conveying voice with writing. Montejo's most "authentic" language, the words and phrases allegedly captured in their purest form on the tape recorder, were deemed inappropriate for the written text.

During the years in which he interviewed Montejo, Barnet studied not only *what* Montejo said but, more importantly, *how* he said it. To convey Montejo's anecdotes in writing, Barnet had, in part, to divest himself of his rigorous discursive training as a cultural anthropologist and become a storyteller. He found that the gesture of storytelling fulfilled the ethnographic promise of recovering collective memory and reformulating it within a present context.

Roger D. Abrahams argues that the act of telling one's story calls for that story to be judged in terms of its believability as well as in terms of its aesthetic value: "Storytelling involves one of the most complicated of all playful complicitous activities, for it allows speakers to use language in a way that immediately denies all claims for veracity."[37] Storytelling requires an ongoing negotiation between storyteller and interlocutor whereby linguistic manipulation can compensate for transparency of verbal expression. Repetitions, interjections, colloquial sayings, and ellipses are some of the means for achieving a mimesis of spoken discourse by creating a rhetorical effect of orality. *Biografía* can be read as a written performance of the stylistics of oral storytelling.

The most significant contributing factor to the literariness of *Biografía* and Barnet's other testimonial novels is their oral quality. Montejo recites his life story in a seamless textual fabric punctuated by moralizing reflections and re-creations of dialogue. How did Barnet create the effect that Montejo was speaking effortlessly through his pen? Through a unique stylistics, he endowed the uniform narrative with an oral rhythm and an intimate tone such that the text is most completely comprehensible when read aloud.

From the opening pages, Montejo is cast as a somewhat crass and opinionated singer of tales. His initial remarks bring to the fore the most pronounced features of oral narration: repetitions, flashbacks, epithets, allusions to multiple variants of myths, false starts, rhetorical questions, digressions, moralistic conclusions, onomatopoeic interjections, temporal imprecision, and syntax and punctuation dictated by oral expression rather than grammatical norms.[38] The opening pages inaugurate us to Montejo's convoluted logic as he attempts to explain the inexplicable. The apocalyptic beginning to Montejo's story—his recollection of a solar eclipse—betrays conventional historic accounts; it leads the reader through a disjointed sequence of observations and culminates in the introduction of slavery, the chapter's theme. Ultimately, Montejo reaches a conclusion that negates all that he has told us up to this point: "La verdad es que yo me pongo a pensar y no doy pie con bola."[39] [The truth is, I start thinking, and I can't make head or tail of it.][40] The opening passage sets the precedent that voice can control and betray meaning.

Biografía is constructed as a performance of oral memory. The supposed origin of the utterance is therefore doubly removed from Barnet, the scribe and editor: a mental performance of Montejo's memories precedes his telling of past experiences. The book portrays memory as an authentic source of voice and an important cultural force. According to Montejo, the extent to which an experience was embedded in a temporal past enhanced its durability throughout time. Time preserves memories, he reflects. One can never remember the recent past.

Montejo appears to be concerned with establishing his position as a long-term witness of events that he perceives to be foreign to the listener. Similarly, as the catalyst of Montejo's memory and the editor of his words, Barnet recognized the need to legitimize the commemorative process as a means for expressing a realist account of past events. The technique for rhetorically sanctioning the veracity of oral memory is even more pronounced in *Gallego* than in *Biografía*. Manuel Ruiz's thoughts on the commemorative process are strikingly reminiscent of Montejo's:

> La memoria, digo yo, es traicionera. Mientras más para atrás se la lleva, más clara se pone. Pero de hoy, vamos, de unos veinte años para acá, voy recordando muy poco, casi nada. Yo digo que se me forma un nido de alacranes en la cabeza y no hay manera de que recuerde. Me preguntan y me quedo en blanco, como si no hubiera sido yo el que soy.[41]

> [Memory, I say, betrays. The farther back you go, the clearer it becomes. But from today back, say twenty years up to the present, I remember very little, almost nothing. I like to say that I have a nest of scorpions in my head and there is no way to remember. They ask me things and I draw a blank, as if I hadn't been who I am.]

When transforming Montejo into a literary figure, Barnet experimented with rhetorical techniques for representing oral memory that he later refined and carried to an extreme in *Canción de Rachel* (Rachel's Song) and *Gallego*.

Essential to the filtering process that converts spoken language into a written aesthetic are certain rhetorical structures that mimic oral noetics. The fact that oral cultures tend to organize their knowledge in thematically based narratives must have been attractive to Barnet in his attempts to achieve a historical interpretation of Montejo's life story. The literary and poetic qualities of the account provided Barnet with a version of Cuba's past that defied, and in his opinion surpassed, conventions of official history. Barnet acknowledged that he significantly altered the order of the transcriptions to construct a chronological story that dovetailed with key moments in Cuban history.

The resulting semblance of linearity, however, conflicts with the natural progression of spoken narrative, which does not tend to obey a chronological sequencing of events. Barnet told us in the introduction that Montejo's story was disjointed. Montejo was not ignorant of the need to fill in historical gaps. Both he and Barnet conspired to transmit recovered history. This act of remembering did not merely repeat memories of the past; its goal was to understand the past within a present context by inscribing the experiences of a previously underrepresented population. Articulation of the past enabled both Montejo and Barnet to define the present and perhaps control the future.

Barnet acknowledged in the prologue of *Biografía* that, had he carried through a faithful transcription of Montejo's language, the resulting text would have been excessively redundant. Barnet excluded information that he deemed superfluous. By paraphrasing much of what Esteban said, Barnet was able to create a clear and coherent narration. But repetition may have been a mnemonic device inextricably linked to the poetics of an oral retelling that formed Montejo's style of narration.

In his 1996 interview, Barnet recalled the memorable day when he presented Montejo with the first edition of the book. Montejo just laughed and remarked that the small book could not possibly contain his entire story. Of course, the three hundred pages of manuscript, practically devoid of corrections, contained Barnet's arrangement of Montejo's biography. Barnet created his own version of Montejo's spoken language; he used what he learned from Montejo about the tropes of oral culture to create a stylistics of the oral. To assume that the editor of *testimonio* is merely an instrument of transcription is to indulge the oral as an unmediated representation of life. The sense of immediate presence that the book conveys is, of course, illusory. As in Cabrera's and Arguedas's writings, voice enters the text by a process of fictionalization.

Barnet constructed *Biografía* as a communicative text by preserving some of Montejo's repetitions to enhance the effect of orality in the narration. Digressions and repetitions, both typical features of speech, are also crucial to Montejo's desire to validate his stories. He obsessively reassures the reader of his reliability as a witness by prefacing his opinions with statements like "The truth is that . . ." and "What I know is that. . . ." At times, he fashions himself as an interlocutor, and offers multiple versions of stories. The middle chapter of the book dramatizes a spiraling progression of oral memory that constantly turns back on itself. The thematic thread of Montejo's experiences as an ex-slave, invented by Barnet, is tangled within a textuality of digressions and flashbacks. In his description of the *bandoleros*, or bandits, Montejo evokes the legend of Manuel García, a Martín Fierro of sorts, whose mysterious death fostered countless stories. Montejo bemoans the lack of clarity of these accounts, and haphazardly stumbles upon the topic of medicine men (*brujos*).

The mention of *brujos* leads him to a tangential discussion of witchcraft, which he links back to the topic of *bandoleros*. Here ensues another digression—a discussion of the extreme heat one must endure in *el monte* —followed by a leap back to the former topic, fear of witchcraft. The narrative transitions into the story of Tajó, another legendary figure of Cuban history who allegedly kidnapped and consumed women. Finally, the mention of women provides Montejo with the perfect segue into his favorite topic: his personal romantic conquests. The dramatic narrative dance informs us of the circuitous logic of Montejo's narrative style and re-creates, in writing, the act of telling.

Montejo, like Barnet, was an anthropologist of sorts, intrigued by the power of stories. His fascination with oral tradition is evident in the episode dedicated to Ma'Lucía, the storyteller of Lucumí descent, whose voice first emerges as a written quotation, highlighting her rustic and colloquial dialect. Montejo's synopses of her stories constitute a brief collection of Afro-Cuban fables. He equivocates about his willingness to believe the stories, saying at first that many of her tales are lies, and later opting to deem the tales as truthful, since he believed Africans to be wise and knowledgeable.

Montejo clearly perceived the fallibility of spoken language and saw the need to portray himself as capable of discerning truth. He differentiated the story of his life—what he saw and what he heard—from stories told by others. Montejo warns his audience that his memory confuses facts, history, and tall tales. He draws a distinction between stories that are intended to entertain and those with a purely didactic function, perhaps to substantiate his own accounts.

Throughout his tale, the ex-slave struggles to control the slipperiness and volatility of spoken discourse. The friction between confession and gossip constitutes a dynamic play of language. Montejo's efforts to censor his words are transparent; and, as a result, he falls victim to the vice he warns against: idle gossip. He portrays himself as a solitary man, a quiet and independent observer rather than a leader and an extrovert, but Barnet's descriptions of their encounters in the barbershop indicate otherwise. By explicitly assuming an exaggeratedly marginal position, Montejo can express himself with greater freedom. He claims to have learned from his elders the dangers of untamed speech. Fortunately, he admits, he has always remained quiet. According to Montejo, excessive talk incites distrust. He expresses his concern that his words might some day be used against him. Nevertheless, he gives in to his desire to relate his exploits, particularly those having to do with countless women. Ironically, Barnet's copious notes and transcriptions are tangible proof of Montejo's irrepressible propensity to tell tall tales, murmur, gossip, joke, and moralize. *Biografía* is a text that relishes in the delight of surprising us with the unbelievable and convincing us of its plausibility.

BARNET'S PILGRIMAGE TO CUBAN IDENTITY

Barnet's knack for using narrative devices to contrive an effect of orality in writing is fully displayed in the final two books of his trilogy of testimonial novels: *Canción de Rachel* (1969) and *Gallego* (1981). In both, the orality of the texts constitutes an important part of the fiction. Rachel is a synthesis of female artists interviewed by Barnet, and Manuel Ruiz's persona is drawn from various written accounts of the *gallego* experience in Cuba. In these texts, Barnet abandoned his role as ethnographer and entered the realm of pure invention.[42] *Casa de las Américas* reviewed *Canción de Rachel* as a comic parody of the mentality of a demimondaine immortalized in Havana's nightlife. The unprepared reader might interpret it as the present-day drama of a single human destiny.[43] A quote cited in the review, drawn from Barnet's brief introduction to the book, reads in toto: "*Canción de Rachel* habla de ella, de su vida, tal y como ella me la contó y tal como yo luego se la conté a ella." [*Canción de Rachel* speaks about her, about her life, just as she told it to me and just as I later told it to her.] The role of the *gestor* evolved significantly in this book; Barnet created a composite literary figure out of multiple informants. He fused the voices of several women into a single monologue, thereby assuming control over the narrative and inventing a fictitious orality.

Canción de Rachel opens *in media res* with a stream of consciousness monologue that immediately establishes the chit-chatty tone of Rachel's confessions. Her voice emerges in rhythmic cadences, punctuated by dramatic interjections and silent ellipses: "Mi madre era húngara y mi padre, alemán. Ella húngara y él alemán. Ella bajita y pecosa, muy jaranera. Una mujercita de temple. Mi padre, no lo sé."[44] [My mother was Hungarian and my father, German. She, Hungarian and he, German. She, short and freckled, a real joker. A strong little woman. My father, I don't know.] Mnemonic devices, crucial to oral retelling, determine the text's syntax and diction. Rachel, like Montejo, appeals to her audience to pardon her digressions; she acknowledges the dangers of gossip. Her reluctance to speak is a rhetorical means of convincing her listener to urge her to continue. As in *Biografía*, these internal contradictions enhance the oral quality of a text that purports to be a single monologue.

Rachel, unlike Montejo, is condemned for her abuse of language. Her confessions are interspersed with secondary accounts, which, according to Barnet, complement the central monologue. But, these supplementary voices undermine the protagonist's narrative. For example, after Rachel vindicates herself from the charge of burning a circus tent, an anonymous voice interjects to say that she tells little white lies. Such interjections point to the fact that the editor ultimately controls the reception of the informant's voice. The polyphonic layering of voices is one of many techniques of oral poetics that enhances the realism of the text. The montage is replete with songs, dramatic interludes, quotations, and sayings.

Rachel's monologue erases gaps in time and space by incorporating direct allusions to her surroundings, as when she guides the listener through her photo album. She announces that she is ugly in one picture, not herself in another, concluding that it is best to destroy pictures or burn them. The scene evolves into the reenactment of her first comedy at the Alhambra, a play entitled *Carne fresca*. As in *Biografía*, the book's ideological claim to represent an exterior reality rests on the premise that the spoken word can endow a text with presentness and authenticity.

The degree of artifice is even more pronounced in *Gallego*, the final book of Barnet's trilogy, published more than a decade after *Canción de Rachel*. Barnet essentially employed the same strategies as he did in *Biografía* to construct a simulacrum of an exceptional informant's oral monologue. Manuel Ruiz, like Rachel, is a composite figure, but his identity is drawn primarily from written sources. The reader learns that Manuel is Antonio, Fabián, José, or any one of many immigrants who abandoned his Galician town in search of a better life.[45] Barnet conducted much of his research in the archives of the Galician collection at Havana's Institute of Literature and Linguistics of the Cuban Academy of Sciences. The book is not parodic, like *Canción de Rachel*; rather, it is a well-documented novel that elaborates one man's account of Cuban culture from the outside perspective of an immigrant.

A close look at the oral tropes that pervade the text reveals lessons Barnet might have learned about writing orality in his previous novels. Like *Biografía*, *Gallego* borrows certain extratextual elements from historiography and ethnography to substantiate the protagonist's account. Heterological operations, like those described by Certeau, are invoked to inscribe the voice of the Other. For example, editorial notes supplement the primary text to clarify the historical context, explain Galician vocabulary, and integrate quotations from archival sources. Barnet chose to revive the voices of Ruiz's compatriots to bolster the protagonist's testimony.

At times the editorial notes are more aesthetic than informative. For example, a strikingly poetic note follows Ruiz's claim to retain in his memory the stories and songs told by his grandfather: "¡Cuánta poesía en las canciones gallegas! ¡Ah, pobre pluma, que no acierta a expresar todo lo que siente un alma gallega cuando se agitan sus alas al pasar por ella el nervioso rumor de muñeira y alalás! Cantad mares y selvas, cantad pájaros, cantad almas enamoradas, cantad poetas... (Isidro Bugellad. Galicia, 1 de diciembre de 1917.)" [There is so much poetry in Galician song! Oh, but the feeble pen is truly inadequate to describe all that one feels, how the Galician heart takes flight in the vibrancy of our *muñeira* {folk dance} and of joyous voices raised in song. Sing, seas and forests; sing, souls entwined; trill, songbirds; sing, poets . . . (Isidro Bugellad. Galicia, December 1, 1917.)] The Galician's realization of the shortcomings of the written word is striking. It seems that only song can completely capture the essence of the Galician's soul. The proclamation confirms the poetic epigraphs that inaugurate each chapter, like Rosalía de Castro's lamentation that opens the book, and is punctuated with the pangs of exile.

The book's self-conscious mimesis of the spoken word, as evidenced in the inaugural epigraph, reflects Barnet's unswaying confidence in the capacity of speech to represent the Other's reality. Ruiz's discourse, like his persona, is a fiction; it reflects a melding of dialects that strives to recreate the bicultural immigrant experience. The narrator-protagonist claims that he took great pains to understand the rapid speech of his acquaintances in Cuba. An editorial note tells the reader that, in comparison with other nationalities that emigrated to Cuba, Galicians assimilated spoken Spanish with ease. In an attempt to further clarify the process of linguistic mediation that the book undertakes, the editor explains that the book seeks to reflect the "linguistic transmutation" that occurred when two languages of ancient origin intersected.[46]

Translation makes it possible to move from one language to another, to create a pervasive sense of immediacy. The text is highly conscious of this ongoing process of mediation. Ruiz assumes the translator's perspective vis-à-vis the very language he struggles to understand, when he offers translations for colloquialisms and Cubanisms. In many ways Ruiz is like Juan Pérez Jolote and, to a certain extent, Montejo; his shifting perspective allows him to move between cultures, as a participant-observer with irrefutable claims of "having been there."

Manuel Ruiz inherits Montejo's penchant for storytelling, his delight in proverbs and sayings, and his notions about the fallibility of memory. *Biografía* served as the proving ground for these tropes of orality that Barnet later refined to endow Ruiz with an authentic voice. Barnet interspersed sayings and moralizing statements throughout Montejo's story to give his testimony a familiar and personal tone. This discursive tactic is so pronounced in *Gallego* that it verges on linguistic parody.

Streams of consciousness, digressions, and repetitions furnish both texts with an undeniably communicative tone. The interpolated tales of Ma'Lucía find their counterpart in the fantastic stories passed on by Ruiz's grandfather. In *Biografía*, Barnet chose to erase concrete references to where and when Montejo told his life story. Only much later do we learn that several of the interviews were conducted in the crowded nursing-home barbershop. In *Gallego*, however, a key mechanism for enhancing the veracity of Ruiz's tale is specific allusions to a tangible Cuban setting in which the informant told his story.

In *La fuente viva*, a collection of Barnet's essays first compiled in 1983, just two years after the publication of *Gallego*, Barnet expressed his conviction that orality granted him access to the Holy Grail of Cuban identity: "La expresión oral, multifacética, su riqueza conceptual, la cosmogonía del hombre cubano, me ha permitido acercarse a esa Meca tan anhelada por todos: la identidad."[47] [Multifaceted oral expression, its conceptual richness and the cosmogony of the Cuban, has allowed me to approach that Mecca so desired by all: identity.] Barnet reached this conclusion at a time when he had set aside his ethnographic guise and discovered that the fictionalization of oral testimony provided him with the most authentic manifestation of the written voice. In this way, he went beyond Cabrera and Arguedas by contriving voice as artifice and creating a fictionalized aesthetic of the oral to capture speech in writing.

His writings of the past two decades reflect a more pronounced division between Barnet the ethnographer and Barnet the fiction writer. Two works are particularly noteworthy, because they are in many ways reminiscent of projects undertaken by Lydia Cabrera. The first, Barnet's 1978 publication of *Los perros mudos* (The Silent Dogs), is essentially an extension of Cabrera's recreations of Afro-Cuban folklore. Barnet tells us that the fables, of African or Spanish origin, have been transformed, respecting the tendencies of the Cuban storytelling tradition.[48] The fables self-consciously re-create the oral language of both white and nonwhite storytellers to dramatize Cuba's rich mythical tradition.

A strikingly different project, *Cultos afrocubanos: La Regla de Ocha; La Regla de Palo Monte* (Afro-Cuban Religions: The Cult of Ocha and the Cult of Palo Monte), was published in 1995. In the introduction, Barnet promises to untangle the complex "jungle" of Cuba's *monte* by focusing on elements of transculturation. The text, a handbook of Cuba's syncretic religions, is essentially an abridged version of *El monte*. Barnet occasionally cites Cabrera, but includes a disclaimer stating his categorical rejection of her political views. Remarkably, he incorporates several quotes from *Biografía*, citing Montejo as a reliable source regarding African religions. *Cultos afrocubanos* thus repeats the ambiguous play between ethnography and literature that canonized *Biografía* as a revolutionary text. Esteban Montejo is immortalized yet again; Barnet reinvents him as an authoritative ethnographer, an expert on the very subject that the informant resisted in their interviews three decades earlier.

RIGOBERTA AND THE TESTIMONIAL CONTRACT

For Barnet, international fame and literary canonization were both unanticipated outcomes of the publication of *Biografía*. Worldwide success also ensued from the publication of another documentary narrative: *Me llamo Rigoberta Menchú y así me nació la conciencia* (1983) (*I, Rigoberta Menchú: An Indian Woman in Guatemala*), the turbulent life story of a woman exiled from a K'iche'-speaking village in Guatemala. Rigoberta, the Indian informant, gained far more celebrity from the book's publication than did Elisabeth Burgos-Debray, the Paris-trained anthropologist who composed the narrative. Burgos, who was born and raised in Venezuela's upper class and later married the Marxist philosopher Régis Debray, interviewed Rigoberta over the course of eight days. Just as Barnet's name graced the cover of *Biografía*, Burgos's name appears on the front cover of the original Spanish version of *Me llamo Rigoberta Menchú*, published by Editions Gallimard in 1983. Ten years after Rigoberta related her story in

Burgos's Paris apartment, the Nobel Committee awarded her the 1992 Peace Prize, in recognition of her work as a cross-cultural mediator and representative of indigenous peoples, and to commemorate the 500th anniversary of the colonization of the Americas. Burgos was not invited to attend the ceremonies.

Fifteen years after its publication, Rigoberta's internationally acclaimed *testimonio* became the subject of significant controversy. A recent study by anthropologist David Stoll has shown that key details of her account are untrue, and indeed betray the indigenous collectivity she purported to represent. Rigoberta's claims of truth in *Me llamo Rigoberta Menchú* are based on her ability to fashion herself rhetorically as an eyewitness and an active participant in the events she recounts. The controversy highlights Western culture's inclination to subscribe to the truth and purity of spoken language. It strikes at the heart of the complex relationship between ethnography and fiction that the genre of *testimonio* revolutionized.

To enhance the realistic quality of the testimony, Burgos, like Barnet, consciously erased her voice from the narrative.[49] Nevertheless, she appears with Rigoberta in a photograph on the inside jacket of the Gallimard edition, and her brief introduction sheds light on the book's production. The book's introduction tells us that when Burgos first met Rigoberta in January 1982, the young Guatemalan woman was dressed in a colorful *huipil*, the native dress of her homeland. Upon meeting her, Burgos was struck by Rigoberta's childlike innocence; but she later found that Rigoberta spoke earnestly about the tragedies her family had endured.

At the time of their first encounter, Burgos was working on her doctoral dissertation and actively collaborating with Guatemalan revolutionaries who resided in Paris. A political exile herself, she identified with their cause, which resembled that of revolutionary movements in her native country. Perhaps this contributed to the instant solidarity between Burgos and Rigoberta, a closeness that was not present in subsequent encounters. Burgos's training with the anthropologist George Devereux had introduced her to an ethnopsychiatric approach that taught her to allow the interviewee's story to take its course by intervening only when necessary.[50] At first, Burgos provided Rigoberta with a general chronological framework for her story: childhood, adolescence, family, political activity, and so on. Rigoberta's story flowed effortlessly, with little prompting from her interviewer.[51]

In the introduction, Burgos explains that Rigoberta used her voice as a mechanism of defense; Rigoberta claims that she learned Spanish so that she could use the language of the oppressor against him. By the time Rigoberta agreed to disclose her past, she had learned how to manipulate the spoken word quite convincingly. As a discursive tool, orality proved to be an ideal means for constructing a collective identity. Rigoberta responded to Western expectations by re-creating her life story in a way that downplayed chronological inconsistencies and factual discrepancies. She understood the impact that telling her story might have as much as she realized the powerful implications of not telling.

Perhaps with the aid of Burgos's editorial touches, Rigoberta strengthened her claims as an eyewitness by explicitly acknowledging that portions of her story were sacred and therefore best kept secret.[52] This deliberate rhetorical strategy is far more effective than simply omitting information. She constructed a realm of knowledge that only she could access and translate for her readership. The final chapter of Rigoberta's testimony concludes as follows: "Todavía sigo ocultando mi identidad como indígena. Sigo ocultando lo que yo considero que nadie sabe, ni siquiera un antropólogo, ni un intelectual, por más que tenga muchos libros, no saben distinguir todos nuestros secretos."[53] [I'm still keeping secret what I think no one should know. Not even anthropologists or intellectuals, no matter how many books they have, can find out all our secrets.][54]

Rigoberta's testimony dramatizes the idea that a literate mentality can never fully access the sacred knowledge enshrined in a predominantly oral culture. The text's treatment of oral discourse as the key to collective expression reflects a belief in a great divide between literacy and orality. This view that privileges the oral and thereby grants spoken words exemption from any review of their truthfulness is suspect. At a practical level, the argument for the incompatibility of oral and literate minds presents a fundamental contradiction insofar as the informant is giving her testimony from within a literate culture and for a reading public. In *Me llamo Rigoberta Menchú,* Burgos and Menchú are coproducers of the book. Both are aware of the rhetorical advantages of affirming an ideological chasm between two cultures, one predominantly oral and the other literate. The text's portrayal of the indigenous world as a collectivity, which celebrates the presentness and sacred powers of oral communication, is really a construction that reflects a Western bias. The ideological construct enables Rigoberta to fashion herself as a cross-cultural mediator. She, like Arguedas, underscores her otherness to convince us of her unique capacity to inscribe the voices of her community.

Rigoberta's story was initially intended as a magazine interview to be published in the Parisian weekly *Le Nouvel Observateur.* According to Burgos, the Canadian medical doctor Marie Tremblay suggested that she write the article. Only after Rigoberta's departure from Paris did Burgos think to transcribe the eighteen and a half hours of taped interviews and compile them into a book. She faced the daunting task of organizing the five-hundred-page manuscript into a coherent narrative. Burgos reached a conclusion similar to Barnet's: a literal transcription, in her opinion, would be illegible. She maintains that she selected some general recurring themes, like "Life in the *finca*," which she believed marked important moments in Rigoberta's story. Then, she endeavored to re-create the nuances of Rigoberta's speech to endow the text with the tone of Guatemalan Spanish. To convey Rigoberta's narrative in writing, Burgos, like Barnet, perceived a necessary conversion: she wanted to become the Other's double, to write from within Rigoberta's memory:

> I allowed her to speak and then became her instrument, her double by allowing her to make the transition from the spoken to the written word. I have to admit that this decision made my task more difficult, as I had to insert linking passages if the manuscript was to read like a monologue, like one continuous narrative.[55]

Burgos describes a mythical transformation to account for the seemingly inexorable challenge of achieving a faithful passage from the oral to the written. For her, the process of transcription differed significantly from Barnet's "decanting" of the spoken word; distortion of the subject's speech might imply betrayal. Burgos aimed to remain faithful to Rigoberta's speech by inscribing each detail and gesture and by simultaneously erasing her own authorial presence from her writing.

Curiously, Rigoberta tells a very different story about the book's conception: she attributes the genesis of the idea for the book to her friend and compatriot Arturo Taracena, a historian working on his doctorate in Paris.[56] This dispute is only one of several that have transpired since the book's publication, many of them hinging on issues of authorship and authority. This controversy highlights several important questions. Who is responsible for the reception and future use of an interviewee's testimony? To what extent did reader expectations and Western ideals shape the way Rigoberta portrayed her life? What dangers are involved in subscribing wholeheartedly to the veracity and historicity of an eyewitness's oral retelling of her experiences?

Perhaps Barnet could have anticipated some of the controversy that has led critics to question Rigoberta's portrait of Guatemalan reality and prompted Rigoberta herself to disown portions of her story. In his 1996 interview, Barnet hailed *Biografía* as the triumph of his career, but also recalled some of the "headaches" that ensued after the book's publication. Members of Montejo's family accosted Barnet when the book first appeared, and Esteban was transformed into a literary character.[57] Montejo's male relatives, in particular, demanded that Barnet grant Montejo authorial rights and compensate him accordingly.

Fortunately for Barnet, and perhaps because the two had forged a lasting friendship, Montejo never challenged him for authorship of the book. Then, three years after the publication of *Biografía*, the daughter of Rosales, an acquaintance of Montejo during the War of Independence and a character in the book, accused Barnet of falsely portraying her father as a deserter and a traitor. Although Barnet responded by attributing the story to Montejo, the conflict escalated into a full-fledged legal battle in which both Barnet and Montejo were ultimately acquitted. The accusation opened the floodgates for numerous other charges against Barnet for misrepresenting people and events.

The slipperiness of authorship with regard to testimonial accounts has similarly plagued *Me llamo Rigoberta Menchú*. Rigoberta has wavered in her claims of authorship: at times she has downplayed Burgos's role in the production of the book, on other occasions she has condemned Burgos for appropriating her story and falsifying her testimony. Initially, Rigoberta actively asserted her role as a partial "author" of the book; in 1991 she asked, "What is effectively a gap in the book is the question of the author, right? Because the authorship of the book really should be more precise, shared, right?"[58] Burgos recognized that *Me llamo Rigoberta Menchú* differed from most examples of *testimonio* because its title contained the name of the protagonist. But she was dismayed that Rigoberta took credit as the winner of the 1983 Casa de las Américas award, when the award, which is typically granted to editors of *testimonio*, actually went to Burgos. Although Burgos initially secured a contract with Editions Gallimard, Rigoberta challenged Burgos to sign over the author's rights once she had been awarded the peace prize and the book had won international acclaim.

Recently, Rigoberta has changed her tune dramatically. In a 1997 article, published in Guatemala's *El Periódico* and entitled "Menchú reniega de *Así me nació la conciencia*" (Menchú Disowns *I, Rigoberta Menchú*), Rigoberta refused any responsibility for the book, accusing Burgos of excluding her from the production process and cheating her out of royalties.[59] Rigoberta criticized the fact that Burgos had organized the text according to her own criteria, forbidding both her and Taracena from commenting on the final version. Then, however, she related a strikingly different version of the editorial process. In the 1998 publication of her life story, *Rigoberta: La nieta de los mayas* (published in English as *Crossing Borders: An Autobiography*), she claimed primary authorship and embellished the role she and Taracena played in the production of *Me llamo Rigoberta Menchú*. She states that both Burgos and Taracena selected and organized the chapters of her testimony. Later, Menchú censured parts of the text that she deemed "imprudent," eliminating details pertaining to her town and her siblings.[60] Rigoberta's ambiguous relationship with her own testimony reflects an underlying tension between creative elaboration and verifiable reality. Questions of authority are highly problematic due to the fact that the imperfect process of writing the oral involves editorial manipulations that inevitably construct the speaker's discourse.

Antonio Vera León points out crucial discrepancies between the transcriber's intentions as outlined in the prologue and the inscribed narration of the informant. Menchú's life story aims to highlight injustices and violence that she and all indigenous peoples have experienced since the time of the Conquest. Burgos writes in the introduction, "The voice of Rigoberta Menchú allows the defeated to speak. . . . In telling the story of her life, Rigoberta Menchú is also issuing a manifesto on behalf of an ethnic group."[61] Nevertheless, as we have seen, her narration deviates significantly from this conception of a cultural totality, and conveys indigenous culture as fragmentary and secret. These inconsistencies reflect the contradictions that underlie *testimonio*. According to Vera León, life is "reinvented" in the process of transcription. It is perceived as a cultural figure into which the transcriber reads the resolution of social and historical tension. This perspective conflicts with the particular life story that the narrator-informant offers.[62] In this context, *testimonio* is best regarded as a complex and rich form of transcultural representation that tells us as much about literate professionals' political goals as it does about native culture.

The anthropologist David Stoll's recent investigations led him to question the way readers interpret Rigoberta's story in their efforts to understand Guatemalan history and, more broadly, universal revolutionary struggles. Since the publication of his book *Rigoberta Menchú and the Story of All Poor Guatemalans* in 1999, a storm of controversy has surrounded Rigoberta's account of Guatemalan indigenous rights, causing intellectuals from a variety of disciplines to debate such issues as oral history and the very definition of *testimonio*. Stoll did not challenge Rigoberta's testimony merely to expose its fallibility. For him, the most important issue was that well-intentioned outsiders could easily misconstrue the political situation in Guatemala by assuming that Rigoberta's story was unassailably truthful. He argues that Rigoberta's discourse appealed to Western audiences because she played to their expectations by painting an idealized portrait of indigenous life.

In light of these recent debates, *Me llamo Rigoberta Menchú* still possesses great value as a powerful account of the recent experiences of Mayan peoples. What is at stake is not a falsification of the suffering and oppression endured by Guatemalans. The controversy raises important issues surrounding the ways we interpret an individual's retelling of past experiences. It exemplifies Western readers' desire to take the oral history of a non-Western subject at face value.

The central issue for Stoll was whether the Guerrilla Army of the Poor (EGP) developed as a reaction of the poor to political oppression that had endured for centuries. According to Rigoberta, the rebel movement grew to fulfill the basic needs of rural Guatemalans. When Stoll visited Uspantán he found a social and ethnic reality that was radically different from that portrayed by Rigoberta:

> Unlike *I, Rigoberta Menchú*, which describes the guerrillas as liberation fighters, my Ixil sources tended to lump soldiers and guerrillas together as threats to their lives. . . . *I, Rigoberta Menchú* presents a titanic struggle between two opposed groups: her own indigenous K'iche' people and the ladinos (of European or mixed descent) who have subjugated them.[63]

The land dispute central to *Me llamo Rigoberta Menchú*, depicted by Rigoberta as a struggle between wealthy landowners and victimized peasants, was, according to Stoll, a prolonged family feud between her father and his in-laws.

Rigoberta told her story in 1982 as a member of the January 31st Popular Front (FP-31), a revolutionary network founded to mobilize Guatemala's masses. According to Stoll, Rigoberta's account of conflict in her community reflected her 1982 political agenda more than the reality of her village. His book invites us to question and challenge the political agenda of the Guatemalan left. Stoll justifies his reassessment of Rigoberta's story in light of the book's repercussions throughout the international community. He outlines three reasons for exposing the limitations of the laureate's testimony: "Doing so can tell us about (1) how the Guatemalan violence was misconstrued, (2) how myths about guerrilla warfare continue to misguide the urban left, and (3) how legitimacy in social sciences and the humanities is being redefined to discourage investigation and debate."[64]

In 2001, Arturo Arias published a collection of scholarly articles that responded to the controversy generated by Stoll's findings. The most significant outcome of this debate has been to compel readers to reconsider the very definition of testimonial literature. By reading Menchú's personal account as verifiable fact, as Stoll did, one fails to appreciate *testimonio* as a rich and complex form of cross-cultural communication. In her response to Stoll's book, Elzbieta Sklodowska stresses the hybridity of the testimonial genre. She underscores the literariness of *testimonio*, seeing a fascinating blend of allegories and metaphors where Stoll might find fabrications.[65] Sklodowska makes a strong case that critics, literary and anthropological, should be wary of reading testimonial texts through a single disciplinary lens, since the genre draws from multiple disciplines. Kay B. Warren also highlights the multidimensional aspects of *testimonio*. She criticizes Stoll for underestimating the openness and flexibility of testimonial literature, and defines *testimonio* as "multiply authored transnational wartime propaganda."[66] Her definition is useful, for it takes into consideration the agendas of both Menchú and Burgos, and urges readers to recall their political motives.

When Stoll subjected Rigoberta's story to critical judgment, he used tools of anthropology. After uncovering inconsistencies in her account, he consulted with John Beverley, a literary critic who has written extensively about *testimonio*. Beverley cited some of Stoll's findings in a 1991 talk at which, to Stoll's chagrin, Rigoberta was an honored guest. Beverley and his colleague Marc Zimmerman accused Stoll of making unverifiable charges against the Nobel laureate. In light of the fact that Beverley and Zimmerman regard *testimonio* as a powerful form of cultural representation and a "means of popular-democratic cultural practice, closely bound with the same forces that produce political and military insurgency," it is not surprising that they condemned Stoll's challenge to the testimonialist's authority.[67]

How, then, can the liberties Rigoberta took with her story be reconciled with *testimonio*'s claims to present an authoritative eyewitness account? Beverley and Zimmerman's narrow definition of *testimonio* as an "extraliterary or even antiliterary form of discourse" erroneously equates literary invention with fictionalization or fabrication. By placing blind faith in the text's ability to "speak directly to us," they ignore the fact that *testimonio* is founded upon a complex sociopolitical negotiation shaped by Western ideological and aesthetic concerns.[68] Although *testimonio* certainly borrows from nonliterary and nonfictitious discourse, it does not promise perfect reliability.

In contrast to Beverley and Zimmerman, Burgos approaches *testimonio* in a way that takes into account the creative aspects involved in the task of telling a life story. Her understanding of the performative nature of story-telling admits that contextual forces can influence the ways testimonialists negotiate their accounts:

> I have become aware that [testimonialists] relate, as their own experiences, what they could not have witnessed directly, what instead happened in proximity to their own histories. It is not that they act in bad faith, nor that

they lie. Instead, they are moved by a feeling of belonging. This feeling of belonging, of identifying with peoples, occurs when they feel empowered to elaborate their own version of history. . . . It is not the same as reflecting on the basis of writing. The act of telling a story orally requires re-creating what happened through images, it requires setting a stage, like a theater director would, and requires what theater does–to demonstrate. Rigoberta's objective with her testimony was to demonstrate, to shake public opinion to the maximum to win support, and that she has accomplished.[69]

Rigoberta's task as a "singer of tales" was to downplay inconsistencies, highlight atrocities and dramatic events, and depict a generalized portrait of the Guatemalan rural experience that her life epitomized. Her story had to be compelling, for she sought to win over a Western public—a readership steeped in postcolonial ideals promoting solidarity and ethnic pride— that championed the voice of a victimized minority.

Although critical readers of *Me llamo Rigoberta Menchú* may concede that the story reflects a personal viewpoint, they run the risk of exaggerating the metonymic function of the narrator's voice and downplaying the literariness of *testimonio* in favor of its claims to document the history of an entire culture. The Menchú-Stoll controversy is a concrete example of the slipperiness of testimonial discourse, a hybrid genre that is best conceived as a literary modality that finds its roots in political discourse and the social sciences. *Testimonio* transforms the voice of the Other into writing in accordance with Western ideals. Its claims to evoke oral truths are crucial to legitimizing the genre. In testimonial novels, orality emerges as the outcome of the transcriber's efforts to reproduce the oral style of the informant. Rather than directly reproducing the reality of the subject's community, the inscription of oral discourse reflects the interests and circumstances of the transcriber who essentially reinvents the life story of the narrator-informant.[70]

When Gallimard published her story in 1983, Rigoberta, like Montejo, was transformed into a figure of literature. Whereas the final chapters of Montejo's story coincided with the last years of his life, Rigoberta's account brought her international recognition during her twenties. Not only did Rigoberta achieve what she intended by publicizing her experiences, but the book's international reception immortalized her as a key figure of Guatemalan history.

Rigoberta has added to her life story in a second book, *Rigoberta: La nieta de los mayas* (1998). As in the case of *Biografía/Autobiography*, the noticeably distinct title of the English translation of Rigoberta's book, *Crossing Borders*, reflects the different intentions of the two versions. The English title smacks of multiculturalism, and brings to mind debates of postmodernism and cultural studies that currently inhabit Western universities. The Spanish version portrays Rigoberta as the chosen descendant of an ancient ethnicity, and compels the reader to regard her as the spokesperson for a cultural identity that transcends national borders. Like *Me llamo Rigoberta Menchú*, the second book is composed entirely in the first person. It differs, however, insofar as it does not purport to re-create an uninterrupted chain of memories; nor does it follow a linear chronology. Rather, each of the ten chapters introduces a general theme that may or may not coincide with the episodes of Rigoberta's life related therein. She alone claims authorship of *Rigoberta: La nieta de los mayas*, although the book's cover acknowledges Dante Liano and Gianni Minà as collaborators.[71]

The chorus of authoritative voices in the many prologues and introductions hails Rigoberta as a poetic storyteller, a privileged heiress of ancestral knowledge, an expert on Western and indigenous value systems, one of countless victims of unspeakable violence, and a staunch defender of human rights. The opening preface, by the writer Eduardo Galeano, establishes that the book is founded on the same premise as *Me llamo Rigoberta Menchú*: Menchú is essentially telling the story of generations of Mayans. Galeano's provocative words ("Voice of voices, time of times, Rigoberta does not speak *about* Mayans, but *from* them")[72] are juxtaposed with torture, violent executions and disappearances described by the director of the Spanish division of Amnesty International, Esteban Beltrán. In Beltrán's words, Rigoberta is a composite *indígena*, a spokesperson for victims of repressive regimes.

The K'iche' poet Humberto Ak'abal's meditations comprise the fourth introductory chapter; he celebrates Rigoberta Menchú Tum's ability to tap ancestral knowledge and to convey the essence of Mayan culture with her poignant words. His description brings to mind the captivating powers of Mario Vargas Llosa's *hablador*: "Rigoberta speaks like our elders, when, at the end of the day, next to the kitchen fire, in front of the cooking stone and pot of boiling *nixtamal,* the family joins together to listen to a grandparent tell his or her story and experiences interspersed with reflections."[73] These introductory essays endorse Rigoberta's authority: as both a poetic voice of her people and as a symbolic leader of worldwide revolutionary struggles.

According to the introduction of *Rigoberta: La nieta de los mayas*, an editorial team was responsible for collaborating with Rigoberta to write the testimony of the years spanning her flight to Mexico and her acceptance of the Nobel Prize. The Italian writer Gianni Minà maintains that he, the Italian publisher Giunti, and the Guatemalan writer Dante Liano asked

Rigoberta to share her story with them for the purpose of producing a second book. In a brief section devoted to acknowledgments, the narrator-protagonist steps into the margins of her text to give thanks to those who facilitated the book's production. Rigoberta's version of the production process differs from Minà's: she describes how she solicited the help of the Guatemalan writer Mario Matute, who listened to hours of her dictated testimony. Minà was in charge of organizing the chapters into coherent wholes, and Liano undertook the very difficult task of translating cultures—he made sure that the Spanish narration respected norms of expression of Rigoberta's native K'iche'.

Rigoberta writes of the obstacles faced by a Maya who endeavors to translate her experience as a native speaker of K'iche' into Spanish. Like Barnet, the editors of *Rigoberta: La nieta de los mayas* deemed certain indigenous terms untranslatable. Therefore, some K'iche' words are italicized and clarified in editorial notes. Black-and-white photographs occupy the middle pages of the book and depict Guatemalan guerrilla activity as well as Rigoberta, accepting the Nobel Prize, and surrounded by her compatriots.

There is a noticeable disconnect in the opening chapter of *Rigoberta: La nieta de los mayas*: the preachy tone of the text is markedly different from the poetic language anticipated in the introductions by Galeano and Ak'abal. Absent are the poetic reflections that endowed the first book with an undeniably oral quality. Instead there is a series of somewhat disjointed anecdotes, interspersed with sections in which Rigoberta moralizes about social responsibility, repeating the phrase "I think." In fact, the spoken language in the second book has little in common with the subtleties of Mayan oral tradition described by Ak'abal. Rather, it is akin to one of Rigoberta's many speeches on her conference tour.

In "El enemigo en casa" (Trouble in the Family: The Enemy Within), the first chapter of *Rigoberta: La nieta de los mayas*, Rigoberta describes a bizarre family crisis that took place in Guatemala. When her family was reunited for a niece's wedding celebration, Pablito, the young son of another niece, was mysteriously kidnapped. Rigoberta immediately interpreted the tragedy as a threatening message directed at her. Eventually, however, it became apparent that the child's own parents, motivated by political objectives, had plotted and carried out the kidnapping. Authorities discovered that the conspirators had hidden Pablito in his grandmother's home, . and the husband and wife were punished.

After enduring this tragedy, Rigoberta felt that she could identify with the mothers of her country's many missing persons. The discourse in Rigoberta's second book is explicitly driven by her political agenda. Each anecdote is followed by a stream of consciousness in which the narrator verbalizes her impressions and judgments. By the time she dictates the second part of her testimony, the storyteller of *Me llamo Rigoberta Menchú* has transformed into an activist speechwriter.

As a woman who has learned firsthand the power of language, Rigoberta negotiates her position vis-à-vis her different audiences. In order to fashion herself as a "granddaughter of the Maya," she affirms her indigenous identity. At the same time, however, she extols her ability to cross borders freely and straddle cultures. Discussion of "Mayanness" did not figure into the first book. Over the course of the fifteen-year period separating the two publications, Rigoberta discovered her indigenous heritage and reinvented herself as an heiress of her ancestors' traditions. She invokes the doctrines of self-identified pan-Mayanists and portrays Indian traditions as an example of a millennial culture, endowed with a particular life vision and a unique philosophy. The anthropologist John M. Watanabe has observed this phenomenon among university-educated and professional Maya who have promoted aspects of their ethnic identity and struggled to have their languages and cultures legitimated in academic circles. Watanabe warns that these practices could ultimately ostracize the indigenous groups they allegedly seek to vindicate:

> By promoting certain "exotic" Maya practices as expressions of ethnic pride and solidarity, they risk "folklorising" themselves into the ersatz Indians that Ladino politicians and tourist guidebooks idealise. . . . Pan-Mayanists appeals to a more generalised, abstract Mayanness could thus easily prove too arbitrary—or too politically self-serving—for local Maya to accept, especially where so-called primordial Maya customs no longer hold sway.[74]

Rigoberta's outright denial that she idealizes her ethnic identity suggests just the opposite. Unlike her testimony in *Me llamo Rigoberta Menchú*, the second book is not shaped by the questions of an interviewer; nor is she committed to relating her life as a story. Rather, a prior challenge to her actions is implicit in Rigoberta's discourse, and her words are marked by a desire to defend a rhetorical position and to reclaim Mayan identity.

Rigoberta: La nieta de los mayas offers a revision of the narrator's first testimony. Rigoberta's symbolic return to her Mayan roots is made possible by exploring memories that she chose to exclude from her first account. When she dictated the first book, Menchú declares, she was so saddened that she could not discuss her mother. Recollections of her relationship with her mother, incorporated into the second book, finally give meaning and sense to the present.

According to Rigoberta, her father was a catechizer in the Catholic Church and her mother subscribed to Mayan religious beliefs. In *Me llamo Rigoberta Menchú*, she focused on her own role as a catechizer, and spoke of her ability to synthesize Catholicism with indigenous religious faith. Given her sensitivity to the concerns of a Western public, Rigoberta was careful in her first testimony to trace parallels between the religious practices of her region and the teachings of the Catholic Church. By the time she delivers her second testimony, however, her agenda has changed significantly. Descriptions of her mother's religious faith and firm beliefs in the powers of nature serve Rigoberta's desire to fashion herself as a profoundly religious member of the Mayan community.

Although Rigoberta frequently alluded to the divine secrets of her ancestors in *Me llamo Rigoberta Menchú*, she opted not to disclose them. Similarly, in her second testimony she seduces the reader by alluding to the sacred knowledge of "our culture": "In my book *I, Rigoberta Menchú*, I said that there were secrets I would not divulge, and I kept some parts of our culture very secret. I still stick to that decision. . . . I didn't want to reveal any secrets, since some people might like to make fun of what we say, but I will tell just one."[75] These confessions appear in the chapter entitled "La madre y la tierra" (The Legacy of My Parents and My Village), the portion of the book that most closely resembles a mimesis of the creative aspects of oral storytelling. The narrator repeats "I remember . . . I remember . . . I remember . . ." in her efforts to make sense of her past by aligning it with the present. The present she wishes to portray comprises a millennial culture imbued with solidarity and ethnic pride.

Rigoberta nostalgically recalls the stories, revelations, and mysteries passed down by her ancestors, and regrets that they will never be equaled in their retelling. She fashions herself as one who can preserve through inscription the vanishing values of the victimized Other. Rigoberta subscribes to the powerful Western allegory of ethnographic salvation that perceives the passage from oral to literate as a story of loss when she observes and speaks about ethnic groups as would an anthropologist. Her second testimony is a poignant defense; it is a revision of her first account, and a referendum on the world's revolutionary and millennial cultures. In both books, Rigoberta's representation of Guatemalans reflects her efforts to control her own identity. The familiar trope of salvation, also manifest in the writings of Cabrera, Arguedas, and Barnet, is used to justify Rigoberta's quest to reclaim Mayan history and oral tradition.

Do recent controversies surrounding Rigoberta's accounts signal a crisis in testimonial discourse? Is any attempt at cross-cultural representation that aims to inscribe the Other's voice futile? The irreducible quality of the paradoxical phrase "oral literature" tells us that *testimonios* are a kind of "re-oralization" of writing. By writing the oral, anthropologist-writers inscribe a sense of difference that renders otherness. Testimonialists, in complicity with their informants, invoke native speech out of a sense of nostalgia and social responsibility. They are aware of their capacity to reinvent the past poetically to give it significance in a present integrally tied to Western sociopolitical aspirations. Books like *Biografía* and *Me llamo Rigoberta Menchú* dramatize the postmodern allegory of resistance and recuperation. They subscribe to the logocentric bias that maintains that writing the oral, and thereby fixing its meaning, enables us to recover the presence of speech and overcome difference.

Testimonio represents the culminating form of an oral aesthetic. Barnet inherited from Cabrera the notion that a fusion of anthropology and poetry could express the voices of Cuba's African inhabitants. Both *Biografía* and *El monte* are based on the premise that orality is central to cultural identity, and uphold the notion that Afro-Cuban oral tradition should be inscribed in official Cuban discourse. Barnet was, however, writing for a different audience than Cabrera. The success of *Biografía* in literary circles showed him the power of invoking fiction to create a writerly orality. The extent to which he fictionalizes the oral implies that telling a story orally involves creative invention. He capitalized on the international recognition of Montejo's story and created a trilogy of Cuban voices. *Rachel* and *Gallego* are books that exploit the aesthetic elements of orality. They are also important texts for understanding works such as *Me llamo Rigoberta Menchú* that purport to re-create the Other's voice. Reading *testimonios* solely in accordance with the editors' and informants' intentions is to fail to appreciate the creative aspects of oral storytelling.

Barnet's essays in *La fuente viva* provide a crucial perspective on his quest to vindicate the other voices of Cuba's heterogeneous population. As an anthropologist, he saw himself as a mediator between cultures. As a poet, he believed he could capture, in writing, the sounds and songs of the Other. Barnet's theories on oral and literate traditions are woven into the pages of his three testimonial novels. His writings indicate, however, that he was not fully aware of the irony of representation that writing orality entailed. Augusto Roa Bastos, Barnet's contemporary, was the Spanish American author who best understood the rhetorical possibilities of inscribing oral tradition.

5

Augusto Roa Bastos's Search
for an Oral Aesthetic

Aɴᴛʜʀᴏᴘᴏʟᴏɢɪᴄᴀʟ ᴅɪsᴄᴏᴜʀsᴇ ᴀɴᴅ sᴘᴀɴɪsʜ ᴀᴍᴇʀɪᴄᴀɴ ɴᴀʀʀᴀᴛɪᴠᴇ ʜᴀᴠᴇ ᴅᴇᴠᴇʟᴏᴘᴇᴅ hand in hand. The end of colonial rule provoked a search for new authoritative discourses. After the beginning of the twentieth century, anthropology shifted from a general science to a method-driven study of cultural practices and daily life. The primary purpose of this new ethnography, a research-oriented science, was salvaging cultural diversity, threatened by global Westernization.[1] The ethnographer could capture in writing the ceremonies, behaviors, and voices of the Other's culture, and portray these cultural practices within the broader context of a coherent world. Like authors of realist texts, anthropologists sought to portray non-Western civilizations as authentic and pure by assembling cultural artifacts that had been collected in the field. Fieldworker-writers place profound emphasis on firsthand experience and the powers of observation. For the ethnographer, as well as the fiction writer, having "been there" granted them the authority to speak for the Other and construct his reality.

Implicit in the ethnographer's interpretive activity was a gesture of cultural comparison that has recently undergone serious revision. Comparative anthropology made it easy for ethnographers to assume an us-them perspective that has perpetuated dichotomizing concepts like orality versus literacy. Whereas both anthropological fieldwork and historical research purportedly generated realist interpretations of culture, the former discipline differed from the latter in its claims to trace cultural origins to oral tradition. Although ultimately embedded in writing, ethnographic discourse was based on the notion of a presentness and purity of speech.

Theorists of orality like Walter J. Ong and Jack Goody told a similar tale of how speech in oral cultures was overcome and altered by the practice of writing, which threatened intimacy and authenticity in a collective oral world. They sought to understand the nonliterate mind, and largely viewed literacy in ethnocentric terms by engaging in comparative analysis. Like many ethnographers in the first half of the twentieth century, theorists of orality tend to stress differences between cultures by conceptualizing them in bipolar terms.

Spanish American narrative followed a parallel evolution. In the 1930s, writers of telluric novels (*novelas de la tierra*) dispelled idealized accounts of natives in their efforts to portray coherent representations of their regions. Like ethnography, regionalist narrative was predicated on synecdoche; individual characters were assumed to be analogous to broader groups in society. Although authors like Rómulo Gallegos and José Eustasio Rivera were not anthropologists by training, their novels borrowed discursive strategies from ethnographic realism to enhance textual veracity. Carlos Alonso proposes that writers of autochthonous texts resolve the predicament posed by Spanish America's introduction into the modern world by celebrating a cultural reality that is at odds with modernity: "The preoccupation with an autochthonous cultural order has consistently served as a vehicle for the validation and generation of intellectual production in Latin America."[2] In a similar fashion, anthropologist-writers invoke oral tradition as a key element of autochthonous culture to express the uniqueness of Spanish American reality.

In the 1930s, a new kind of Spanish American writer emerged who straddled anthropology and literature. This synthesis of two disciplines that share the desire to understand and represent other cultures by searching for origins is not surprising. Lydia Cabrera inaugurated this trend, which developed over the following decades. She, like many participants in the phenomenon of ethnographic surrealism, was both a scientific observer and an artist. Cabrera's probe into Cuban reality drew on both disciplines. Inspired by colleagues who explored African art forms and beliefs, her cross-cultural analysis critiqued contemporary society from the vantage point of what she perceived to be a more vital Other. Cabrera's dedication to fieldwork and her profound knowledge of Afro-Cuban religions distinguished her from the other surrealists who frequented the avant-garde exhibitions in Paris. *El monte* is perhaps the greatest example of Spanish American narrative that is not a novel.

José María Arguedas engaged in a similar form of cultural criticism by juxtaposing Quechuan and Hispanic concepts in his effort to vindicate the indigenous components of mestizo identity. Artistic techniques helped him to revisit his past and articulate Peruvian consciousness. *Los ríos profundos* (*Deep Rivers*), his most poetic novel, reflects his belief in the ideological power of music and orality, and the possibility of fusing Quechuan and

Spanish voices. In contrast, *El zorro de arriba y el zorro de abajo* (*The Fox from Up Above and the Fox from Down Below*), left incomplete by Arguedas's suicide, reflects the author's realization of the irreducible nature of oral literature. Although Arguedas's anthropological writings never appealed aesthetically in the same way that Cabrera's did, he nevertheless conveyed his profound spiritual connection to Quechua reality in his expository pieces. His ethnographies are literary insofar as they are infused with a plurality of voices; his narrative is anthropological in its pursuit of authentic representation of an uprooted, dominated culture. Arguedas's tragic personal quest was driven by a nostalgic yearning for a world of voices that anthropology and writing, the very disciplines he practiced, threatened to annihilate.

In the 1950s, a crisis in the status of anthropology caused anthropologists to reflect critically on fieldwork practices and ethnographic writing.[3] Although Arguedas did not participate in these theoretical discussions, he was anxiously aware that cultural analysis is by no means innocent. Mario Vargas Llosa's *El hablador* (*The Storyteller*) captures this shift in anthropology by problematizing the nature of fieldwork and the concept of culture. The novel epitomizes Arguedas's dilemma: must one completely become the Other in order to tell his stories and sing his songs; or does one do violence to the Other by seeking to preserve and inscribe his culture? While *El hablador* offers two extreme examples—the mysterious Machiguenga storyteller and the intellectual and Westernized narrator—Arguedas struggled to inhabit a middle ground by forging an identity that could mediate between what he perceived to be two incompatible worlds.

Cross-cultural mediation was canonized as a form of literary expression with the 1966 publication of Miguel Barnet's *Biografía de un cimarrón* (*The Autobiography of a Runaway Slave*). *Testimonio*, which purports to give voice to the Other, involves a constructive negotiation between two politically aware subjects. *Biografía* was published in the wake of the Cuban revolution, at a time when official accounts of culture were deemed insufficient. Barnet used anthropology to escape the constraints of novelistic and historical discourse and legitimize his desire to retell Esteban Montejo's story. Barnet's introduction to the book points to his initial perception of a modern division between anthropology and art. He later recanted, however, and celebrated the transparency of the ethnographic and metanarrative aspects of *Biografía* as evidence of a postmodern poetics. Although Barnet claimed to erase his voice from Montejo's narrative in the same way that Cabrera granted complete authority to her informants, the book contains a shuffling and shifting of voices. Barnet invented a literary language that transmitted the nuances of spoken language. That it is virtually impossible to separate Barnet's rhetoric from Montejo's in *Biografía* illustrates that cultural relations are matters of power and authority. *Biografía* is the outcome of a complex process of negotiation, rather than a translation of the Other's experience.

Writers of testimonial novels share with anthropologists the desire to faithfully represent non-Western cultural traditions. They invoke native voices as a means of reproducing life stories that purport to represent collective reality. *Testimonios* masquerade as scientific discourse and appeal to Western audiences. Recent controversies surrounding choices Rigoberta Menchú made when recounting her experiences are cause to reconsider the definition of *testimonio*, taking into account the fictional aspects of the genre.

The notion of cultural dualism—upheld to some extent by each of these writers—served the Western rhetorical goal of incorporating cultural diversity into a modern context. Cabrera, Arguedas, and Barnet felt themselves to be marginal, but were ultimately committed to Western intellectual enterprises. All three had a striking tendency to dichotomize the human condition as a means of legitimizing their own roles as cultural mediators. In this regard, the ethnographic vantage point proved to be advantageous. Anthropologist-writers are painfully conscious both of the ephemeral nature of orally transmitted knowledge and of the fact that they are inescapably bound to scriptural culture. In order to sidestep this dilemma, they portray themselves as practitioners of cultural redemption. The allegory of salvation is found in the invention of an "oralized" writing.

"Oralized" writing is as much a construction as the premise upon which it is founded: the great divide between orality and literacy. All of these writers tended to emphasize the opposition between speech and writing. Treating speech and writing like mutually exclusive domains serves the authors' needs to establish themselves as authoritative cross-cultural mediators. In fact, their writings prove that the onset of scriptural culture does not cause the demise of oral tradition. The theoretical claim that writing displaces spoken language presupposes that oral tradition retains the purity of a desired origin, one that has been compromised by written discourse. But the notion of an origin, buried in oral memory, is as much a fiction as the idea that orality authenticates writing. Ultimately, we must ask whether oral tradition exists outside the practice that seeks to transcribe and interpret it.

Critical readings of works like *Los cuentos negros de Cuba* (Black Stories of Cuba), *Los ríos profundos*, and *Biografía de un cimarrón* are also predicated on the notion of a conflict between speech and writing. Angel Rama regards writers like Arguedas, Augusto Roa Bastos, Juan Rulfo,

Gabriel García Márquez, and João Guimarães Rosa as "transculturadores" [cultural mediators], a concept that is largely based on each one's sanction of the marginalized oral traditions of his respective nation.[4] Carlos Pacheco, recognizing the ideological importance of orality in these writers' texts and drawing on Rama's thesis, has described specific strategies for fictionalizing oral discourse.[5] In both Pacheco and Rama, however, textual analysis fails to scrutinize dichotomizing concepts—inside/outside; orality/ writing; authenticity/artifice.

By dismantling binary distinctions that stem from biases in Western thought, we can better understand the great divide between orality and literacy as a rhetorical device, implicit in Spanish American narrative's nostalgic yearning for authentic knowledge and truth. Reading this problematic into the works of anthropologist-writers like Cabrera, Arguedas, and Barnet allows a richer understanding of the relation between orality and writing. By creating a poetic effect of orality in their ethnographies and narratives, these writers play the role of the quintessential Spanish American writer: they inscribe the mythical world of a vanishing Other. Though these texts indeed satisfy Western expectations of authenticity and pureness, they are valuable examples of an innovative form of literary expression.

No Spanish American writer was more aware of the rhetorical possibilities of these theories on orality and literacy than Augusto Roa Bastos. Roa Bastos differs from Cabrera, Arguedas, and Barnet insofar as he did not invoke anthropology as a means of mediating between what he perceived to be the conflicting realms of Paraguay's bipolar culture. His theories on orality, and the practice of these theories in his narrative, however, reveal a master trope in the discourse of orality and literacy that informs the ethnographic and literary works of each one of these anthropologist-writers. Roa Bastos has expressed better than any Spanish American author a coherent theory of the relation between orality and literacy, and has articulated the writer's task of creating an "oralized" writing. His narrative contains the implementation and evolution of these ideas.

Roa Bastos describes how, with the onset of the colonial period and the ensuing process of *mestizaje*, the Other's speech entered into perpetual conflict with that of the dominant culture. In his essays, Roa Bastos invoked a system of binary oppositions to describe Paraguay's multifaceted culture. According to him, the oppositions writing/orality and dominant culture/dominated culture function between the "axes" of Spanish and Guaraní that distort the structures of expression and communication. This conception of cultural dualism informs all of his fiction and mimics Guaraní cosmology and popular tradition.[6] More significantly, Roa Bastos used essentialist rhetoric to come to terms with his nation's turbulent history and to describe the divided identity of the Paraguayan self. Like many Spanish American writers, he invoked exile and displacement as fundamental tropes in his writings.

In Roa Bastos's opinion, the oppositional relation between Guaraní orality and Spanish literacy accounted for his nation's "absent literature." In a sense, he argues, the presence of a vigorous popular literature could compensate for the lack of written literature.[7] He regarded Paraguayan writing as lifeless, and asserted the redemptive powers of speech. This argument turns on a view that privileges orality over literacy. Roa Bastos's conception of the binary distinctions embedded in Paraguayan culture enabled him to fashion himself as a cross-cultural mediator and a savior of oral tradition.

Roa Bastos attributed Paraguay's "cultural backwardness" to the fact that it was the only truly bilingual country in Spanish America, and observed an ongoing state of mutual linguistic invasion. He criticized Paraguayan writers for suppressing Guaraní oral culture, which permeated every aspect of the nation's emotional life. Like most Paraguayan writers, he was not a direct descendant of tribal Guaraní culture, but his everyday use of Guaraní and his immersion in Paraguay's mestizo culture provided him with a profound understanding of Guaraní oral culture.

The task of infusing the written with the oral is manifest in Roa Bastos's narrative creations. He maintained that spoken language best expresses Paraguayan social reality. Roa Bastos condemned writing in much the same way as Plato did; yet both were necessarily bound to it. Both Roa Bastos and Plato portrayed writing as a powerful tool that can betray the living presence of collective speech with its arbitrary and lifeless signs.[8] Roa Bastos claimed that, in opposition to the power of writing, the spoken word of the "antiestablishment" imposes the tone and the interior modulation of Paraguayan culture. [9] When Roa Bastos wrote this he was driven, like Cabrera, Arguedas, and Barnet, by the desire to designate an origin for truth and knowledge. The mystique of origins was attractive for each of these writers, in his or her individual quest to transform contemporary intellectual trends by exploring marginalized discourses.

Although Roa Bastos's formal education ended when he was fifteen, he was already producing poems and short fiction that played an important role in his subsequent literary creations. His first writings demonstrate early attempts to achieve syncretism by combining sacred writings with "the spirit" of oral tradition. In these early writings, he realized that, in order to write, it was essential that he first "read" a nonwritten text.[10] His eclectic library reflected his affinity for oral literature. Roa Bastos was decisively influenced by John the Theologian, who preferred the spoken word over pen and ink; by Leonardo da Vinci, who depicted the world as an image in movement; and by *Ayvu Rapyta*, the mythical texts of the Mby'a-guaraní of Guairá, compiled by León Cadogan.[11]

Roa Bastos's primary inspiration derived from Guaraní oral discourse, but he broadened his reading public by writing in Spanish. Sounds and voices, in his opinion, most perfectly expressed Paraguayan reality. From the language of oral culture emerges that primary text that one reads and hears simultaneously, in its elements of phonic, rather than alphabetical, signification. This primary text is archaic and free, saturated with the feelings of social life.[12] Roa Bastos's preference for phonocentric language reveals an underlying set of assumptions that link his project to Western ideology. He implicitly treated voice as a metaphor for truth and Paraguayan identity. Yet insofar as Roa Bastos sought to uphold the authenticity and ideality of speech, he was inescapably committed to writing. Paradoxically, in his attempts to transgress Western literary norms, he privileged orality as a means of accessing truth, a bias that originates in Western culture.

Roa Bastos acknowledged that, by choosing to write in Spanish, he assumed—consciously or unconsciously—an ideological position upheld by Paraguayan dominant culture. He reasoned that, by using Spanish, the writer invokes elements of this culture linguistically, psychologically and ideologically. Writing attempts to grasp and "translate" the intonation and modulation of the oral system of Guaraní, or "Ava–ñe–ê" [the language of the common man].[13] Unlike Plato, Saussure, and Lévi-Strauss, who have fallen prey to what Derrida denounces as a phonocentric bias by treating writing as a merely supplemental activity, Roa Bastos maintained that oral texts are already inhabited by writing, and should be read as well as heard. As a bicultural writer, he defined his role as a mediator between Spanish and Guaraní, and emphasized his capacity to expose the nuances of an eclipsed oral text. For Roa Bastos, the "absent" oral text is already written; it is up to the intellectual, who inhabits written culture, to rescue and translate the latent rhythms of speech.

In Roa Bastos's initial attempts at bilingual writing, his search for a narrative voice followed a similar trajectory as Arguedas's. He described the task of infusing Spanish with a Guaraní "atmosphere" as "devilishly difficult."[14] His early works, like *El trueno entre las hojas* (The Thunder among the Leaves), a collection of stories published in 1953, incorporate and explain Guaraní expressions and terms in the Spanish text. Aware of the limitations of this approach, Roa Bastos formulated a more cohesive narrative style in his first novel, *Hijo de hombre* (*Son of Man*), first published in 1960 and later in 1982 in a revised edition. He, like Arguedas in

Los ríos profundos, suggested that the protagonists spoke in Guaraní, but he dramatically reduced the quantity of Guaraní terms accompanied by Spanish translations. He felt that he could achieve a more expressive literary language than in his prior writings by overcoming a simple mixing of vocabulary and syntax. Roa Bastos claimed that *Hijo de hombre* permitted him to study in depth a quest for the fusion of two linguistic hemispheres of Paraguayan culture in literary language.[15]

Hijo de hombre was Roa Bastos's first novelistic attempt to represent Paraguay's traumatic history of social repression. He sought to show how Paraguay's history was driven by the clashing forces of a dualistic culture. The book opens with two epigraphs: the first is a series of biblical verses taken from Ezekiel, and echoes the novel's title; the second is a fragment from the Guaraní *Himno de los Muertos* (Hymn of the Dead): "My voice shall be heard again among the dead . . . / And my word shall once more be made flesh . . . / When this age is over and a new age begins. . . ."[16] This juxtaposition of textual traditions suggests Roa Bastos's fundamental view of the confrontation between opposing cultural universes underlying Paraguayan social reality: Guaraní/Spanish; orality/writing; dominated culture/ dominant culture. The complex interplay between shifting narrative perspectives and the book's mythic undertones distinguish it from Spanish American realist texts that have dealt with similar subject matter.

When Roa Bastos revised *Hijo de hombre* in 1982, he redefined the novel as an exposition of his theories on orality and bilingual literature. Several of the ideas outlined in the "Author's Note," absent from the 1960 version, were later reiterated in Roa Bastos's 1987 article "Una cultura oral." In the "Author's Note," Roa Bastos reflected on the complex process undertaken by Paraguayan writers who endeavor to interpret Guaraní culture and mythology in Spanish. He wrote that his narrative texts were based on the primacy of Guaraní oral tradition. Roa Bastos reasoned that unwritten texts underlie the Spanish-Guaraní linguistic universe. They are texts about which the writer does not think, but rather that approach the writer from within. Therefore, the linguistic presence of Guaraní imposes itself from within the emotional world of Paraguayans. It shapes everyday colloquial expression, as well as the symbolic expression of social myths and individual and collective experiences.[17] Roa Bastos's words in the "Author's Note" are suffused with the trope of salvation and recuperation. His desire to recover the past, which he believed to inhabit texts marked by the authenticity and interiority of speech, signifies his discontent with writing as a form of expression.

Hijo de hombre opens with tales of Macario Francia, a paradigmatic singer of tales and hero of Guaraní oral tradition. Macario's stories, which proliferate in poetic variations, derive from a mythic subtext of Paraguayan lore. Macario is a storyteller par excellence, and would be a likely bedfellow of Montejo or Mascarita. As his name suggests, however, he is also the offspring of the nation's official history. His multiple retellings of the epic tale of the leper Gaspar Mora are woven into Miguel Vera's narration of the fantastic history of Itapé. The narrator relishes the captivating tonalities of Macario's stories, and struggles to emulate him as he writes his testimony:

> He was a living history-book of the village and had some knowledge of events which had taken place outside it as well. . . . He always spoke in Guaraní. The soft, slurring Indian language made the horror bearable, domesticated it. Echoes of echoes. Shadows of shadows. Reflections of reflections. Perhaps not the truth about events, but certainly their fascination.[18]

These poetic words are an ode to the oral. Macario's tales embody a form of storytelling that highlights the shortcomings of written memory. He and María Rosa, the babbling *chipera* (bread maker) who lives on the hill of Caveroní, are the final guardians of the oral memories of Itapé. María Rosa speaks an archaic Guaraní that is incomprehensible: in her delusional state, she wanders the streets of the town, singing a refrain from the *Himno de los muertos* and echoing the book's poetic epigraph.

The conclusion of *Hijo de hombre* states that Miguel Vera wrote his story in manuscript form and sent it to Rosa Monzón to solicit her advice. Rosa Monzón copied the script, without changing a single comma. Vera, in striking contrast to Macario, epitomizes literate culture; he struggles to convey truth through writing. His own narration of Macario's tales reveals his awareness of the complexity of passing from the oral to the written:

> [Macario] was not interested in the comet in so far as it was connected with the story of his leprous nephew. Each time he told the story, he changed it slightly. He telescoped events, altered names, dates and places, as perhaps I am doing now without realising it, for my uncertainty is greater than was the old dotard's. At least his heart was pure.[19]

Whereas Vera believes that inconsistencies and alterations in a story reflect features of an oral culture, he fears that they might undermine the veracity of his written account. He, like Montejo, cautions that the spoken word can betray the truth.

Miguel Vera's desire to preserve the popular history of Itapé and weave it into official accounts corresponds to Roa Bastos's overall reinterpretation of Paraguay's history, inspired by oral memory. *Hijo de hombre* is marked by allusions to historic events, such as the War of the Triple Alliance, the Chaco War, and the 1947 civil uprising, yet the complex textuality, interspersed with oral accounts and flashbacks, defies norms of written history and realist texts. In the "Author's Note," Roa Bastos claims to identify ideologically with Macario. Over the course of his life, he writes, he has unknowingly imitated Macario. In his opinion, all authors should adhere to the ethics and poetics of variation.[20] Although Roa Bastos may attribute his inspiration to Guaraní oral tradition, his task of rewriting historic discourse by deconstructing its linearity is similar to that of the book's principal narrator, Miguel Vera. Both imbue their writing with oral nuances in order to give form to popular knowledge.

In *Hijo de hombre*, Roa Bastos demonstrated his conviction that oral texts can tell us many tales with many voices. The first chapter of the modified edition contains a brief epigraph by W. B. Yeats (which did not appear in the 1960 version) in which the poet claims that when he revises his works, he, in essence, revises himself.[21] Roa Bastos undertook the transgressive task of modifying a work that had already achieved international critical acclaim. The introductory "Author's Note" inaugurated the 1982 edition as an entirely new work, one of many possible versions that a singer of tales could conceive. This essay, as well as the addition of the ninth chapter, some minor textual alterations, and the deletion of the book's final paragraphs compose a fictionalization of orality. Roa Bastos compares *Hijo de hombre* to a living oral text, and emulates Macario by inventing a "poetics of variation." He believes that a creative and free author can vary a text indefinitely, enriching it rather than causing it to lose its original form.[22] According to Roa Bastos, the novel's configuration originates in a matrix of orality. His efforts to modify *Hijo de hombre* reflect a desire to overturn norms of novelistic discourse that associate writing with textual fixation. Roa Bastos offered his public a second performance of a well-known piece.

Roa Bastos's remarks on a "poetics of variation" echo the Spanish philologist Ramón Menéndez Pidal's famous adage: "To live is to vary."[23] The medievalist, who lamented the gradual decline of the tradition of the *romancero*, cast himself as the last *juglar*. His attempt to inscribe what he perceived to be the fluidity and freedom of orality is expressed most succinctly in his personal collection, *Flor nueva de romances viejos* (New Flower of Old Ballads). Menéndez Pidal regarded multiple manuscripts of a poem as poetic variations rather than inexact copies of a supposed original. He embraced these variations as manifestations of a dynamic written tradition analogous to oral tradition.

Roa Bastos applied theories of orality to narrative discourse and sought to infuse his writing with salient features of Guaraní oral culture. His efforts to retrieve the collective nature of oral tradition by varying the 1960 version of *Hijo de hombre* can be read as a part of the fiction. In this context, the authoritative tone of the introductory "Author's Note" is conspicuous, for it signals Roa Bastos's acute awareness of the need to define his "poetics of variation" as a stylistic gesture.

Roa Bastos's revisions reveal his awareness of the poststructuralist debates surrounding speech and writing that took place in the late 1960s. Theorists of writing deemed the role and nature of writing in Western culture to be tied to structures of authority. Within this context, Roa Bastos was trapped in a dialectic that pitted the culture of variation, associated with oral performance, against literate culture's quest for authentic and original texts. The second version of *Hijo de hombre* was not intended to replace the universally acclaimed 1960 edition. Rather, Roa Bastos sought to invoke the ethics of variation, prevalent in oral culture, by treating his text as one of multiple performances.

There is a certain irony embedded in this gesture of variation. Roa Bastos consistently prized voice as the key to virtuous and authentic expression. He argued for the preeminence of a latent primary text that one simultaneously hears and reads. But the concepts of authenticity and origins are foremost products of Western literate culture. Within an oral culture of variation, the search for origins is meaningless. When he produced a variation of *Hijo de hombre*, Roa Bastos bypassed the dilemma faced by writers caught between an aesthetics that privileges fixed forms and one that values variation. His compromise was to invent a new poetics that would undermine a literate culture's impulse to fix an immutable text.

In 1971, when the magazine *Alcor* resumed its publication after a lapse of almost two decades, a special issue focused on "El génesis de los guaraníes," a poetic series conceived by Roa Bastos between 1947 and 1949 and never before published as a whole. In the opening article, Rubén Bareiro Saguier distinguishes the extensive poem as the first valid attempt to approach an indigenous mythical-religious text in Spanish. "El génesis" is based on several myths collected by the ethnographer Curt Unkel, published in a German magazine, and later translated by Francisco Recalde into Spanish. Unkel lived among members of a Guaraní tribe in the early 1900s, and was ultimately honored with the Guaraní name Nimuendalú. His story is strikingly similar to that of Vargas Llosa's enigmatic storyteller or Fred Murdock's in Borges's story "El etnógrafo" (The Ethnographer): Nimuendalú Unkel was reluctant to betray his fellow tribesmen by divulging their mythical secrets. Ultimately, he chose to retell their foundational story, with the hopes that the mythical voices might somehow humanize Western society.

Roa Bastos decided to collaborate in this mission of salvation by transforming elements of the foundational myths of the Apapokuva-Guaraní into a lengthy poem. He describes "El génesis" as a free and imaginative version of some of the songs found in Unkel's collection of legends. The poem was one of Roa Bastos's early attempts to infuse his writing with the spoken nuances of Guaraní culture. As in the early works of Arguedas and Barnet, poetry provided an ideal medium for creating an effect of orality.

Roa Bastos's quest to bring together Guaraní and Spanish in a synthesized poetic language culminated in *Yo el Supremo* (*I the Supreme*), the most theoretical of his novels with regard to discourse on orality and writing. The 1974 book, written in Buenos Aires, evokes the remains of the 1960s debates in France surrounding the practice of writing. *Yo el Supremo* dramatizes the productive conflict of inscribing the oral that was at the core of the literary projects of Cabrera, Arguedas, and Barnet. It carries the ambiguous relationship between speech and writing to an extreme. Roa Bastos admits that the book practices the "Writing of Power" in its attempts to find an alphabet whereby letters become objects and meaning is obscured.[24] The Supremo attributes primacy to writing, and derives his authority from the power implicit in language.

Both *Hijo de hombre* and *Yo el Supremo* deal manifestly with the myth of authority in Paraguayan history. With *El fiscal* (1993) (The Prosecutor), they form Roa Bastos's "Paraguayan Trilogy," inspired by his nation's society and history. In *Yo el Supremo* Roa Bastos goes beyond showing that mythical forces drive his country's history to consider the issue of the power of language. The book demystifies the nineteenth-century dictator, Dr. Francia, by reinterpreting his role in Paraguay's turbulent history. As in *Hijo de hombre*, Roa Bastos transforms this notorious historical figure into the protagonist of the narrative.

Yo el Supremo is composed of numerous texts, written by or about the Supremo, which have been arranged and annotated by a "compiler" who tells the story of the book's creation in a series of editorial notes. It is essentially a mock critical edition. The book concludes with the editor's disclaimer, similar to that of Rosa Monzón, which states that he faithfully copied and compiled the polemical written texts of Paraguayan history and supplemented this collection of heterogeneous written accounts with multiple oral texts derived from taped interviews and Paraguayan oral tradition.

The editor declares that he transcribed and compiled original texts: "The reader will already have noted that, unlike ordinary texts, this one was read first and written later. Instead of saying and writing something new, it merely faithfully copies what has already been said and composed by others."[25] This disclaimer highlights the ambiguities that subtend similar statements in Lydia Cabrera's introduction of *El monte* and Miguel Barnet's preface to *Biografía*. In *Yo el Supremo*, Roa Bastos dramatizes the predicament faced by writers whose authority is founded upon the faithful representation of oral truths.

The Supremo's anxiety with writing as a source of betrayal stems from his belief in the power implicit in language.[26] The novel opens with the transcription of a mysterious pasquinade that announces the Supremo's death and instructs that his remains be cremated and the ashes thrown into a river. The emphatic "Yo" (I) that inaugurates the text and echoes the book's title is essentially an oral enunciation transcribed into longhand. The flowing calligraphy of the pasquinade represents an intermediate stage on the continuum between oral and print cultures. The story told in the book's opening pages involves the Supremo's attempt to discover the identity of the pasquinade's authors. The Supremo asks Patiño, his defenseless secretary and scribe, if the handwriting might be the dictator's own: "Dime, ¿la letra del pasquín no es la mía? [...] De lo imposible sale lo posible. Fíjate ahí, bajo la marca de agua, el florón de las iniciales ¿no son las mías? Son suyas Señor; tiene razón. El papel, las iniciales verjuradas también."[27] [Tell me, isn't the handwriting of the pasquinade mine? . . . The possible is a product of the impossible. Look here, underneath the water mark, the flourish of the initials. Aren't they mine? They are yours, Sire; you are quite right. The paper, the verjured initials as well.][28] Patiño remarks that, although the handwriting is a perfect copy of His Exellency's, the "spirit" of the writing is distinct. The mystery of the pasquinade introduces the fundamental notion that the dictator cannot control written language. It presents the problem of writing as a form of deception and falsification.

In *Yo el Supremo*, multiple voices intersect and the author evokes the rhythm of popular Guaraní speech. What follows the pasquinade is essentially a reproduction of the dictator's conversation with Patiño. The most oral moments in the book occur in the pages that imitate the record of a dialogue. Long, unbroken paragraphs of the transcription mimic oral discourse by omitting quotation marks to create the effect of a witty debate. The first line of the dialogue reads, "Where was this found? Nailed to the door of the cathedral, Excellency."[29] The reader must infer the identity of the speaker. These rambling conversations include interjections and expletives ("Hum. Ah," "Bah," "¡eh!"). Roa Bastos, who studied characteristics of the dictator's speech, re-creates his use of vulgar and abusive language.

The two characters' use of wordplay (expressions with multiple meanings, misspellings, interior monologues, neologisms, etc.) as well as popular sayings enhances the dialogic aura of the text:[30] "Aunque mal tiro sería para ellos meterse en estos negocios del peje-vigüela, ahora que están mejor que nunca. No les conviene un nuevo Gobierno de gente yente-viniente. Se le acabará su bigua salutis. ¡Bien dicho Patiño! Te corono rey de las inteligencias."[31] [Though it would be bad business for them to get mixed up in these fish-and-fowl affairs now that they're better off than ever. A new government of people coming and going isn't in their interest. That would be the end of their bigua salutis. Well put, Patiño! I crown you king of wits.][32] Roa Bastos's sonorous writing is replete with examples of onomatopoeia, alliteration, assonance and consonance, used to create a literary illusion of orality.

Another strategy for infusing the Supremo's speech with oral nuances was to enact the agglutinative properties of Guaraní in Spanish (el anteojo de ver-lejos, memoria-juicio, El-sin-muerte, El-sin-sueño). Roa Bastos admits that he struggled to evoke the bilingual roots of the Supremo's speech, a "ghostly" idiom that corresponds with the dictator's delirium. The protagonist's language returns to its roots by invoking the syncretic elements of Guaraní mythology and orality.[33] Like Arguedas, who devoted much of his career to developing a written Andeanized Spanish, Roa Bastos created an artificial literary language that was infused with characteristics of Guaraní speech.

Augusto Roa Bastos maintains that these devices for invoking the oral in writing are intended to rescue "the living word." The Supremo's obsession with language reflects the author's quest to express orality by means of what he perceives to be the difficult art of writing. Recovery of native speech forms part of a nostalgic attempt to resurrect an ephemeral past and to save a future from the illness, or "deathlike fixity," of writing.[34] Whereas Cabrera, Arguedas, and Barnet were committed to this quest, Roa Bastos realized that any attempt to recover an oral past was fraught with ambiguity.

More than polyphonic, *Yo el Supremo* is polyscriptural and polygraphic; various forms of writing overlap, and interlinear commentary runs throughout the novel. Embedded in the record of the Supremo's conversations with his scribe are transcriptions of the "Perpetual circular," an official document that the Supremo dictates to Patiño. It is the dictator's attempt to establish his own absolute version of Paraguayan history. The circular transgresses norms of historical discourse. It contains numerous anachronisms and shows how an oral retelling of history differs from a written account. The literary version of Dr. Francia's reign transcends official historiography and, like *Hijo de hombre*, attempts to create "counterhistory."[35] *Vigilia del Almirante* (The Admiral's Vigil), Roa Bastos's 1992 novel, is a direct descendant of this kind of inventive historical narrative.

The dictator's private notebook appears along with these other texts. It is ostensibly the Supremo's secret diary. But it, too, has been edited by an unknown hand. Originally intended as a log of treasury accounts, the notebook also includes the aging dictator's incoherent reflections on a variety of topics. Whereas the "Perpetual circular" offers the Supremo's official view of history, the notebook is, in a sense, its inversion. The Supremo uses these private writings to bypass the predicament of misinterpretation and to preserve his memory. By avoiding the stage of oral dictation, he aims to control language completely: "In the beginning I did not write; I only dictated. Now I must dictate/write; note it down somewhere. That is the only way I have of proving that I still exist."[36] The Supremo naively fuses speech and writing ("dictate/write") in his efforts to avoid falling into the "great divide" that he believes separates the two processes.

Yo el Supremo is, in many ways, an annotated manuscript. Even the private notebook, initially intended as an official register, contains editorial comments that respond to and contradict the dictator's musings. The editor compares the notebook to the polyphonic score of a musical piece. This observation is just one example of the abundance of interlinear commentary found in the book. In addition to the footnotes, one reads descriptions of damaged paper as well as notes that indicate commentary in the margins. Although *Yo el Supremo* is primarily concerned with the manipulation of writing, the heterogeneity of the physical text suggests affinities with oral culture.

Commentary in the margins of a manuscript highlights oral analogues to the process of textual compilation. John Dagenais, who has made important observations regarding medieval manuscript culture, writes:

> One way of getting a grip on the physical texts is, paradoxically, by viewing the manuscript text as a variety of oral performance. Curiously, that most ephemeral of literary events, an oral performance, comes closest to imitating that solidly physical text we seek: in its uniqueness, in the impossibility of its iteration, in its vulnerability to accidents of time and environment. A physical text, a manuscript . . . is in fact an oral performance.[37]

The marginal comments, complex layers, and editorial notes that make up *Yo el Supremo* are important parts of textual production in a manuscript culture. *Yo el Supremo* demands an active reader who, like the editor, can compile the diverse fragments of the book. This kind of reading is similar to the give-and-take of oral discourse.

In one of the book's longest footnotes, found in the pages of the private notebook, the editor tells the story of how he came to possess the Supremo's pen from a descendant of Patiño. This unique pen simultaneously writes and projects interlinear photographs of "optical metaphors." At one time, the editor explains, the pen was capable of reproducing sound in writing:

> I believe that at one time the pen must also have possessed a third function: reproducing the phonic space of writing, the sound-text of the visual images; which could have been the *spoken time* of those words without forms, of those forms without words, that allowed *El Supremo* to conjoin the three texts in a fourth intemporal dimension turning around the axis of an undifferentiated point between the origin and the extinction of writing; that thin shadow between tomorrow and death.[38]

Like the editor, the Supremo yearns for an ideal world in which a pen contains a perfect memory and writing can capture the elusive dimension of spoken language. As the dictator writes in his diary, however, he realizes that he cannot control the artificial nature of writing. The Supremo tells his secretary that dictated words possess a meaning that the written word can never capture.

Patiño is a curious choice for a scribe. Although he knows by heart all official documents of the republic, he is also a "singer of tales," and tells the Supremo a series of oral legends. In his private notebook the dictator criticizes the scribe's inability to faithfully record the spoken word: "Le cuesta a Patiño subir la cuesta del contar y escribir a la vez; oír el son-ido de lo que escribe; trazar el signo de lo que escucha."[39] [It costs Patiño an effort not to allow himself merely to coast downhill, to follow instead the uphill path of the telling and write at the same time; to hear the dispari-son of what he writes: to trace the sign of what his ear is taking in.][40] Patiño seems fated to fail in his endeavors as a faithful scribe, due to the dictator's obsession with the power of writing. The friction between the two dramatizes the notion of a "great divide" between oral and literate cultures. Their debates are reminiscent of Don Quixote and Sancho Panza's rambling conversations about writing.

In the dialogues between the dictator and his scribe, Roa Bastos stages the dilemma we have seen as underlying the writings of Cabrera, Arguedas, and Barnet. In the Supremo's diatribe against scriptural culture, he reprimands Patiño for corrupting his words and staunchly defends the virtues of spoken language: "No has arruinado todavía la tradición oral sólo porque es el único lenguaje que no se puede saquear, robar, repetir, plagiar, copiar. Lo hablado vive sostenido por el tono, los gestos, los movimientos del rostro, las miradas, el acento, el aliento del que habla. En todas las lenguas las exclamaciones más vivas son inarticuladas."[41] [You have not yet destroyed oral tradition only because it is the one language that cannot be sacked, robbed, repeated, plagiarized, copied. What is spoken remains alive, sustained by the tone, the gestures, the facial expressions, the gaze, the accent, the breath of the speaker. In all languages the most forceful exclamations are not articulated.][42] The Supremo fears the dispersion and eventual loss of his memories if they are merely transmitted orally. Yet his only recourse is to set them down in writing, an inadequate form that threatens to undermine his absolute power. Cabrera, Arguedas, and Barnet were caught in a similar paradox: each, working from within literate culture, sought to defend oral culture from contamination by writing.

After *Yo el Supremo*, Roa Bastos did not publish another novel until 1992, when *Vigilia del Almirante* coincided with the fifth centennial celebration of the "Discovery" of the Americas. Roa Bastos set aside the initial outline and notes for this novel more than forty years earlier, and decided to complete the project as the anniversary approached. *Vigilia* informs and borrows from Roa Bastos's trilogy of dictator novels. The novel is composed of a collection of documents including the Almirante's memoirs, logs, personal papers, and a narrator's commentary.

In the preface, Roa Bastos describes the book as a mock historical account. In the pages of *Vigilia* Pedro Mártir de Anglería and Pedro Páramo converge. Roa Bastos essentially writes against the grain of official historical discourse, demonstrating how fiction and history intermingle. In Roa Bastos's novels, writing empowers and threatens authority figures. The Almirante is both writer and protagonist of *Vigilia*. He is in many ways the predecessor to, and descendant of, the Supremo. Both depend on writing as a source of authority, but realize their inability to control the power implicit in language.

The story of *Vigilia* turns on the Almirante's anxiety about Alonso Sánchez, an apocryphal explorer whose voyage preceded his. The oral legend of the unknown navigator haunts the Almirante. The narrator, who cites various written accounts verifying the legend of the "prediscoverer," defends oral tradition as the ultimate source of truth, the only source that cannot be "sacked, robbed or erased."[43] His words echo almost verbatim those of the Supremo. The Almirante frantically tries to invoke the power of writing to undo these spoken truths. He, like the Supremo, wants reality to match what he writes. For both, absolute power depends on the existence of absolute writing.

This obsession with the power of writing, and the notion that writing can steal, manipulate, and deform reality, are important themes of *El fiscal*, published a year after *Vigilia*. With *El fiscal* Roa Bastos completed his trilogy surrounding "the 'monotheism' of power."[44] The first version of the book was written in the 1980s, but had to be destroyed for political reasons. Roa Bastos returned to the book after several years and, in the context of a changed world, composed a new version in just four months.

El fiscal, like *Hijo de hombre* and *Yo el Supremo*, deals manifestly with the figure of a dictator, Alfredo Stroessner. It is the story of a Paraguayan intellectual, the victim of political oppression and severe torture, exiled in France. The exiled protagonist changed his name to Félix Moral and became an associate professor at the "University of X." Obsessed with the idea of returning to his homeland, Moral devises an intricate plan to reenter Paraguay to assassinate Stroessner.

The writer-editor who assumed the author function in *Yo el Supremo* is replaced in *El fiscal* by the protagonist, who essentially writes his own posthumous papers. The past and present merge in the writing process, reflecting a narrative structure similar to that of *Hijo de hombre*. *El fiscal*, like its predecessor, resists literary norms. It pretends to mimic, in writing, the immediacy of oral memory. Whereas the Supremo's private notebook was designated for a broad audience, Moral writes to his wife, Jimena Tarsis, a French intellectual who specializes in the mythology of America's "primitive" cultures. Moral's letters, which contain anachronisms and interlinear commentary, represent a textualization of oral memory. In *El fiscal* Roa Bastos invokes many of the same literary devices as in his other novels to create the effect of an uninterrupted confession.

Moral writes with a special fountain pen, crafted from the root of the "amorphophallus," an extinct plant from Indochina. The name of the plant, which combines the prefix "amorpho" with the suffix "phallus," suggests that the pen symbolizes a shapeless, dysfunctional male sexual organ. The special pen, which writes by mirror in the dark, essentially disempowers the act of writing.[45] Moral's friend Clovis offers it to him, explaining that it is perfect for writing clandestine documents or secret love letters. When Moral writes, he marvels at the point of shimmering phosphoric light that imprints a trace that immediately dries and vanishes. By writing in the dark, Moral feels less threatened by the truths revealed in his written confessions. His invisible inscriptions mimic the immediacy of the spoken word.

El fiscal is divided into three sections. The first two contain Moral's letters to Jimena, relating the events leading up to the attempted assassination of Stroessner; the third is a letter written by Jimena to Moral's mother, describing Moral's imprisonment, attempted escape and death. As in Roa Bastos's other novels, the figure of the uncertain writer replaces that of the great author. Like the Supremo, Moral questions the relationship between writing and reality and feels threatened by the power of written language.

Moral, who survived years of torture and forced confession, essentially writes about his own death by composing posthumous papers. His written confession to Jimena describes his depraved and violent encounters with Leda Kautner, a graduate student. However, at the same time that these events are textualized, he questions whether they really occurred. Moral's death is analogous to that of the Supremo; both are absent from the end, and thus unable to claim absolute authority over their written lives.

Roa Bastos's novels marvelously dramatize the orality/writing debate. They highlight important issues faced by Cabrera, Arguedas, and Barnet, who struggled to preserve the immediacy and interiority of oral language in their writing. Like the protagonists of Roa Bastos's novels, these anthropologist-writers perceived an inequality in the relationship between the oral and the written that could result in the demise of the oral cultures they defended. When Roa Bastos revolutionized Paraguayan literary expression, he struggled with the same dilemma that Cabrera, Arguedas, and Barnet encountered: How can one pretend to express the intimate tones and intonations of the Other's culture when the interiority attributed to orality is constructed from the hierarchy of writing one seeks to topple?

For Roa Bastos, the answer did not lie in the intermingling of ethnographic and literary discourses. He, like the others, invented a poetics of orality as a means of creating a fictional orality effect. Roa Bastos argues that present-day Spanish American writers should rescue the "inferior hemisphere" of their bilingual world by incorporating and infusing the voice of orality into written Spanish.[46] He invoked orality as an authentic form of knowledge. In his opinion, spoken language expressed collective values and a conception of the universe that offered an alternative to Western ideology. All of his writings are marked by the modernist desire to salvage oral tradition by inscribing it. In his novels, the voice of the Other emerges from an artistic process whereby orality becomes part of the fiction. Cabrera, Arguedas, and Barnet engaged in a similar gesture; they combined the idea of *poesis* with anthropology, demonstrating their discontent with the capacity of scientific writing to capture the presence of collective native speech.

Although Roa Bastos and Barnet can be considered contemporaries, only Roa Bastos's writings reflect an acute awareness of the philosophical debates surrounding writing and speech that came to prominence in the 1960s. He, like many intellectuals exiled in Argentina, participated in theoretical discussions about writing that were spurred by an important theoretical revolution in France. Roa Bastos's novels dramatize multiple versions of a contentious encounter between the ephemeral nature of speech and the recourse to writing as a means of fixing authentic language. He analyzed Paraguayan reality in terms of binary oppositions, but was ultimately caught in a dialectic that he believed arose from incompatible cultural forces. Whereas Cabrera, Arguedas, and Barnet were naively caught in the orality-versus-literacy debate, Roa Bastos consciously attempted to stage the predicament in his narrative. His awareness of poststructuralist discussions enabled him to confront the question directly, in ways that the others could not. For this reason, Roa Bastos's writings enact the dilemma faced by Spanish American anthropologist-writers and authors who attempted to inscribe the voices of other peoples.

The complexity of novels like *Yo el Supremo* derives from the paradox that Spanish American literary tradition is filled with written texts that privilege speech. Writers like Cabrera, Arguedas, Barnet, and Roa Bastos, who perceived themselves as marginalized vis-à-vis national culture, tended to regard their worlds as organized hierarchically—dominant culture versus oppressed culture; Spanish versus native language. They deemed the relationship between writing and speech to be structured similarly: writing was seen as a fixed supplement, whereas speech was seen as the ideal stronghold of authentic culture. Only Roa Bastos was fully aware of the underlying paradox of this dialectic: writers who seek to vindicate an oral poetics are ultimately bound to literate culture. As Derrida has explained, the immediacy and presentness associated with speech are illusory, and the notion of "oralized" writing comprises part of a book's fiction. This reading allows us to see how fictionalized orality is a rhetorical strategy that enables one to make legitimate claims as a cross-cultural mediator. These books seek to transform Western literary norms by revealing the poetic capacity of non-Western discursive forms.

Lydia Cabrera and Augusto Roa Bastos both invoked native spoken language because of their discontentment with ways other cultures were portrayed in existing discourse. Miguel Barnet responded to revolutionary ideology and sought to expand notions of Cuban culture to include his nation's marginalized groups. For José María Arguedas, oralization of writing stemmed from his personal awareness of the contradictions inherent in his bicultural upbringing. His quest to salvage Quechuan orality arose from a critical need to piece together his fragmented identity.

Roa Bastos's novels enact a quest for recovery and salvation of oral tradition that closely resembles the projects of Spanish American anthropologist-writers in the twentieth century. Each of the writers considered here turned to speech out of a longing for a past that preceded the modernization symbolized by writing. Ultimately, it was for personal and political reasons that they sought to represent native speech in writing. The notion that orally infused writing captures the interiority of a culture is fraught with a sense of alienation: the author or anthropologist, although motivated by nostalgia or poetic innovation, composes within the context of literate culture. For all of these writers, spoken language, associated with the image of interiority and wholeness, was rich material as they undertook rewritings of their respective cultures.

Can anthropology really grant us access to the timeless stories told by Spanish America's native inhabitants of the postcolonial world? Does the oralization of writing fulfill Spanish American narrative's quest for collective identity and self-knowledge by dismantling biases inherent in Western thought? Or, does it merely reinforce these ethnocentric tendencies? Will the musicologist of Alejo Carpentier's *Los pasos perdidos* (*The Lost Steps*) ever gain passage to the elusive origin at Santa Mónica to recover the songs of a traditional oral culture? Since this mythic return has not yet occurred, the stories told here, by writers who straddle anthropology and literature, are about a process toward creating faithful representation of an origin different from that of the West. Cabrera, Arguedas, and Barnet were essentially archaeologists of the oral: they sidestepped the predicament faced by the nostalgic narrator-protagonist of Carpentier's novel by inventing, in writing, an artistic effect of orality.

Notes

Chapter 1. Anthropologist-Writers as Singers of Tales

1. Garcilaso de la Vega, *Comentarios reales* (Mexico City: Porrúa, 1990), 132.

2. Roberto González Echevarría, *Myth and Archive: A Theory of Latin American Narrative* (New York: Cambridge University Press, 1990).

3. Daphne Patai expresses this idea with regard to *testimonio* in the wake of the Rigoberta Menchú controversy. "Whose Truth? Iconicity and Accuracy in the World of Testimonial Literature," in *The Rigoberta Menchú Controversy*, ed. Arturo Arias (Minneapolis: University of Minnesota Press, 2001), 284.

4. According to Carlos Alonso, the same is true of the autochthonous literary text in Spanish America. See *The Spanish American Regional Novel: Modernity and Autochthony* (Cambridge: Cambridge University Press, 1998) 67.

5. Josefina Ludmer writes that the gauchesque genre necessarily deals with borders and alliances between the voice and the written. *El género gauchesco: Un tratado sobre la patria* (Buenos Aires: Editorial Sudamericana, 1988), 44.

6. Ibid., 75–76.

7. Aníbal González, *Killer Books: Writing, Violence, and Ethics in Modern Spanish American Narrative* (Austin: University of Texas Press, 2001), 5.

8. The concept of "transculturación" was first put forward by Fernando Ortiz to describe a complex process whereby a culture undergoes a transition characterized by the simultaneous loss of cultural practices and the creation of new cultural phenomena. Fernando Ortiz, *Contrapunteo del tabaco y el azúcar* (Caracas: Biblioteca Ayacucho, 1978), 86.

9. Angel Rama, *Transculturación narrativa en América Latina* (Mexico City: Siglo XXI, 1982), 95.

10. Martin Lienhard, *La voz y su huella: Escritura y conflicto étnico-social en América Latina 1492–1988* (Hanover, NH: Ediciones del Norte, 1991) 55.

11. Antonio Cornejo Polar, *Escribir en el aire: Ensayo sobre la heterogeneidad socio-cultural en las literaturas andinas* (Lima: Editorial Horizonte, 1994).

12. Carlos Pacheco, *La comarca oral: La ficcionalización de la oralidad cultural en la narrativa latinoamericana contemporánea* (Caracas: Ediciones de La Casa de Bello, 1992), 51.

13. Ibid., 59.

14. Paul Zumthor, *Oral Poetry: An Introduction*, trans. Kathryn Murphy-Judy, foreword by Walter J. Ong (Minneapolis: University of Minnesota Press, 1990). The quotation

is on p. 22. Zumthor writes: "Performance is the complex action by which a poetic message is simultaneously transmitted and perceived in the here and now. Speaker, receiver(s) of the message, circumstances (which the text with the help of linguistic means represents or does not represent) are concretely confronted, are indisputable." Ibid., 22–23.

15. Carlos Pacheco, "Sobre la construcción de lo rural y lo oral en la literatura hispanoamericana," *Revista de Crítica Literaria Latinoamericana* 21, no. 42 (Segundo semestre 1995): 60.

16. González, *Killer Books*, 3–4.

17. Jack Goody, *The Domestication of the Savage Mind* (1968; reprint, Cambridge: Cambridge University Press, 1977).

18. Brian Street, *Social Literacies: Critical Approaches to Literacy in Development, Ethnography and Education* (New York: Longman, 1995), 65–66.

19. Walter J. Ong, *Orality and Literacy: The Technologizing of the Word* (New York: Methuen, 1982). Ong also discusses the salient features of oral cultures in *Interfaces of the Word: Studies in the Evolution of Consciousness and Culture* (Ithaca, NY: Cornell University Press, 1977) and *The Presence of the Word: Some Prolegomena for Cultural and Religious History* (New Haven, CT: Yale University Press, 1967).

20. Jacques Derrida, *Of Grammatology*, trans. Gayatri Chakravorty Spivak (Baltimore: Johns Hopkins University Press, 1976). Also see Christopher Norris, *Deconstruction: Theory and Practice* (New York: Routledge, 1982).

21. Street, *Social Literacies*. In particular, see pp. 29, 74, 158, and 175.

22. Jorge Marcone, *La oralidad escrita: Sobre la reivindicación y re-inscripción del discurso oral* (Lima: Pontificia Universidad Católica del Perú, Fondo Editorial, 1997), 47.

23. Augusto Roa Bastos, ed., *Culturas condenadas* (Mexico City: Siglo XXI, 1978), 14. Also see Augusto Roa Bastos, "Una cultura oral," *Hispamérica* 46–47 (1987): 85–112.

24. Michel de Certeau, *The Writing of History*, trans. Tom Conley (New York: Columbia University Press, 1988), 2–3. Also see Michel de Certeau, *Heterologies: Discourse on the Other*, trans. Brian Massumi (Minneapolis: University of Minnesota Press, 1986).

25. Michel de Certeau, *The Practice of Everyday Life*, trans. Steven Rendall (Berkeley: University of California Press, 1984), 159.

26. See James Clifford, Clifford Geertz, Marc Manganaro, and George E. Marcus.

27. George E. Marcus and Michael M. J. Fischer write: "Ethnographic poetics tries to establish culturally authentic ways to read indigenous oral narratives as literary forms." *Anthropology as Cultural Critique* (Chicago: University of Chicago Press, 1986), 73.

28. Clifford Geertz, *Works and Lives: The Anthropologist as Author* (Stanford, CA: Stanford University Press, 1988), 16.

29. Carlos Alonso, *The Burden of Modernity: The Rhetoric of Cultural Discourse in Spanish America* (New York: Oxford University Press, 1998), 26.

30. Alonso, *Spanish American Regional Novel*, 3.

31. Ibid., 7–9.

32. Ibid., 31. Also, see pp. 15–16.

33. Alonso, *Burden of Modernity*, 21.

34. María Rosa Menocal traces the ascendance of the concept of an authentic original to the advent of print, and aptly suggests that purist notions of originality are at odds with a culture of variation and performance. "The Flip Side," in *Mapping Benjamin: The Work of Art in the Digital Age*, ed. H. U. Gumbrecht and M. Marrinam (Stanford, CA: Stanford University Press, 2003), 291–300.

35. James Clifford, "On Ethnographic Allegory," in *Writing Culture: The Poetics and*

Politics of Ethnography, ed. James Clifford and George E. Marcus (Berkeley: University of California Press, 1986), 101.

36. Denis Donoghue, *The Practice of Reading* (New Haven, CT: Yale University Press, 1999), 112.

37. Roland Barthes, *The Rustle of Language*, trans. Richard Howard (Oxford: Basil Blackwell, 1986), 148.

CHAPTER 2. ORAL POETICS IN LYDIA CABRERA'S *EL MONTE*

1. Lydia Cabrera. "Asociación de Arte Retrospectivo," *Diario de la Marina*, June 1922, 12.

2. Rosario Hiriart, *Lydia Cabrera: Vida hecha arte* (New York: Eliseo Torres & Sons, 1978), 72.

3. Ibid., 22–23.

4. Alejo Carpentier, "Los *Cuentos negros* de Lydia Cabrera," *Carteles* 28, no. 41 (Oct. 11, 1936): 40.

5. Isabel Castellanos, *Páginas sueltas* (Miami: Ediciones Universal, 1994), 39.

6. Alejo Carpentier, "Ortega y Gasset," *El Nacional*, 22 Oct. 1955, 16.

7. Roberto González Echevarría, *Alejo Carpentier: The Pilgrim at Home* (Ithaca, NY: Cornell University Press, 1977), 55.

8. Frobenius, the founder of an institute for Africanist studies in Berlin, was one of the first anthropologists to reject the portrayal of Africans as savage people who were in need of salvation on Western terms, and his works proclaimed the value of African art forms. Readers of Frobenius and Maurice Delafosse responded to the breakdown of positivist thinking and evolutionist doctrines by abandoning previously held ideas of cultural dominance. See Lilyan Kesteloot, *Black Writers in French: A Literary History of Negritude*, trans. Ellen Conroy Kennedy (Philadelphia: Temple University Press, 1974), xvii.

9. Christopher Miller, *Blank Darkness: Africanist Discourse in French* (Chicago: University of Chicago Press, 1985), 5, 15.

10. James Clifford, *The Predicament of Culture: Twentieth-Century Ethnography, Literature, and Art* (Cambridge, MA: Harvard University Press, 1988), 130, 147. For a discussion of ethnographic surrealism, refer to ibid., 117–51. James Clifford's definition of "surrealism" extends beyond the artistic and literary movement outlined by Breton and others: "I am using the term surrealism in an obviously expanded sense to circumscribe an aesthetic that values fragments, curious collections, unexpected juxtapositions–that works to provoke the manifestation of extraordinary realities drawn from the domains of the erotic, the exotic and the unconscious." See James Clifford, *Routes: Travel and Translation in the Late Twentieth Century* (Cambridge, MA: Harvard University Press, 1997), 118.

11. For a detailed discussion of Paris at the turn of the century, see Roger Shattuck, *The Banquet Years: The Origins of the Avant-Garde in France, 1885 to World War I* (New York: Vintage Books, 1968), 144.

12. Lydia Cabrera, "Notas sobre Africa, la Negritud y la actual poesía yoruba," *Revista de la Universidad Complutense* 24, no. 95 (1975): 9–59.

13. Spurred on by European postwar passion for African cultures, these Martiniquans were avid readers of Frobenius's *Histoire* and Maurice Delafosse's *Les négres*, works that valued the social and artistic contributions of African civilizations. This vocal group of Parisian students vowed not to be suppressed by the capitalistic tendencies that could be

blamed for the disgraces of their time. They embraced surrealism and Communism, and rejected the bourgeois society of which they were, ironically, a product.

14. L. S. Senghor, "Rapport sur la doctrine et le programme du parti," paper delivered at the Constitutive Congress of the African Assembly Party, Paris, France, 1959, 59.

15. Lydia Cabrera, "Damas," *Journal of Caribbean Studies* 1 (1980): 1.

16. Castellanos, *Páginas sueltas*, 251–53.

17. Aimé Césaire, *Notebook of a Return to the Native Land,* trans. and ed. Clayton Eshleman and Annette Smith (Middletown, CT: Wesleyan University Press, 2001), 36–39.

18. Carpentier, "Los *Cuentos negros*," 40.

19. Fernando Ortiz established the journal *Archivos del Folklore Cubano*, which first appeared in 1927, and ten years later became president of the Sociedad de Estudios Afrocubanos, which published the inaugural issue of its quarterly magazine in 1937, followed by three more numbers until its termination in 1940. The group aspired to study phenomena of reciprocal, racial interactions, and derided tendencies of ethnophobia that had characterized years of relations between Cubans. The society's emblem, which appeared on the cover of each issue, depicted a Greek chalice adorned with the side-by-side profiles of two women, one black and one white, which harked back to an historic vase crafted by Charinus in the sixth century. Although this icon is indeed emblematic of the coexistence of blacks and whites, it also suggests that the movement's ideology ultimately sought to absorb black culture by conceiving it on Western terms. Fernando Ortiz, "La Sociedad de Estudios Afrocubanos Contra los Racismos: Advertencia, comprensión y designio," *Estudios Afrocubanos* 1, no. 1 (1937): 4–11.

20. Fernando Ortiz, review of *Contes nègres de Cuba*, by Lydia Cabrera, trans. Francis de Miomandre, *Estudios Afrocubanos* 12, no. 1 (1938): 133–35.

21. Rómulo Lachatañeré, *¡¡Oh, mío Yemaya!!* (1938; reprint, Havana: Editorial de Ciencias Sociales, 1992), 3.

22. Clifford, *The Predicament of Culture*, 218. For a detailed description of Clifford's theory of "culture collecting," see his chapter in *The Predicament* entitled "On Collecting Art and Culture," 215–51.

23. Fernando Ortiz, introduction to *¡¡Oh, mío Yemaya!!* by Rómulo Lachatañeré, *Revista Bimestre Cubana* 70 (1955): 86, 90.

24. Street, *Social Literacies*, 158.

25. Ortiz, introduction, 91.

26. Lino Novás-Calvo, "Los cuentos de Lydia Cabrera," *Exilio* 3, no. 2 (1969): 18.

27. Ibid., 18.

28. Jorge Castellanos and Isabel Castellanos, *Cultura afrocubana*, vol. 3 (Miami: Ediciones Universal, 1971), 101–6.

29. Lydia Cabrera, *Cuentos negros de Cuba* (Havana: La Verónica, 1940), 25.

30. Lydia Cabrera, *Ayapá: Cuentos de Jicotea* (Miami: Ediciones Universal, 1971), 14.

31. Lydia Cabrera, *El monte: Igbo finda, ewe orisha, vititi nfinda (Notas sobre las religiones, la magia, las supersticiones y el folklore de los negros criollos y del pueblo de Cuba)* (1954; reprint, Miami: Ediciones C.R., 1968), 217.

32. Ramón Menéndez Pidal, *Flor nueva de romances viejos* (1928; reprint, Madrid: Espasa-Calpe, 1969), 40.

33. Lydia Cabrera, "Un gran pintor: Wifredo Lam," in Castellanos, *Páginas sueltas*, 222.

34. Lydia Cabrera, "Wifredo Lam," in Castellanos, *Páginas sueltas*, 264.

35. Lydia Cabrera, "Eggüe o Vichichi Finda," *Revista Bimestre Cubana* 60 (1947): 47–120. This article represents a preliminary version of Cabrera's definitive volume *El monte*, published eight years later by Ediciones C.R. in the Colección de Chicherekú, a series of publications initiated by Lydia and Titina, and later transplanted to Miami and renamed Colección de Chicherekú en el Exilio. Lydia Cabrera explains that a *chicherekú* is a wooden doll into which a *Santero* breathes life. Since the gods were exiled with those who worshipped them, why not the chicherekús as well? It occurred to her that it would be a good idea to give her series of books the same name. Hence the name "Chicherekús in Exile." Hiriart, *Lydia Cabrera*, 92.

36. Lydia Cabrera, "La ceiba y la Sociedad Secreta Abakuá," *Orígenes* 7, no. 25 (1950): 16–47.

37. Cabrera, "Eggüe," 47.

38. "Cuatro años" (editorial), *Orígenes* 12 (1947): 46.

39. María Zambrano, "Lydia Cabrera, poeta de la metamorfosis," *Orígenes* 25 (1950): 12–13.

40. Cabrera, *El monte*, 7.

41. James Clifford, "On Ethnographic Authority," *Representations* 1, no. 2 (1983): 120.

42. Marcus and Fischer, *Anthropology as Cultural Critique*, 22–23.

43. Cabrera, *El monte*, 10.

44. Clifford, "On Ethnographic Authority," 140.

45. Clifford Geertz maintains that ethnography is "thick description": "What the ethnographer is in fact faced with . . . is a multiplicity of complex conceptual structures, many of them superimposed upon or knotted into one another, which are at once strange, irregular, and inexplicit, and which he must contrive somehow first to grasp and then to render." See Clifford Geertz, *The Interpretation of Cultures: Selected Essays by Clifford Geertz* (New York: Basic Books, 1973), 10–11.

46. Ludmer, *El género gauchesco*, 71–72.

47. Cabrera, *El monte*, 32.

48. Cabrera, *Ayapá*, 14.

49. Menéndez Pidal, *Flor nueva*, 40.

50. Cabrera, *El monte*, 66.

51. Wilhelm Dilthey, *Wilhelm Dilthey: Selected Writings*, ed. H. P. Rickman (Cambridge: Cambridge University Press, 1976), 187.

52. Cabrera, *El monte*, 27.

53. Geertz, *Works and Lives*, 84.

54. Cabrera, *El monte*, 9.

55. Dilthey, *Wilhelm Dilthey*, 228.

56. Miguel Acosta Saignes, review of *El monte*, by Lydia Cabrera, *Revista Bimestre Cubana* 71 (1956): 286–87.

57. Francis de Miomandre, "Sobre 'El monte,'" *Orígenes* 39 (1955): 75.

58. Lino Novás-Calvo, review of *El monte*, by Lydia Cabrera, *Exilio*, Sept. 1968, 298.

59. Cabrera, *El monte*, 354–55.

60. Lydia Cabrera, *Por qué... Cuentos negros de Cuba* (1948; reprint, Miami: Ediciones C.R., 1972), 55.

61. Ibid., 56.

62. Cabrera, *El monte,* 14.

63. Ibid., 147.

64. Ibid., 194.

65. Ibid., 287.

66. Lydia Cabrera, *Anagó: Vocabulario lucumí (el yoruba que se habla en Cuba)* (Miami: Ediciones C.R., 1970), 13.

67. Ibid., 15.

68. Lydia Cabrera, *Reglas de congo: Palo Monte-Mayombe* (Miami: Ediciones C.R., Colección del Chicherekú en el exilio, 1979), 18–19.

69. Cabrera, *El monte*, 286.

70. Lydia Cabrera, *Otán Iyebiyé: Las piedras preciosas* (Miami: Ediciones C.R., 1970), 66.

71. Eugene Vance, "Roland and the Poetics of Memory," in *Textual Strategies*, ed. Josué Harari (Ithaca, NY: Cornell University Press, 1979), 374.

72. Lydia Cabrera, *Koeko iyawó, aprende novicia: Pequeño tratado de regla lucumí* (Miami: Ediciones C.R., 1980), 6.

73. Cabrera, *Anagó*, 17.

74. Clifford, "On Ethnographic Allegory," 99.

75. Ibid., 115–17.

76. Lydia Cabrera, "Religious Syncretism in Cuba," ed. and trans. "from a talk given by the late LC in Miami, FL, 1979 (ORD)," *Journal of Caribbean Studies* 10, nos. 1–2 (1994): 93.

77. Cabera, *Ayapá*, 10.

78. Ibid., 15–16.

79. Ibid., 21.

80. Ibid., 51.

81. Lydia Cabrera, *Animales en el folklore de Cuba* (Miami: Ediciones Universal, 1988), 11.

82. Lydia Cabrera, introduction to *La religión afrocubana*, by Mercedes Cros Sandoval (Madrid: Playor, 1975), 5.

83. Lydia Cabrera, *La laguna sagrada de San Joaquín* (Madrid: Ediciones Madrid, 1973), 16.

84. This quote can be found on the back cover of *La laguna*.

CHAPTER 3. ECHOES FROM *LOS RÍOS PROFUNDOS*

1. José María Arguedas, *Agua* (1948; reprint, Lima: Universidad Nacional Mayor de San Marcos, 1974), 15.

2. José María Arguedas, "Alrededor de este nudo de la vida," interview with Chester Christian, *Revista Iberoamericana* 49, no. 122 (1983): 221–28.

3. José María Arguedas, "Ensayo sociológico," in *Arguedas: Documentos inéditos*, ed. Roland Forgues (Lima: Empresa Editora Amauta, 1955), 58.

4. Mario Vargas Llosa, *La utopía arcaica y las ficciones del Indigenismo* (Mexico City: Fondo de Cultura Económica, 1996), 75–77.

5. Alberto Flores Galindo, *Buscando un inca: Identidad y utopía en los Andes* (Lima: Editorial Horizonte, 1988), 338–39.

6. Ibid., 21.

7. Alberto Escobar, *Arguedas o la utopía de la lengua* (Lima: Instituto de Estudios Peruanos, 1984), 46.

8. José María Arguedas, "La colección de Alicia Bustamante y la Universidad," *El Comercio*, 12 Jan. 1969, 30.

9. Clifford, *The Predicament of Culture*, 218, 231.

10. Rolena Adorno, "La soledad de Waman Puma de Ayala y José María Arguedas," *Revista Iberoamericana* 122 (1983): 147.

11. Murra is surprised by two shortcomings in Arguedas scholarship: the limited use of his ethnologic production in the study of his artistic writing and the lack of interest in the role played by Santiago, Chile, in his artistic works. John Murra, "José María Arguedas: Dos imágenes," *Revista Iberoamericana* 122 (1983): 46. Surprisingly few critics have focused their attention on Arguedas's literary and ethnographic texts in conjunction. However, the topic has been addressed by Alberto Flores Galindo in *Buscando un inca*; by Silverio Muñoz in *José María Arguedas y el mito de la salvación por la cultura* (Lima: Editorial Horizonte, 1987); and in a few articles: Antonio Melis, "Escritura antropológica y escritura narrativa en Arguedas," *Hoja Naviera*, Nov. 1993, 26–34; William Rowe, "Arguedas: El narrador y el antropólogo frente al lenguaje," *Revista Iberoamericana* 122 (1993): 97–109; idem, *Ensayos arguedianos* (Lima: SUR, 1996); and Silvia Spitta, "Hacia una nueva lectura del mestizo en la obra de José María Arguedas," *Hispamérica* 24, no. 72 (1995): 15–26.

12. José María Arguedas, *Canto kechwa con un ensayo sobre la capacidad de creación artística del pueblo indio y mestizo* (Lima: Editorial Horizonte, 1989), 7.

13. Ibid., 12. The *wayno* is the most popular song and dance of the Peruvian *sierra*. As Arguedas explains, it is essentially a Quechua song that has been enriched with Spanish elements. He claims that the indigenous *wayno* is epic and simple, and the mestizo form is more melodic and soft. Ibid., 14.

14. Ibid., 22.

15. Clifford, *The Predicament of Culture*, 94. For a detailed description of fictional self-fashioning, see Stephen Greenblatt, *Renaissance Self-Fashioning: From More to Shakespeare* (Chicago: University of Chicago Press, 1980).

16. Alejandro Ortiz Rescaniere, ed., *José María Arguedas, recuerdos de una amistad* (Lima: Fondo Editorial de la Pontificia, 1996), 245.

17. Murra, "José María Arguedas," 45, 52.

18. Arguedas, *Canto kechwa*, 23.

19. The subject has received little critical attention. The best exposition of the confluence of literature and ethnography in Arguedas's writings, and the problematics involved, can be found in William Rowe's essays. For Rowe, the concept of an invented poetics encompasses a common ground of mutual transformations shared by the two discourses. See Rowe, *Ensayos arguedianos*, 16.

20. José María Arguedas, "Simbolismo y poesía de dos canciones populares quechuas," in *Indios, mestizos y señores,* ed. Sybila Arredondo de Arguedas (Lima: Editorial Horizonte, 1989), 22.

21. José María Arguedas, "Entre el kechwa y el castellano la angustia del mestizo," in *Indios, mestizos y señores*, 26.

22. Escobar, *Arguedas*, 70.

23. Ibid., 101.

24. Ibid., 103–4.

25. José María Arguedas, "Fiesta en Tinta," in *Indios, mestizos y señores*, 59. This article first appeared in *La Prensa* on October 20, 1940.

26. José María Arguedas, "El wayno: La canción popular mestiza en el Perú, su valor

documental y poético," *La Prensa*, 18 Aug. 1940. This article also appears in José María Arguedas, *Nuestra música popular y sus intérpretes* (Lima: Mosca Azul & Horizonte Editores, 1977); and idem, *Indios, mestizos y señores*.

27. José María Arguedas, *Canciones y cuentos del pueblo quechua* (Lima: Editorial Huascarán, 1949), 68, 13.

28. Roland Forgues, *José María Arguedas, la letra inmortal: Correspondencia con Manuel Moreno Jimeno* (Lima: Ediciones de Los Ríos Profundos, 1993), 78.

29. José María Arguedas, "El libro 'Canto de amor' y el fanatismo Indigenista," *El Comercio* 17, no. 6 (June 17, 1956).

30. Arguedas, *Canciones*, 11.

31. Alberto Flores Galindo studies various models of Peruvian utopia in his book *Buscando un inca*.

32. Muñoz, *José María Arguedas*, 48.

33. José María Arguedas, "Yawar (Fiesta)," *Revista Americana de Buenos Aires* 156 (1937).

34. Muñoz, *José María Arguedas*, 163.

35. José María Arguedas, *Yawar fiesta* (1941; reprint, Santiago: Editorial Universitaria, 1968), 18.

36. José María Arguedas, "La novela y el problema," in ibid., 16.

37. Rita de Grandis has studied the combination and contamination of languages in Arguedas's writings in her article, "Los *Zorros* de Arguedas: Una traducción mestiza," in *Dos estudios sobre textos de Arguedas* (Lima: CICOSUL, 1990), 9–17.

38. José María Arguedas, "Evolución de las comunidades indígenas: El valle del Mantaro y la ciudad de Huancayo; Un caso de fusión de culturas no comprometida por la acción de las instituciones de origen cultural," in *Formación de una cultura nacional indoamericana*, ed. Angel Rama (1956; reprint, Mexico City: Siglo XXI, 1975), 45, 79.

39. Murra, "José María Arguedas," 44. In his compilation of correspondence with Arguedas, Murra writes that between approximately 1942 and 1956, Arguedas published no artistic texts. This, however, was the period of his greatest anthropologic production. The two forms complemented one another: when he wrote things of an anthropologic nature, this coincided with "sterile" periods of artistic writing, and vice versa. John V. Murra, "Semblanza de Arguedas," in *Las cartas de Arguedas*, ed. John V. Murra and Mercedes López-Baralt (Lima: Pontificia Universidad Católica del Perú, 1996), 288.

40. Murra, "Semblanza," 287.

41. According to Pinilla, Arguedas found that Dilthey's theories complemented his own perspectives regarding his connection to the indigenous community. Carmen María Pinilla, *Arguedas: Conocimiento y vida* (Lima: Fondo Editorial de la Pontificia Universidad Católica del Perú, 1994), 94. Pinilla's most compelling arguments with regard to Arguedas's contact with Dilthey's theories can be found in the first chapter, "Biografía, experiencia y conocimiento en José María Arguedas."

42. Dilthey, *Wilhelm Dilthey*, 218.

43. José María Arguedas, "Algunas consideraciones acerca del contenido y la finalidad de este libro," in *Mitos, leyendas y cuentos peruanos*, ed. José María Arguedas and Francisco Izquierdo Ríos (Lima: Ediciones de la Dirección de Educación Artística y Extensión Cultural, 1947), 16.

44. José María Arguedas, "El Ollantay: Lo autóctono y lo occidental en el estilo de los dramas coloniales quechuas," *Letras Peruanas* 2, no. 8 (1952): 114.

45. González Echevarría, *Myth and Archive*, 153. James Clifford's ideas surrounding

ethnographic representation complement this theory. He assumes "that the poetic and the political are inseparable, that science is in, not above, historical and linguistic processes[,] . . . that academic and literary genres interpenetrate and that the writing of cultural descriptions is properly experimental and ethical." James Clifford, "Introduction: Partial Truths," in Clifford and Marcus, *Writing Culture*, 2.

46. Ariel Dorfman has studied this aspect of the novel in "Puentes y padres en el infierno: *Los ríos profundos*," *Revista de Crítica Literaria Latinoamericana* 12 (1980): 91–137.

47. José María Arguedas, *Cusco* (Lima: Ediciones Contur, 1947), 1.

48. José María Arguedas, *Los ríos profundos*, ed. Ricardo González Vigil (1958; reprint, Madrid: Cátedra, 1995), 144.

49. José María Arguedas, *Deep Rivers*, trans. Frances Horning Barraclough (Austin: University of Texas Press, 1978), 7.

50. On this topic, see Julio Ortega, *Texto, comunicación y cultura*; and Angel Rama, "Los ríos profundos del mito y de la historia," *Revista de Crítica Literaria Latinoamericana* 2 (1980): 69–90.

51. M. M. Bakhtin, "Discourse in the Novel," in *The Dialogic Imagination: Four Essays by M. M. Bakhtin*, ed. Michael Holquist (Austin: University of Texas Press, 1981), 262–63.

52. Arguedas, *Los ríos profundos*, 149.

53. Arguedas, *Deep Rivers*, 9.

54. Arguedas, *Cusco*, 5.

55. Arguedas, *Los ríos profundos*, 155.

56. Arguedas, *Deep Rivers*, 13.

57. Arguedas, *Los ríos profundos*, 171–72.

58. Arguedas, *Deep Rivers*, 23.

59. According to Rowe, sound becomes the "soul" of objects; it embodies a magical substance. William Rowe, "La música como espacio sonoro: La evolución de la reflexión de Arguedas sobre la música andina," in *Ensayos arguedianos*, 51. In a separate article, Rowe argues similarly that sound embodies a plurality of levels in the novel *El zorro de arriba y el zorro de abajo*. William Rowe, "Deseo, escritura y fuerzas productivas en *El zorro de arriba y el zorro de abajo*," in *Ensayos arguedianos*, 118.

60. Arguedas, "El Ollantay," 139.

61. Arguedas, *Los ríos profundos*, 156.

62. Arguedas, "El Ollantay," 139.

63. Arguedas, *Los ríos profundos*, 249–51.

64. Arguedas, *Deep Rivers*, 74–75.

65. In his article "Escritura antropológica y escritura narrativa en Arguedas," Antonio Melis has studied the "circularity" and "intersection" between Arguedas's literary and ethnographic production with regard to chapter 6 of *Los ríos profundos* and the piece published in *La Prensa*.

66. Arguedas, *Los ríos profundos*, 235.

67. José María Arguedas, "La literatura quechua en el Perú," *Mar del Sur* 1, no. 1 (1948): 50.

68. Arguedas, *Los ríos profundos*, 240–41.

69. Arguedas, *Deep Rivers*, 67–68.

70. Arguedas, *Los ríos profundos*, 363.

71. Arguedas, *Deep Rivers*, 160.

72. Arguedas, *Los ríos profundos*, 379.

73. Arguedas, *Deep Rivers*, 172.

74. González Echevarría, *Myth and Archive*, 158.

75. Murra, "Semblanza," 293.

76. José María Arguedas, "París y la patria," *El Comercio*, suplemento dominical, 7 Dec. 1958, 2.

77. Alberto Flores Galindo, "Los últimos años de Arguedas (intelectuales, sociedad e identidad en el Perú)," paper presented at the conference *Literatura e identidad nacional en el Perú*, Jauja, Perú, 8–12 Aug. 1988.

78. José María Arguedas, "Reflexiones peruanas sobre un narrador mexicano," *El Comercio*, suplemento dominical, 4 Oct. 1964, 3.

79. José María Arguedas, "Cuentos religioso-mágicos quechuas de Lucanamarca," *Folklore Americano* 8–9 (1960–61): 143–44.

80. Ibid., 215–16.

81. The letter was written by Arguedas in the winter of 1969 and sent to Ortiz from Santiago, Chile. Ortiz Rescaniere, *José María Arguedas, recuerdos*, 280.

82. Murra and López-Baralt, *Las cartas de Arguedas*, 66.

83. Martin Lienhard, *Cultura andina y forma novelesca: Zorros y danzantes en la última novela de Arguedas* (Lima: Editorial Horizonte, 1990), 139.

84. José María Arguedas, *La agonía de Rasu-Ñiti* (Lima: Taller de Artes Gráficas Ícaro, Camino del Hombre, 1962), 13–14.

85. José María Arguedas, *Temblar: El sueño del pongo* (Havana: Casa de las Américas, 1976), 53–54.

86. José María Arguedas, *Katatay: Temblar* (Lima: Editorial Horizonte, 1984), 59.

87. Ibid., 59.

88. José María Arguedas, *Las comunidades de España y del Perú* (Lima: Universidad Nacional Mayor de San Marcos, 1968), 5.

89. Murra, "José María Arguedas"; and idem, "Semblanza."

90. For a transcription of the discussion in its entirety, refer to José María Arguedas, *¿He vivido en vano? Mesa Redonda sobre Todas las sangres, 23 de junio de 1965* (Lima: Instituto de Estudios Peruanos, 1985). Pinilla has written a chapter entitled "Mesa redonda sobre *Todas las sangres* y el encuentro de dos modos de conocimiento de la realidad social" that can be found in Pinilla, *Arguedas*.

91. Arguedas, *¿He vivido en vano?* 36.

92. Vargas Llosa, *La utopía*, 262.

93. Ibid., 263.

94. Flores Galindo, "Los últimos años," 21.

95. Luis E. Valcárcel and Carlos Araníbar, "La colección de fuentes e investigaciones para la historia del Perú," in *Dioses y hombres de Huarochirí: Edición bilingüe*, trans. José María Arguedas (Lima: Museo Nacional de Historia e Instituto de Estudios Peruanos, 1966), 8.

96. José María Arguedas, introduction to Valcárcel and Araníbar, *Dioses y hombres de Huarochirí*, 10.

97. Ibid.

98. Vargas Llosa, *La utopía*, 298.

99. González Echevarría, *Myth and Archive*, 145, 174.

100. Mario Vargas Llosa, *El hablador* (Barcelona: Seix Barral, 1987), 77.
101. Marcone, *La oralidad escrita* (1997), 194. For a discussion of *El hablador*, see pp. ibid., 165–213.
102. Vargas Llosa, *El hablador* 152.

Chapter 4. Barnet and Burgos as Ghostwriters

1. Miguel Barnet, *La fuente viva* (Havana: Editorial Letras Cubanas, 1983), 43.
2. Miguel Barnet, "Confesiones con palabras no escritas," interview by Alberto Batista Reyes, *Letras Cubanas* 3 (1987): 132.
3. Miguel Barnet, *La piedra fina y el pavorreal* (Havana: Ediciones Unión, 1963), 7.
4. Elzbieta Sklodowska focuses on the tendency of prologues to configure readers' expectations, thereby authoritatively predetermining the reception of a text. *Testimonio hispanoamericano: Historia, teoría, poética* (New York: Peter Lang, 1992), 7–9, 139.
5. Kay B. Warren, "Telling Truths: Taking David Stoll and the Rigoberta Menchú Exposé Seriously," in Arias, *Rigoberta Menchú Controversy*, 201.
6. Antonio Vera León, "Hacer hablar: La transcripción testimonial," *Revista de Crítica Literaria Lationamericana* 18, no. 36 (1992): 184–85.
7. Marcone, *La oralidad escrita* (1997), 215.
8. Sklodowska argues that Barnet and Elisabeth Burgos opt to sidestep the problem of translation/betrayal of the voice of the Other by following the classic model of realist ethnography. She observes that Barnet, like Burgos, erases any tension associated with writing the Other's voice by suppressing metadiscursive tools and projecting a harmonious relationship between ethnographer and informant, a contract based on mutual consent. Sklodowska, *Testimonio hispanoamericano,* 118.
9. See Marcus and Fischer, *Anthropology as Cultural Critique*, 16.
10. Miguel Barnet, *Biografía de un cimarrón* (1966; reprint, Havana: Editorial Letras Cubanas, 1980), 9.
11. In *Myth and Archive* Roberto González Echevarría examines the proclivity of contemporary Latin American novels to imitate nonfictitious discursive practices.
12. Miguel Barnet, introduction to *The Autobiography of a Runaway Slave*, by Esteban Montejo, trans. Jocasta Innes (New York: Pantheon Books, 1968), 8–11.
13. Sklodowska, *Testimonio hispanoamericano*, 16.
14. Ibid., 85–86. In his review of *Testimonio hispanoamericano*, González Echevarría deems this observation to be Sklodowska's most insightful. He argues that, upon turning voice into writing, *testimonio* "occidentalizes" what it intends to preserve of the Other, in an act complicit with processes of colonization. Exploitation of the "informant" is undeniable. González Echevarría, review of *Testimonio hispanoamericano: Historia, teoría, poética*, by Elzbieta Sklodowska, *Bulletin of Hispanic Studies* 71 (1994): 515.
15. Elzbieta Sklodowska, "The Poetics of Remembering, the Politics of Forgetting: Rereading *I, Rigoberta Menchú*," in Arias, *Rigoberta Menchú Controversy*, 254–56.
16. Barnet, *La fuente viva*, 27.
17. Lucille Kerr, "Gestures of Authorship: Lying to Tell the Truth in Elena Poniatowska's *Hasta no verte Jesús mío*," *MLN* 106 (1991): 390.
18. Barnet, *La fuente viva*, 23.
19. Ibid., 36–37.
20. Vera León, "Hacer hablar," 191.

21. González Echevarría, *Myth and Archive*, 122.

22. Miguel Barnet, "Para llegar a Esteban Montejo: Los caminos del cimarrón," *Contracorriente* 6 (1996): 29–32.

23. Ibid., 44.

24. Ibid., 33.

25. Geertz, *Works and Lives*, 16.

26. Barnet, *Biografía*, 47.

27. Barnet, introduction, 47–48.

28. Barnet, *Biografía*, 124.

29. Barnet, introduction, 132.

30. Clifford, "Introduction," 2.

31. Barnet, "Para llegar," 35, 40.

32. See Marc Manganaro, James Clifford, Clifford Geertz, and George E. Marcus.

33. Miguel Barnet, "Miguel Barnet: 'Con Esteban Montejo había que jugar limpio,'" in *Miguel Barnet: Rescate e invención de la memoria*, by Abdeslam Azougarh (Geneva: Editions Slatkine, 1996), 217.

34. Barnet, *La fuente viva*, 30.

35. Certeau, *Practice of Everyday Life*, 159–61. Sklodowska notes that recent trends in interpretive ethnography (Geertz, Clifford, Marcus, and others) can be inscribed in the series of discourses Certeau refers to as "heterologous." Sklodowska, *Testimonio hispano-americano*, 112. Also see Sklodowska's article "Máscaras y simulacros: El arte del *storyteller* en la cuentística de Jesús Gardea y Eraclio Zepeda," in *Literatura mexicana/Mexican literature*, ed. José Miguel Oviedo (Philadelphia: University of Pennsylvania Press, 1993), 114–26.

36. Barnet, introduction, 7 (emphasis added).

37. Roger D. Abrahams, "Complicity and Imitation in Storytelling: A Pragmatic Folklorist's Perspective," *Cultural Anthropology* 1, no. 2 (1986): 233.

38. Stephanie Merrim has analyzed the oral qualities of *Grande sertão: Veredas* and *Tres tristes tigres*, concluding that both texts are linguistically self-conscious insofar as they are predominantly arranged according to patterns of oral language: "Oral language therefore serves both the ecological and regionalist designs of the work by allowing the lost world to speak directly to us, immortalizing a marginal language as a literary language, and giving voice to the 'other' of society—the sertão and the nightworld." Merrim, *Logos and the Word: The Novel of Language and Linguistic Motivation in "Grande sertão: Veredas" and "Tres tristes tigres"* (New York: Peter Lang, 1983), 88.

39. Barnet, *Biografía*, 16.

40. Barnet, introduction,16.

41. Miguel Barnet, *Gallego* (Madrid: Ediciones Alfaguara, 1981), 24.

42. The pervasive fictionality of *Canción de Rachel* has been studied by Sklodowska in "La forma testimonial y la novelística de Miguel Barnet," *Revista/Review Interamericana* 12, no. 3 (1982): 375–84; and Bensa Vera, "La *Canción de Rachel*: La literariedad de su testimonio," *Revista/Review Interamericana* 19, nos. 1–2 (1989): 65–76.

43. Oscar Collazos, review of *Canción de Rachel*, by Miguel Barnet, *Casa de las Américas* 59 (1970): 192.

44. Miguel Barnet, *Canción de Rachel* (Barcelona: Editorial Laia, 1979), 9, 11.

45. Barnet, *Gallego*, 12.

46. Ibid., 25, 62.

47. Barnet, *La fuente viva*, 5.

48. Miguel Barnet, *Los perros mudos* (Havana: Alfaguara, 1978), 11. This collection

was also published in the same year with the title *Akeké y la jutía* (Havana: Unión de Escritores y Artistas de Cuba, 1978).

49.   Sklodowska traces parallels between *Me llamo Rigoberta Menchú* and *Biografía*, and concludes that both invoke the tools of ethnographic realism to sidestep the dangers of translation/betrayal involved in representing the Other's voice. She argues that Burgos and Barnet convey a sense of harmony with regard to the ethnographer-informant relationship by portraying the writing process as the result of a consensual dialogue. See chapter 3 of Sklodowska, *Testimonio hispanoamericano*.

50.   David Stoll, *Rigoberta Menchú and the Story of All Poor Guatemalans* (Boulder, CO: Westview Press, 1999), 184–85.

51.   In spite of Burgos's explicit remarks about letting Rigoberta control the structure of the text, Jorge Marcone notes that the reorganization of enunciations to follow a certain chronology betrays characteristics of oral retelling. Marcone, *La oralidad escrita* (1997), 227.

52.   Dorris Sommer writes that Rigoberta's explicit negation is an example of a "performative": it constructs the apparent cause of denial, which is the reader's desire to know. By controlling the information she discloses, Rigoberta is maintaining a safe distance between her world and that of her readers. Sommer, "Sin secretos," *Revista de Crítica Literaria Latinoamericana* 36 (1992): 137. Whereas Sommer regards Rigoberta's secrets as more "literary" than "real," Sklodowska offers a slightly different analysis: she considers Rigoberta's negations to be important aspects of the "literaturization" of discourse. Sklodowska, *Testimonio hispanoamericano*, 129.

53.   Elisabeth Burgos, *Me llamo Rigoberta Menchú y así me nació la conciencia* (Barcelona: Editorial Argas Vergara, 1983), 271.

54.   Elisabeth Burgos-Debray, *I, Rigoberta Menchú: An Indian Woman in Guatemala*, trans. Ann Wright (London: Verso, 1983), 247.

55.   Ibid., xx.

56.   Rigoberta Menchú, *Rigoberta: La nieta de los mayas,* with Dante Liano and Giovanni Minà (Mexico City: Aguilar, 1998), 253.

57.   Barnet, "Para llegar," 39–42.

58.   Alice A. Brittin, "Close Encounters of the Third World Kind: Rigoberta Menchú and Elisabeth Burgos's *Me llamo Rigoberta Menchú*," *Latin American Perspectives* 22, no. 4 (Fall 1995): 110–11.

59.   David Stoll's translation of Rigoberta's allegation reads: "'[T]hat is not my book. . . . It is a book by Elisabeth Burgos. It is not my work; it is a work that does not belong to me morally, politically, or economically. . . . Anyone who has doubts about the work should go to Ms. Burgos.'" Stoll, preface to *Rigoberta Menchú and the Story of All Poor Guetemalans*, xi. The article originally appeared under the title "Menchú reniega de '*Así me nació la conciencia*,'" *El Periódico*, 10 Dec. 1997.

60.   Menchú, *Rigoberta*, 253–54.

61.   Burgos-Debray, *I, Rigoberta Menchú*, xi–xiii.

62.   Vera León, "Hacer hablar," 195.

63.   Stoll, *Rigoberta Menchú*, 8, 16.

64.   Ibid., 274.

65.   Sklodowska, "Poetics," 256.

66.   Warren, "Telling Truths," 205.

67.   Marc Zimmerman, "*Testimonio* in Guatemala: Payeras, Rigoberta, and Beyond," *Latin American Perspectives* 18, no. 4 (1991): 22.

68. John Beverley and Marc Zimmerman, *Literature and Politics in the Central American Revolutions* (Austin: University of Texas Press, 1990), 178. They write, "Because [*testimonio*] is the discourse of a witness who is not a fictional construct, *testimonio* in some sense or another speaks directly to us, as an actual person might. To subsume *testimonio* under the category of literary fictionality is to deprive it of its power to engage the reader in the ways indicated, to make of it simply another form of literature." Ibid., 177.

69. Stoll, *Rigoberta Menchú*, 198–99. In his book, Stoll includes this quote drawn from personal correspondence with Burgos (Jan. 28, 1997).

70. Jorge Marcone denotes the activity of transferring discourse from one medium and context to another medium and context "citing," emphasizing the important distinction that, in contrast to "repeating" foreign discourse, "citing" implies a discursive activity motivated by the writer's own circumstances and interests. *La oralidad escrita: Novela y discurso en "Canto de sirena," "El hablador" y "La última mudanza de Felipe Carrillo"* (Ann Arbor, MI: UMI Dissertation Services, 1992), 210.

71. In *Crossing Borders*, the English edition of *Rigoberta: La nieta de los mayas* published by Verso, neither Minà's work nor Liano's is recognized. Rigoberta is acknowledged as the author, and Ann Wright as the book's translator. In the translator's introduction, Wright describes the great pains she took to translate the testimony. Minà and Liano did not become aware of the omission of their names from the English edition until the book appeared in stores. Ann Wright responded to accusations of piracy by alleging that, when she was commissioned by the publisher to translate and reorganize the book, she received only the manuscript. Absent were the five introductory essays that eventually inaugurated the Spanish edition. Her inquiries regarding the book's compilation, addressed to the publisher and the Menchú Foundation in Guatemala, were never answered. According to Wright, she only learned of Minà and Liano's collaboration five months after having submitted her translation of the text. She lamented the fact that the English version failed to appropriately acknowledge those involved in the book's production. The controversy points to complex issues of authorship and authority that underlie testimonial discourse. These findings are based on transcriptions of electronic correspondence between Arturo Arias, Marc Zimmerman, and Ann Wright, and forwarded to Roberto González Echevarría in October 1998.

72. Eduardo Galeano, "Prefacio," in Menchú, *Rigoberta*, 7.

73. Humberto Ak'abal, "Introducción," in Menchú, *Rigoberta*, 21.

74. John M. Watanabe, "Unimagining the Maya: Anthropologists, Others, and the Inescapable Hubris of Authorship," *Bulletin of Latin American Research* 14, no. 1 (1995): 37–38.

75. Rigoberta Menchú, *Crossing Borders*, trans. Ann Wright (New York: Verso, 1998), 81–82.

CHAPTER 5. AUGUSTO ROA BASTOS'S SEARCH FOR AN ORAL AESTHETIC

1. Marcus and Fischer, *Anthropology as Cultural Critique*, 24.

2. Alonso, *Spanish American Regional Novel*, 17.

3. See Clifford, *Predicament of Culture*, 41; and Marcus and Fischer, *Anthropology as Cultural Critique*, 25–26.

4. Rama, *Transculturación narrativa*.

5. Pacheco, *La comarca oral*.

6. Augusto Roa Bastos, "La narrativa paraguaya en el contexto de la narrativa hispanoamericana actual," in *Augusto Roa Bastos y la producción cultural americana*, ed. Saúl Sosnowski (Buenos Aires: Ediciones de la Flor, 1986), 130. Carlos Pacheco examines Roa Bastos's use of binarisms in "La binariedad como modelo de concepción estética en la cuentística de Augusto Roa Bastos," in *Las voces del karaí: Estudios sobre Augusto Roa Bastos*, ed. Fernando Burgos (Madrid: Edelsa, 1988).

7. Roa Bastos, "Una cultura oral," 85.

8. Aníbal González discusses writing's relation to violence in his influential work *Killer Books*.

9. Roa Bastos, "Una cultura oral," 99.

10. Augusto Roa Bastos, "Algunos núcleos generadores de un texto narrativo," in *L'Ideologique dans le texte (Textes hispaniques)* (Toulouse: Université de Toulouse–Le Mirail Services de Publications, 1978), 73.

11. Augusto Roa Bastos, "El texto cautivo (apuntes de un narrador sobre la producción y la lectura de textos bajo el signo del poder cultural)," *Hispamérica* 30 (1981): 6 n. 1.

12. Roa Bastos, "La narrativa paraguaya," 131–32.

13. Ibid.

14. Rubén Bareiro Saguier, "Estratos de la lengua guaraní en la escritura de Augusto Roa Bastos," *Revista Iberoamericana* 19 (1984): 36. In this article, Bareiro Saguier traces Roa Bastos's various approaches to bilingual expression from *El trueno entre las hojas* (1953) through *Yo el Supremo* (1974).

15. Augusto Roa Bastos, "Nota del autor," in *Hijo de hombre* (Madrid: Espasa Calpe, 1993), 32. The author's note does not appear in the 1960 edition of *Hijo de hombre*. Roa Bastos composed it in Toulouse in 1982, and it introduces all revised editions published after that year.

16. Augusto Roa Bastos, *Son of Man*, trans. Rachel Caffyn (New York: Monthly Review Press, 1988), 14.

17. Roa Bastos, "Nota del autor," 31.

18. Roa Bastos, *Son of Man*, 18.

19. Ibid., 23. In the opening pages of the first chapter, Miguel Vera questions the accuracy of his memory, and confesses that his testimony is not altogether reliable. See ibid., 18.

20. Roa Bastos, "Nota del autor," 33.

21. "Cuando retoco mis obras es a mí a quien retoco." Roa Bastos, *Hijo de hombre*, 35.

22. Roa Bastos, "Nota del autor," 32.

23. Menéndez Pidal, *Flor nueva*, 40.

24. Roa Bastos, "Algunos núcleos," 85.

25. Augusto Roa Bastos, *I the Supreme*, trans. Helen Lane (New York: Alfred A. Knopf, 1986), 435.

26. Jorge Marcone argues that, in the Supremo's critique of Patiño's inscription of the words he dictates, one encounters a general critique of the notion of "transparency" as a key to interpreting an inscription of oral discourse. Marcone, *La oralidad escrita* (1997), 73–74.

27. Augusto Roa Bastos, *Yo el Supremo*, ed. Milagros Ezquerro (1974; reprint, Madríd: Cátedra, 1987), 167.

28. Roa Bastos, *I the Supreme*, 63–64.

29. Ibid., 3.

30. For a reading of *Yo el Supremo* that considers Bakhtin's theories, see Helene Carol Weldt-Basson, *Augusto Roa Bastos's "I the Supreme": A Dialogic Perspective* (Columbia: University of Missouri Press, 1993). On page 43 she looks specifically at the use of word-play in the novel as a characteristic of the polyphonic novel. Carlos Pacheco has also discussed *Yo el Supremo* as a dialogic novel, and notes that Roa Bastos was not aware of Bakhtin's theories until after the novel was published. Carlos Pacheco, "Yo/El: Primeras claves para una lectura de la polifonía en *Yo el Supremo*," in Sosnowski. *Augusto Roa Bastos*, 153–78.

31. Roa Bastos, *Yo el Supremo*, 107–8.

32. Roa Bastos, *I the Supreme*, 15.

33. Roa Bastos, "Algunos núcleos," 82.

34. Augusto Roa Bastos, "Notas sobre *Yo el Supremo*." Excerpts from these unpublished notes are printed in Bareiro Saguier, "Estratos," 44–45.

35. Roa Bastos, "Algunos núcleos," 78.

36. Roa Bastos, *I the Supreme*, 45.

37. John Dagenais, "That Bothersome Residue: Toward a Theory of the Physical Text," in *Vox Intexta: Orality and Textuality in the Middle Ages*, ed. Algeri Nicholas Doane and Carol Braun Pasternack (Madison: University of Wisconsin Press, 1991), 255.

38. Roa Bastos, *I the Supreme*, 197; italics in original.

39. Roa Bastos, *Yo el Supremo*, 111.

40. Roa Bastos, *I the Supreme*, 18.

41. Roa Bastos, *Yo el Supremo*, 158.

42. Roa Bastos, *I the Supreme*, 56.

43. Augusto Roa Bastos, *Vigilia del Almirante* (Buenos Aires: Editorial Sudamericana, 1992), 79.

44. Augusto Roa Bastos, *El fiscal* (Madrid: Alfaguara, 1993), 9.

45. Ibid., 245.

46. Roa Bastos, "La narrativa paraguaya," 133–34.

Bibliography

PRIMARY SOURCES

Books

Arguedas, José María. "Acerca del intenso significado de dos voces quechuas." 1948. Reprinted in *Indios, mestizos y señores*, edited by Sybila Arredondo de Arguedas, 147–49. Lima: Editorial Horizonte, 1989.

———. *La agonía de Rasu-Ñiti*. Lima: Taller de Artes Gráficas Ícaro, Camino del Hombre, 1962.

———. *Agua*. 1935. Reprint, Lima: Universidad Nacional Mayor de San Marcos, 1974.

———. "La canción popular mestiza en el Perú y su valor documental y poético." 1940. Reprinted in *Indios, mestizos y señores*, edited by Sybila Arredondo de Arguedas, 71–74. Lima: Editorial Horizonte, 1989.

———. "La canción popular mestiza en el Perú y su valor documental y poético." 1941. Reprinted in *Indios, mestizos y señores*, edited by Sybila Arredondo de Arguedas, 49–55. Lima: Editorial Horizonte, 1989.

———. *Canciones y cuentos del pueblo quechua*. Lima: Editorial Huascarán, 1949.

———. *Canto kechwa con un ensayo sobre la capacidad de creación artística del pueblo indio y mestizo*. 1938. Reprint, Lima: Editorial Horizonte, 1989.

———. "El carnaval de Tambobamba." 1942. Reprinted in *Indios, mestizos y señores*, edited by Sybila Arredondo de Arguedas, 117–20. Lima: Editorial Horizonte, 1989.

———. *Las comunidades de España y del Perú*. Lima: Universidad Nacional Mayor de San Marcos, 1968.

———. *Cusco*. Lima: Ediciones Contur, 1947.

———. *Deep Rivers*. Translated by Frances Horning Barraclough. Austin: University of Texas Press, 1978.

———. *Diamantes y pedernales: Agua*. Lima: Juan Mejía Baca and P. L. Villanueva Editores, 1954.

———. "Ensayo sociológico." In *Arguedas: Documentos inéditos*, edited by Roland Forgues, 55–65. Lima: Empresa Editora Amauta, 1955.

———. "Entre el kechwa y el castellano la angustia del mestizo." 1939. Reprinted in *Indios, mestizos y señores*, edited by Sybila Arredondo de Arguedas, 25–28. Lima: Editorial Horizonte, 1989.

———. "Evolución de las comunidades indígenas: El valle del Mantaro y la ciudad de Huancayo; Un caso de fusión de culturas no comprometida por la acción de las instituciones de origen colonial." In *Formación de una cultura nacional indoamericana*, edited by Angel Rama, 80–147. Mexico: Siglo XXI, 1975.

———. "Fiesta en Tinta." 1940. Reprinted in *Indios, mestizos y señores*, edited by Sybila Arredondo de Arguedas, 57–60. Lima: Editorial Horizonte, 1989.

———. *¿He vivido en vano? Mesa Redonda sobre Todas las sangres, 23 de junio de 1965*. Lima: Instituto de Estudios Peruanos, 1985.

———. *Indios, mestizos y señores*. Edited by Sybila Arredondo de Arguedas. Lima: Horizonte, 1989.

———. Introduction to *Dioses y hombres de Huarochirí: Edición bilingüe*, translated by José María Arguedas, 9–15. Lima: Museo Nacional de Historia e Instituto de Estudios Peruanos, 1966.

———. *Katatay: Temblar*. 1972. Reprint, Lima: Editorial Horizonte, 1984.

———. *Nuestra música popular y sus intérpretes: De lo mágico a lo popular*. Lima: Mosca Azul & Horizonte Editores, 1977.

———. *Primer encuentro de narradores peruanos: Arequipa 1965*. Edited by Antonio Cornejo Polar. Lima: Casa de la Cultura del Perú, 1969. Arguedas's interventions, 36–43.

———. "Puquio, una cultura en proceso de cambio." 1956. Reprinted in *Formación de una cultura nacional indoamericana*, edited by Angel Rama, 34–79. Mexico City: Siglo XXI, 1975.

———. "Respuestas a Castro Klarén." Interview by Sara Castro Klarén. In *Texto, comunicación y cultura: "Los ríos profundos" de José María Arguedas*, edited by Julio Ortega, 101–12. Lima: CEDEP, 1982.

———. *Los ríos profundos*. 1958. Reprint, edited by Ricardo González Vigil. Madrid: Cátedra, 1995.

———. *El Sexto*. Lima: Juan Mejía Baca, 1961.

———. "Simbolismo y poesía de dos canciones populares quechuas." 1938. Reprinted in *Indios, mestizos y señores*, edited by Sybila Arredondo de Arguedas, 21–24. Lima: Editorial Horizonte, 1989.

———. *Temblar: El sueño del pongo*. Havana: Casa de las Américas, 1976.

———. *Todas las sangres*. Buenos Aires: Losada, 1964.

———. *Yawar fiesta*. 1941. Reprint, Santiago: Editorial Universitaria, 1968.

———. *El zorro de arriba y el zorro de abajo*. Buenos Aires: Editorial Losada, 1971.

Arguedas, José María, and Francisco Izquierdo Ríos, eds. *Mitos, leyendas y cuentos peruanos*. Lima: Ediciones de la Dirección de Educación Artística y Extensión Cultural, 1947.

Asturias, Miguel Angel. *Leyendas de Guatemala*. Madrid: Alianza Editorial, 1981.

Barnet, Miguel. *Akeké y la jutía*. Havana: Unión de Escritores y Artistas de Cuba, 1978.

———. *Biografía de un cimarrón*. 1966. Reprint, Havana: Editorial Letras Cubanas, 1980.

———. *Canción de Rachel*. Barcelona: Editorial Laia, 1979.

———. *Cultos afrocubanos: La Regla de Ocha; La Regla de Palo Monte*. Havana: Ediciones Unión, 1995.

————. *La fuente viva.* Havana: Editorial Letras Cubanas, 1983.

————. *Gallego.* Madrid: Ediciones Alfaguara, 1981.

————. Introduction to *The Autobiography of a Runaway Slave*, by Esteban Montejo. Translated by Jocasta Innes. New York: Pantheon Books, 1968.

————. "Miguel Barnet: 'Con Esteban Montejo había que jugar limpio.'" Interview by Abdeslam Azougarh. In *Miguel Barnet: Rescate e invención de la memoria*, by Abdeslam Azougarh, 211–26. Geneva: Editions Slatkine, 1996.

————. *Los perros mudos.* Havana: Alfaguara, 1978.

————. *La piedra fina y el pavorreal.* Havana: Ediciones Unión, 1963.

Borges, Jorge Luis. "El etnógrafo." In *Elogio de la sombra*, 59–61. Buenos Aires: Emecé Editores, 1969.

Burgos, Elisabeth. *Me llamo Rigoberta Menchú y así me nació la conciencia.* Barcelona: Editorial Argas Vergara, 1983.

Burgos-Debray, Elisabeth. *I, Rigoberta Menchú: An Indian Woman in Guatemala.* Translated by Ann Wright. London: Verso, 1984.

————. "Testimonio del testimonio." Paper delivered at Yale University, New Haven, CT, 1998.

Cabrera, Lydia. *Anagó: Vocabulario lucumí (el yoruba que se habla en Cuba).* Miami: Ediciones C.R., Colección del Chicherekú en el exilio, 1970.

————. *Animales en el folklore de Cuba.* Miami: Ediciones Universal, 1988.

————. *Ayapá: Cuentos de Jicotea.* Miami: Ediciones Universal, 1971.

————. *Consejos, pensamientos y notas de Lydia E. Pinbán.* Edited by Isabel Castellanos. Miami: Ediciones Universal, 1993.

————. *Contes nègres de Cuba.* Translated by Francis de Miomandre. Paris: Editions Gallimard, 1936.

————. *Cuentos negros de Cuba.* Havana: La Verónica, 1940.

————. *Cuentos para adultos, niños y retrasados mentales.* Miami: Ultra Graphic Corp., Colección del Chicherekú en el exilio, 1983.

————. Introduction to *La religión afrocubana*, by Mercedes Cros Sandoval, 3–8. Madrid: Playor, 1975.

————. *Koeko iyawó, aprende novicia: Pequeño tratado de regla lucumí.* Miami: Ediciones C.R., 1980.

————. *La laguna sagrada de San Joaquín.* Madrid: Ediciones Madrid, 1973.

————. *La lengua sagrada de los ñáñigos.* Miami: Ediciones C.R., 1988.

————. *La medicina popular en Cuba.* Miami: Ediciones Universal, 1984.

————. *El monte: Igbo finda, ewe orisha, vititi nfinda (Notas sobre las religiones, la magia, las supersticiones y el folklore de los negros criollos y del puebo de Cuba).* 1954. Reprint, Miami: Ediciones C.R., 1968.

————. *Otán Iyebiyé: Las piedras preciosas.* Miami: Ediciones C.R., Colección del Chicherekú en el exilio, 1970.

————. *Por qué... Cuento negros de Cuba.* 1948. Reprint, Miami: Ediciones C.R., Colección del Chicherekú en el exilio, 1972.

————. *Refranes de negros viejos.* Havana: Ediciones C.R., 1955.

————. *Reglas de congo: Palo Monte-Mayombe*. Miami: Ediciones C.R., Colección del Chicherekú en el exilio, 1979.

————. *La sociedad secreta Abakuá (narrada por viejos adeptos)*. Miami: Ediciones C.R., Colección del Chicherekú en el exilio, 1970.

Carpentier, Alejo. *¡Ecué-Yamba-O!* 1946. Reprint, Barcelona: Bruguera, 1979.

————. *Los pasos perdidos*. Edited by Roberto González Echevarría. Madrid: Ediciones Cátedra, 1985.

Césaire, Aimé. *Notebook of a Return to the Native Land*. Translated and edited by Clayton Eshelman and Annette Smith. Middletown, CT: Wesleyan University Press, 2001.

Guimarães Rosa, João. *Grande sertão: veredas*. Rio de Janeiro: J. Olympio, 1956.

Lachatañeré, Rómulo. *¡¡Oh, mío Yemaya!!* 1938. Reprint, Havana: Editorial de Ciencias Sociales, 1992.

Mariátegui, José Carlos. *Mariátegui total*. Edited by Sandro Mariátegui Chiappe. Lima: Empresa Editora Amauta, 1994.

Menchú, Rigoberta. *Crossing Borders*. With Dante Liano and Gianni Minà. Translated by Ann Wright. New York: Verso Books, 1998.

————. *Rigoberta: La nieta de los mayas*. With Dante Liano and Giovanni Minà. Mexico City: Aguilar, 1998.

Menéndez Pidal, Ramón. *Flor nueva de romances viejos*. 1928. Reprint, Madrid: Espasa-Calpe, 1969.

————. *Poesía popular y poesía tradicional en la literatura española*. Oxford: Imprenta Clarendoniana, 1924.

Ortiz, Fernando. *La africanía de la música folklórica de Cuba*. Havana: Editora Universitaria, 1965.

————. *Contrapunteo del tabaco y el azúcar*. 1940. Reprint, Caracas: Biblioteca Ayacucho, 1978.

————. *Hampa afro-cubana: Los negros brujos; Apuntes para un estudio de etnología criminal*. 1906. Reprint, edited by Alberto N. Pamies. Miami: Ediciones Universal, 1973.

————. Introduction to *Cuentos negros de Cuba*, by Lydia Cabrera, 7–11. Havana: Imprenta La Verónica, 1940.

Ortiz Rescaniere, Alejandro. *De Adaneva a Inkarrí (una visión indígena del Perú)*. Lima: Ediciones Retablo de Papel, 1973.

————. *Huarochirí 400 años después*. Lima: Pontificia Universidad Católica del Perú, 1980.

————, ed. *José María Arguedas, recuerdos de una amistad*. Lima: Fondo Editorial de la Pontificia, 1996.

Parra, Teresa de la. *Obra (Narrativa, ensayos, cartas)*. Caracas: Biblioteca Ayacucho, 1982.

Pérez de la Riva, Juan. *El barracón: Esclavitud y capitalismo en Cuba*. Havana: Editorial de Ciencias Sociales, 1975.

Pozas, Ricardo. *Juan Pérez Jolote: Biografía de un tzotzil*. Mexico City: Fondo de Cultura Económica, 1952.

Roa Bastos, Augusto. "Algunos núcleos generadores de un texto narrativo." In *L'Ideologique dans le texte (Textes hispaniques)*. Toulouse: Université de Toulouse-Le Mirail Services de Publications, 1978.

——. *Contravida*. Madrid: Alfaguara, 1994.

——, ed. *Culturas condenadas*. Mexico City: Siglo XXI, 1978.

——. *El fiscal*. Madrid: Alfaguara, 1993.

——. *Hijo de hombre*. 1960. Reprint, Madrid: Espasa Calpe, 1993.

——. *I the Supreme*. Translated by Helen Lane. New York: Alfred A. Knopf, 1986.

——. *Madama Sui*. Buenos Aires: Seix Barral, 1995.

——. *Metaforismos*. Buenos Aires: Seix Barral, 1996.

——. "La narrativa paraguaya en el contexto de la narrativa hispanoamericana actual." In *Augusto Roa Bastos y la producción cultural americana*, edited by Saúl Sosnowski, 119–38. Buenos Aires: Ediciones de la Flor, 1986.

——. *Son of Man*. Translated by Rachel Caffyn. New York: Monthly Review Press, 1988.

——. *El trueno entre las hojas*. Buenos Aires: Losada, Colección Novelistas de España y América, 1953.

——. *Vigilia del Almirante*. Buenos Aires: Editorial Sudamericana, 1992.

——. *Yo el Supremo*. 1974. Reprint, edited by Milagros Ezquerro. Madrid: Cátedra, 1987.

Valcárcel, Luis E., and Carlos Araníbar. "La colección de fuentes e investigaciones." In *Dioses y hombres de Huarochirí: Edición bilingüe*, translated by José María Arguedas, 7–8. Lima: Museo Nacional de Historia e Instituto de Estudios Peruanos, 1966.

Vargas Llosa, Mario. *El hablador*. Barcelona: Seix Barral, 1987.

——. *La utopía arcaica y las ficciones del indigenismo*. Mexico City: Fondo de Cultura Económica, 1996.

Vega, Garcilaso de la. *Comentarios reales*. Mexico City: Porrúa, 1990.

Articles

Arguedas, José María. "Alrededor de este nudo de la vida." Interview by Chester Christian. *Revista Iberoamericana* 49, no. 122 (1983): 221–28.

——. "Cátedra de investigaciones: Plan de trabajo para el verano de 1967." *Runa* 6 (November 1977).

——. "La colección de Alicia Bustamante y la Universidad." *El Comercio*, 12 January 1969, 30.

——. "Cuentos mágico-realistas y canciones de fiestas tradicionales del valle del Mantaro, provincias de Jauja y Concepción." *Folklore Americano* 1, no. 1 (1953): 101–293.

——. "Cuentos religioso-mágicos quechuas de Lucanamarca." *Folklore Americano* 8–9 (1960–61): 142–216.

——. "El libro 'Canto de amor' y el fanatismo indigenista." *El Comercio*, June 17, 1956.

——. "La literatura quechua en el Perú." *Mar del Sur* 1, no. 1 (1948): 46–54.

——. "La novela y el problema de la expresión literaria en el Perú." *Mar del Sur* 3, no. 9 (1950): 66–72.

——. "El Ollantay: lo autóctono y lo occidental en el estilo de los dramas coloniales quechuas." *Letras Peruanas* 2, no. 8 (1952): 1, 114–16, 139–40.

——. "París y la patria." *El Comercio*, suplemento dominical, 7 December 1958, 2.

———. "Reflexiones peruanas sobre un narrador mexicano." *El Comercio*, suplemento dominical, 4 October 1964, 3.

———. "El wayno: La canción popular mestiza en el Perú, su valor documental y poético." *La Prensa*, 18 August 1940.

———. "Yawar (Fiesta)." *Revista Americana de Buenos Aires* 14, no. 156 (1937).

Barnet, Miguel. "Confesiones con palabras no escritas." Interview by Alberto Batista Reyes. *Letras Cubanas* 3 (1987): 131–41.

———. "Para llegar a Esteban Montejo: Los caminos del cimarrón." *Contracorriente* 6 (1996): 29–44.

Cabrera, Lydia. "Asociación de Arte Retrospectivo." *Diario de la Marina*, June 1922, 12.

———. "La ceiba y la sociedad secreta Abakuá." *Orígenes* 25 (1950): 16–47.

———. "Damas." *Journal of Caribbean Studies* 1, no. 1 (1980): 1–2.

———. "Eggüe o Vichichi finda." *Revista Bimestre Cubana* 60 (1947): 47–120.

———. "Un gran pintor: Wifredo Lam." In *Páginas sueltas*, edited by Isabel Castellanos, 221–26. Miami: Ediciones Universal, 1994.

———. "Notas sobre Africa, la Negritud y la actual poesía yoruba." *Revista de la Universidad Complutense* 24, no. 95 (1975): 9–59.

———. "Religious Syncretism in Cuba." *Journal of Caribbean Studies* 10, no. 1–2 (1994): 89–94.

———. "El sincretismo religioso de Cuba: Santos, orishas, ngangas, lucumís y congos." *Orígenes* 36 (1954): 8–20.

———. "Wifredo Lam." In *Páginas sueltas*, edited by Isabel Castellanos, 262–66. Miami: Ediciones Universal, 1994.

Carpentier, Alejo. "Ortega y Gasset." *El Nacional*, 22 October 1955, 16.

———. "Los *Cuentos negros* de Lydia Cabrera." *Carteles* 28, no. 41 (11 October 1936): 40.

Menchú, Rigoberta. "Carta de Rigoberta Menchú." *El Periódico*, 12 December 1997.

———. "Menchú reniega de *Así me nació la conciencia*." *El Periódico*, 10 December 1997.

Ortiz, Fernando. Introduction to *¡¡Oh, mío Yemaya!!* by Rómulo Lachatañeré. *Revista Bimestre Cubana* 70 (1955): 85–96.

———. Review of *Contes négres de Cuba*, by Lydia Cabrera, translated by Francis de Miomandre. *Estudios Afrocubanos* 2, no. 1 (1938): 133–38.

———. "La Sociedad de Estudios Afrocubanos Contra los Racismos: Advertencia, comprensión y designio." *Estudios Afrocubanos* 1, no. 1 (1937): 3–6.

Roa Bastos, Augusto. "Una cultura oral." *Hispamérica* 46–47 (1987): 85–112.

———. "Cultura oral y literatura ausente." *Quimera* 61 (1986): 38–53.

———. "La escritura como proceso mítico." Interview by Jorge Fernando Aguadé. *Sendero*, 30 April 1982, 12.

———. "El génesis de los Apapokuva-Guaraní." *Alcor* 1 (1971): 22–23.

———. "El texto cautivo (apuntes de un narrador sobre la producción y la lectura de textos bajo el signo del poder cultural)." *Hispamérica* 30 (1981): 3–28.

Vargas Llosa, Mario. "José María Arguedas y el indio." *Casa de las Américas* 26 (1964): 139–47.

Secondary Sources

Books

Adorno, Rolena. *Guaman Poma: Writing and Resistance in Colonial Peru.* Austin: University of Texas Press, 1986.

Alonso, Carlos. *The Burden of Modernity: The Rhetoric of Cultural Discourse in Spanish America.* New York: Oxford University Press, 1998.

———. *The Spanish American Regional Novel: Modernity and Autochtony.* Cambridge: Cambridge University Press, 1990.

Azougarh, Abdeslam. *Miguel Barnet: Rescate e invención de la memoria.* Geneva: Editions Slatkine, 1996.

Bakhtin, M. M. *The Dialogic Imagination: Four Essays by M. M. Bakhtin.* Edited by Michael Holquist. Translated by Caryl Emerson and Michael Holquist. Austin: University of Texas Press, 1981.

Balansa de Ocampos, Margarita, Ramiro Domínguez, Adriano Irala Burgos, Josefina Plá, and Beatriz Alcalá de González Oddone. *Comentarios sobre "Yo el Supremo."* Asunción: Club del Libro, 1975.

Bareiro Saguier. Prologue to *Antología personal*, by Augusto Roa Bastos, 9–24. Mexico City: Editorial Nueva Imagen, 1980.

Barthes, Roland. *The Rustle of Language.* Translated by Richard Howard. Oxford: Basil Blackwell, 1986.

Beverley, John. *Against Literature.* Minneapolis: University of Minnesota Press, 1993.

Beverley, John, and Marc Zimmerman. *Literature and Politics in the Central American Revolutions.* Austin: University of Texas Press, 1990.

Burgos, Fernando, ed. *Las voces del karaí: Estudios sobre Augusto Roa Bastos.* Madrid: Edelsa, 1988.

Castellanos, Isabel, and Lydia Cabrera. *Páginas sueltas.* Miami: Ediciones Universal, 1994.

Castellanos, Isabel, and Josefina Inclán, eds. *En torno a Lydia Cabrera: cincuentenario de Cuentos negros de Cuba (1936–1986).* Miami: Ediciones Universal, 1987.

Castellanos, Jorge, and Isabel Castellanos. *Cultura afrocubana.* Vol. 3. Miami: Ediciones Universales, 1971.

Cavell, Stanley. *A Pitch of Philosophy: Autobiographical Exercises.* Cambridge, MA: Harvard University Press, 1994.

Certeau, Michel de. *Heterologies: Discourse on the Other.* Translated by Brian Massumi. Minneapolis: University of Minnesota Press, 1986.

———. *The Practice of Everyday Life.* Translated by Steven Rendall. Berkeley: University of California Press, 1984.

———. *The Writing of History.* Translated by Tom Conley. New York: Columbia University Press, 1988.

Clifford, James. "On Ethnographic Allegory." In *Writing Culture: The Poetics and Politics of Ethnography*, edited by James Clifford and George E. Marcus, 98–121. Berkeley: University of California Press, 1986.

———. *The Predicament of Culture: Twentieth-Century Ethnography, Literature, and Art.* Cambridge, MA: Harvard University Press, 1988.

———. *Routes: Travel and Translation in the Late Twentieth Century.* Cambridge, MA: Harvard University Press, 1997.

Clifford, James, and George E. Marcus, eds. *Writing Culture. The Poetics and Politics of Ethnography.* Berkeley: University of California Press, 1986.

Cornejo Polar, Antonio. *Escribir en el aire: Ensayo sobre la heterogeneidad socio-cultural en las literaturas andinas.* Lima: Editorial Horizonte, 1994.

———. *Literatura y sociedad en el Perú: La novela indigenista.* Lima: Lasontay, 1980.

———. *Los universos narrativos de José María Arguedas.* Buenos Aires: Editorial Losada, 1973.

Coulthard, G. R. *Race and Colour in Caribbean Literature.* London: Oxford University Press, 1962.

Cros Sandoval, Mercedes. *La religión afrocubana.* Madrid: Playor, 1975.

Cuervo Hewitt, Julia. "Yoruba Presence: From Nigerian Oral Literature to Contemporary Cuban Narrative." In *Voices from Under: Black Narrative in Latin America and the Caribbean,* edited by William Luis. 65–85. Westport CT: Greenwood Press, 1984.

Dagenais, John. "That Bothersome Residue: Toward a Theory of the Physical Text." In *Vox Intexta: Orality and Textuality in the Middle Ages,* edited by Algeri Nicholas Doane and Carol Braun Pasternack, 246–59. Madison: University of Wisconsin Press, 1991.

———. *The Ethics of Reading in Manuscript Culture.* Princeton, NJ: Princeton University Press, 1994.

Derrida, Jacques. *Of Grammatology.* Translated by Gayatri Chakravorty Spivak. Baltimore: Johns Hopkins University Press, 1976.

Dilthey, Wilhelm. *Wilhelm Dilthey: Selected Writings.* Edited by H. P. Rickman. Cambridge: Cambridge University Press, 1976.

Donoghue, Denis. *The Practice of Reading.* New Haven, CT: Yale University Press, 1999.

Emery, Amy Fass. *The Anthropological Imagination in Latin American Literature.* Columbia: University of Missouri Press, 1996.

Escobar, Alberto. *Arguedas o la utopía de la lengua.* Lima: Instituto de Estudios Peruanos, 1984.

Fabian, Johannes. *Time and the Other: How Anthropology Makes Its Object.* New York: Columbia University Press, 1983.

Fischer, Michael M. J. "Ethnicity and the Post-Modern Arts of Memory." In *Writing Culture: The Poetics and Politics of Ethnography,* edited by James Clifford and George E. Marcus. Berkeley: University of California Press, 1986.

Flores Galindo, Alberto. *Buscando un inca: Identidad y utopía en los Andes.* Lima: Editorial Horizonte, 1988.

Foley, John Miles, ed. *Oral Tradition in Literature: Interpretation in Context.* Columbia: University of Missouri Press, 1985.

Forgues, Roland. *José María Arguedas, la letra inmortal: Correspondencia con Manuel Moreno Jimeno.* Lima: Ediciones de Los Ríos Profundos, 1993.

———. "El mito del monolingüismo quechua de Arguedas." In *José María Arguedas: Vida y obra,* edited by Roland Forgues, Hildebrando Pérez, and Carlos Garayar, 47–58. Lima: Amaru Editores, 1991.

Forgues, Roland, Hildebrando Pérez, and Carlos Garayar, eds. *José María Arguedas: Vida y obra*. Lima: Amaru Editores, 1991.

Frye, Northrop. *The Educated Imagination*. Bloomington: Indiana University Press, 1964.

Geertz, Clifford. *The Interpretation of Cultures: Selected Essays by Clifford Geertz*. New York: Basic Books, 1983.

———. *Works and Lives: The Anthropologist as Author*. Stanford, CA: Stanford University Press, 1988.

González, Aníbal. *Killer Books: Writing, Violence, and Ethics in Modern Spanish American Narrative*. Austin: University of Texas Press, 2001.

González Echevarría, Roberto. *Alejo Carpentier: The Pilgrim at Home*. Ithaca, NY: Cornell University Press, 1977.

———. *Myth and Archive: A Theory of Latin American Narrative*. New York: Cambridge University Press, 1990.

———. *"Biografía de un cimarrón and the Novel of the Cuban Revolution."* In *The Voice of the Masters: Writing and Authority in Modern Latin American Literature*, 110–23. Austin: University of Texas Press, 1985.

González Vigil, Ricardo. Introduction to *Los ríos profundos*, by José María Arguedas, 11–111. Madrid: Cátedra, 1995.

Goody, Jack. *The Domestication of the Savage Mind*. 1968. Reprint, Cambridge: Cambridge University Press, 1977.

———. *The Interface between the Written and the Oral*. New York: Cambridge University Press, 1987.

Grandis, Rita de. *"Los Zorros de Arguedas: Una traducción mestiza."* In *Dos estudios sobre textos de Arguedas*, 9–17. Lima: CICOSUL, 1990.

Greenblatt, Stephen. *Renaissance Self-Fashioning: From More to Shakespeare*. Chicago: University of Chicago Press, 1980.

Gutiérrez, Mariela. *Lydia Cabrera: Aproximaciones mítico-simbólicas a su cuentística*. Madrid: Editorial Verbum, 1997.

Havelock, Eric A. *Preface to Plato*. Cambridge, MA: Harvard University Press, 1963.

Hiriart, Rosario. *Lydia Cabrera: Vida hecha arte*. New York: Eliseo Torres & Sons, 1978.

Holquist, Michael, ed. Introduction to *The Dialogic Imagination*, by Mikhail M. Bakhtin. Translated by Caryl Emerson and Michael Holquist. Austin: University of Texas Press, 1981.

Johnson, Barbara. *"Writing."* In *Critical Terms for Literary Study*, edited by Frank Lentricchia and Thomas McGlaughlin, 39–49. Chicago: University of Chicago Press, 1990.

Kesteloot, Lilyan. *Black Writers in French: A Literary History of Negritude*. Translated by Ellen Conroy Kennedy. Philadelphia: Temple University Press, 1974.

Kristal, Efraín. *Una visión urbana de los Andes: Génesis y desarrollo del indigenismo en el Perú, 1848–1930*. New York: Peter Lang, 1989.

Kutzinski, Vera. *Sugar's Secrets: Race and the Erotic of Cuban Nationalism*. Charlottesville: University Press of Virginia, 1993.

Lewis, Bernard. *History: Remembered, Recovered, Invented*. Princeton, NJ: Princeton University Press, 1975.

Lienhard, Martin. *Cultura andina y forma novelesca: Zorros y danzantes en la última novela de Arguedas*. Lima: Editorial Horizonte, 1990.

———. "Sobre la complejidad semántica de la poesía de Arguedas." In *José María Arguedas: Vida y obra*, edited by Roland Forgues, Hildebrando Pérez, and Carlos Garayar, 215–26. Lima: Amaru Editores, 1991.

———. *La voz y su huella: Escritura y conflicto étnico-social en América Latina, 1492–1988*. Hanover, NH: Ediciones del Norte, 1991.

Lira, Jorge A. *Diccionario kkechuwa-español*. 2nd ed. Bogota: Editora Guadalupe, 1982.

Lord, Albert B. *The Singer of Tales*. Cambridge, MA: Harvard University Press, 1960.

Ludmer, Josefina. *El género gauchesco: Un tratado sobre la patria*. Buenos Aires: Editorial Sudamericana, 1988.

———. "Las tretas del débil." In *La sartén por el mango*, edited by Patricia Elena Gonalez and Eliana Ortega, 47–54. Río Piedras, Puerto Rico: Huracán, 1985.

Luis, William. "Latin American (Hispanic Caribbean) Literature Written in the United States." In *Cambridge History of Latin American Literature*, edited by Roberto González Echevarría and Enrique Pupo-Walker, 526–56. Cambridge: Cambridge University Press, 1996.

———. *Literary Bondage: Slavery in Cuban Narrative*. Austin: University of Texas Press, 1990.

Manganaro, Marc, ed. *Modernist Anthropology: From Fieldwork to Text*. Princeton, NJ: Princeton University Press, 1990.

Marcone, Jorge. *La oralidad escrita: Novela y discurso en "Canto de sirena," "El hablador" y "La última mudanza de Felipe Carrillo."* Ann Arbor, MI: UMI Dissertation Services, 1992.

———. *La oralidad escrita: Sobre la reivindicación y re-inscripción del discurso oral*. Lima: Pontificia Universidad Católica del Perú, Fondo Editorial, 1997.

Marcus, George E. *Rereading Cultural Anthropology*. Durham, NC: Duke University Press, 1992.

Marcus, George E., and Michael M. J. Fischer. *Anthropology as Cultural Critique*. Chicago: University of Chicago Press, 1986.

Marín, Gladys C. *La experiencia americana de José María Arguedas*. Buenos Aires: Fernando García Cambeiro, 1973.

Menocal, María Rosa. *Exile and the Origins of the Lyric*. Durham, NC: Duke University Press, 1994.

———. "The Flip Side." In *Mapping Benjamin: The Work of Art in the Digital Age*, edited by H. U. Gumbrecht and M. Marrinam, 291–300. Stanford, CA: Stanford University Press, 2003.

Merino de Zela, Mildred E. "Cronología." In *Los ríos profundos*, by José María Arguedas, 295–446. Caracas: Biblioteca Ayacucho, 1978.

Merrim, Stephanie. *Logos and the Word: The Novel of Language and Linguistic Motivation in "Grande sertão: Veredas" and "Tres tristes tigres."* New York: Peter Lang, 1983.

Miller, Christopher. *Blank Darkness: Africanist Discourse in French*. Chicago: University of Chicago Press, 1985.

Montoya, Rodgrido, ed. *José María Arguedas, veinte años después: Huellas y horizonte, 1969–1989*. San Marcos, Peru: Escuela de Antropología de la Universidad Nacional Mayor de San Marcos, 1991.

Muñoz, Silverio. *José María Arguedas y el mito de la salvación por la cultura.* Lima: Editorial Horizonte, 1987.

Murra, John, and Mercedes López-Baralt, eds. *Las cartas de Arguedas.* Lima: Pontificia Universidad Católica del Perú, 1996.

Norris, Christopher. *Deconstruction: Theory and Practice.* New York: Routledge, 1982.

———. *Derrida.* Cambridge, MA: Harvard University Press, 1987.

Ong, Walter J. *Interfaces of the Word: Studies in the Evolution of Consciousness and Culture.* Ithaca, NY: Cornell University Press, 1977.

———. *Orality and Literacy: The Technologizing of the Word.* New York: Methuen, 1982.

———. *The Presence of the Word: Some Prolegomena for Cultural and Religious History.* New Haven, CT: Yale University Press, 1967.

Ortega, Julio, ed. *Texto, comunicación y cultura: "Los ríos profundos" de José María Arguedas.* Lima: CEDEP, 1982.

Pacheco, Carlos. "La binariedad como modelo de concepción estética en la cuentística de Augusto Roa Bastos." In *Las voces del karaí: Estudios sobre Augusto Roa Bastos,* edited by Fernando Burgos, 173–86. Madrid: Edelsa, 1988.

———. *La comarca oral: La ficcionalización de la oralidad cultural en la narrativa latinoamericana contemporánea.* Caracas: Ediciones de La Casa de Bello, 1992.

———. "Yo/El: Primeras claves para una lectura de la polifonia en *Yo el Supremo.*" In *Augusto Roa Bastos y la producción cultural americana,* edited by Saúl Sosnowski, 153–78. Buenos Aires: Ediciones de la Flor, 1986.

Patai, Daphne. "Whose Truth? Iconicity and Accuracy in the World of Testimonial Literature." In *The Rigoberta Menchú Controversy,* edited by Arturo Arias, 270–87. Minneapolis: University of Minnesota Press, 2001.

Perera, Hilda. *Idapo: El sincretismo en los "Cuentos negros" de Lydia Cabrera.* Miami: Ediciones Universales, 1971.

Pinilla, Carmen María. *Arguedas: Conocimiento y vida.* Lima: Fondo Editorial de la Pontificia Universitaria Católica del Perú, 1994.

Prieto, René. "The Literature of *Indigenismo.*" In vol. 2 of *Cambridge History of Latin American Literature,* edited by Roberto González Echevarría and Enrique Pupo-Walker, 138–63. Cambridge: Cambridge University Press, 1996.

———. *Miguel Angel Asturias's Archaeology of Return.* Cambridge: Cambridge University Press, 1993.

Rama, Angel. *La ciudad letrada.* Montevideo: Fundación Internacional Angel Rama, 1984.

———, ed. *Formación de una cultura nacional indoamericana.* Mexico City: Siglo XXI, 1975.

———, ed. *Señores e indios: Acerca de la cultura quechua.* Buenos Aires: Arca/Calicanto, 1976.

———. *Transculturación narrativa en América Latina.* Mexico City: Siglo XXI, 1982.

Richard, Renaud. "El zumbayllu, objeto emblemáctico de *Los ríos profundos.*" In *José María Arguedas: Vida y obra,* edited by Roland Forgues, Hildebrando Pérez, and Carlos Garayar, 181–94. Lima: Amaru Editores, 1991.

Richardson, Michael, ed. *Refusal of the Shadow: Surrealism and the Caribbean.* Translated by Krzysztof Fijalkowski and Michael Richardson. New York: Verso, 1996.

Romualdo, Alejandro. "Arguedas: Poesía de la resistencia." In *José María Arguedas: Vida y obra*, edited by Roland Forgues, Hildebrando Pérez, and Carlos Garayar, 207–14. Peru: Amaru Editores, 1991.

Rosemont, Franklin, ed. *What is Surrealism? Selected Writings of André Breton*. London: Pluto Press, 1978.

Rowe, William. *Ensayos arguedianos*. Lima: SUR, 1996.

———. *Mito e ideología en la obra de José María Arguedas*. Lima: Instituto Nacional de Cultura, 1979.

Segundo seminario sobre "Yo el Supremo." Poitiers: Publications du Centre de Recherches Latino-Americaines de l'Université de Poitiers, 1980.

Seminario sobre "Yo el Supremo" de Augusto Roa Bastos. Poitiers: Publications du Centre de Recherches Latino-Americaines de l'Université de Poitiers, 1976.

Shattuck, Roger. *The Banquet Years: The Origins of the Avant-Garde in France., 1885 to World War I*. New York: Vintage Books, 1968.

Sklodowska, Elzbieta. "Máscaras y simulacros: El arte del *storyteller* en la cuentística de Jesús Gardea y Eraclio Zepeda." In *Literatura mexicana/Mexican literature*, edited by José Miguel Oviedo, 114–26. Philadelphia: University of Pennsylvania Press, 1993.

———. "The Poetics of Remembering, the Politics of Forgetting: Rereading *I, Rigoberta Menchú*." In *The Rigoberta Menchú Controversy*, edited by Arturo Arias, 251–69. Minneapolis: University of Minnesota Press, 2001.

———. *Testimonio hispanoamericano: Historia, teoría, poética*. New York: Peter Lang, 1992.

Sosnowski, Saúl, ed. *Augusto Roa Bastos y la producción cultural americana*. Buenos Aires: Ediciones de la Flor, 1986.

Soto, Sara. *Magia e historia en los "Cuentos negros," "Por qué" y "Ayapá" de Lydia Cabrera*. Miami: Ediciones Universal, 1988.

Spengler, Oswald. *The Decline of the West.*. 1917. Reprint, translated and edited by Charles Francis Atkinson. New York: Knopf, 1950.

Staples, Lindsay. *Wilderness and Storytelling*. Ottawa: Canadian Center for Folk Culture Studies, 1981.

Stephen, Ruth, ed. *The Singing Mountaineers: Songs and Tales of the Quechua People*. Collected by José María Arguedas. Austin: University of Texas Press, 1957.

Stoll, David. *Rigoberta Menchú and the Story of All Poor Guatemalans*. Boulder, CO: Westview Press, 1999.

Street, Brian, ed. *Cross-Cultural Approaches to Literacy*. Cambridge: Cambridge University Press, 1993.

———. *Literacy in Theory and Practice*. New York: Cambridge University Press, 1984.

———. *Social Literacies: Critical Approaches to Literacy in Development, Ethnography and Education*. New York: Longman, 1995.

Thomas, Hugh. *Cuba: The Pursuit of Freedom*. New York: Harper & Row, 1971.

Tyler, Stephen. "On Being without Words." In *Rereading Cultural Anthropology*, edited by George E. Marcus, 1–7. Durham, NC: Duke University Press, 1992.

Valdés-Cruz, Rosa. "Los cuentos de Lydia Cabrera, ¿transposiciones o creaciones?" In *Homenaje a Lydia Cabrera*, edited by Reinaldo Sánchez and José Antonio Madrigal, 93–99. Miami: Ediciones Universal, 1977.

Vance, Eugene. "Roland and the Politics of Memory." In *Textual Strategies*, edited by Josué Harari, 374–403. Ithaca, NY: Cornell University Press, 1979.

Verger, Pierre. *Dílógún: Brazilian Tales of Yorùbá Divination Discovered in Bahia.* Translated and edited by Willfried F. Feuser and José Marianno Carneiro da Cunha. Nigeria: Center for Black and African Arts and Civilization, 1989.

———. *Orixás: Deuses iorubás na Africa e no novo mundo.* Translated by Maria Aparecida de Nóbrega. El Salvador: Editora Corrupio Comércio, 1981.

Warren, Kay B. "Telling Truths. Taking David Stoll and the Rigoberta Menchú Exposé Seriously." In *The Rigoberta Menchú Controversy*, edited by Arturo Arias, 198–218. Minneapolis: University of Minnesota Press, 2001.

Weldt-Basson, Helene Carol. *Augusto Roa Bastos's "I the Supreme": A Dialogic Perspective.* Columbia: University of Missouri Press, 1993.

Zumthor, Paul. *Oral Poetry: An Introduction.* Translated by Kathryn Murphy-Judy. Foreword by Walter J. Ong. Minneapolis: University of Minnesota Press, 1990.

Articles

Abrahams, Roger D. "Complicity and Imitation in Storytelling: A Pragmatic Folklorist's Perspective." *Cultural Anthropology* 1, no. 2 (1986): 223–37.

Achugar, Hugo. "Historias paralelas/historias ejemplares: La historia y la voz del otro." *Revista de Crítica Literaria Latinoamericana* 36 (1992): 49–71.

Acosta Saignes, Miguel. Review of *El monte*, by Lydia Cabrera. *Revista Bimestre Cubana* 71 (1956): 286–87.

Adorno, Rolena. "La soledad de Waman Puma de Ayala y José María Arguedas." *Revista Iberoamericana* 122 (1983): 143–48.

Bareiro Saguier, Rubén. "Estratos de la lengua guaraní en la escritura de Augusto Roa Bastos." *Revista Iberoamericana* 19 (1984): 35–45.

Beverley, John. "'Through All Things Modern': Second Thoughts on *Testimonio.*" *Boundary 2* 18, no. 2 (1991): 1–21.

Brittin, Alice A. "Close Encounters of the Third World Kind: Rigoberta Menchú and Elisabeth Burgos's *Me llamo Rigoberta Menchú.*" *Latin American Perspectives* 22, no. 4 (Fall 1995): 110–14.

Clifford, James. "Fieldwork, Reciprocity and the Making of Ethnographic Texts: The Example of Maurice Leenhardt." *Man* 15 (1980): 518–32.

———. "On Ethnographic Authority." *Representations* 1, no. 2 (1983): 118–46.

Collazos, Oscar. Review of *Canción de Rachel*, by Miguel Barnet. *Casa de las Américas* 59 (1970): 190–92.

Cornejo Polar, Antonio. "José María Arguedas: Las nuevas dimensiones del indigenismo." *Insula* 29 (1974): 11, 22.

"Cuatro años." Editorial. *Orígenes* 12 (1947): 46.

Miomandre, Francis de. "Sobre 'El monte.'" *Orígenes* 39 (1955): 75.

Dorfman, Ariel. "Puentes y padres en el infierno: *Los ríos profundos.*" *Revista de Crítica Literaria Latinoamericana* 12 (1980): 91–137.

Duchesne, Juan. "Etnopoética y estrategias discursivas en *Canto de sirena.*" *Revista de Crítica Literaria Latinoamericana* 20 (1984): 189–205.

Fabian, Johannes. "Presence and Representation: The Other and Anthropological Writing." *Critical Inquiry* 16, no. 4 (1990): 768.

Flores Galindo, Alberto. "Los últimos años de Arguedas (intelectuales, sociedad e identidad en el Perú)." *Literatura e identidad en el Perú* (Jauja, Perú), 8–12 August 1988.

Geertz, Clifford. "Blurred Genres: The Refiguration of Social Thought." *American Scholar* 49, no. 2 (1980): 165–72.

Golden, Tim. "Guatemala Indian Wins the Nobel Peace Prize." *New York Times*, 17 October 1992, 1.

González Echevarría. "Criticism and Literature in Revolutionary Cuba." *Cuban Studies/ Estudios Cubanos* 11, no. 1 (1980): 1–17.

———. Review of *Testimonio hispanoamericano: Historia, teoría, poética*, by Elzbieta Sklodowska. *Bulletin of Hispanic Studies* 71 (1994): 514–16.

Herzberg, Julie. "Wifredo Lam: Return to Havana and the Afro-Cuban Tradition." *Review* 37 (1987): 22–30.

Kerr, Lucille. "Gestures of Authorship: Lying to Tell the Truth in Elena Poniatowska's *Hasta no verte Jesús mío.*" *MLN* 106 (1991): 370–94.

Levine, Suzanne Jill. "A Conversation with Lydia Cabrera." *Latin American Literature & Arts Review* 31 (1982): 13.

Lienhard, Martin. "Apuntes sobre los desdoblamientos, la mitología y la escritura en 'Yo el Supremo.'" *Hispamérica* 19 (1978): 3–12.

———. "La función del danzante de tijeras en tres textos de José María Arguedas." *Revista Iberoamericana* 122 (1983): 149–57.

———. "Una intertextualidad 'indoamericana' y *Moriencia*, de Augusto Roa Bastos." *Revista Iberoamericana* 127 (1984): 505–23.

Luis, William. "The Politics of Memory and Miguel Barnet's *The Autobiography of a Runaway Slave.*" *MLN* 104, no. 2 (1989): 475–91.

March, Kathleen. "El bilingüismo literario y la verosimilitud." *Anales de Literatura Hispanoamericana* 13 (1984): 195–201.

Meliá, Bartolomeu. "Del buen uso de los mitos (en que el etnógrafo pretende justificarse llorando como un caimán)." *Alcor* 1 (1971): 8–17.

Melis, Antonio. "Escritura antropológica y escritura narrativa en Arguedas." *Hoja Naviera* Nov. 1993: 26–34.

Miller, Christopher L. "Theories of Africans: The Question of Literary Anthropology." *Critical Inquiry* 13, no. 1 (1986): 120–39.

Murra, John. "José María Arguedas: Dos imágenes." *Revista Iberoamericana* 122 (1983): 43–54.

Niño, Hugo. "Escritura contra oralidad: ¿Y dónde está el documento?" *Casa de las Américas* 213 (1998): 79–85.

Novás-Calvo, Lino. "Los cuentos de Lydia Cabrera." *Exilio* 3, no. 2 (1969): 17–20.

———. Review of *El monte*, by Lydia Cabrera. *Exilio*, September 1968, 298.

Ochando Aymerich, Carmen. "Antropoesía cubana: Lydia Cabrera." *Quimera* 123 (1994): 8–9.

Pacheco, Carlos. "*Hijo de hombre*: El escritor entre la voz y la escritura." *Escritura* 30 (1990): 401–19.

———. "Sobre la construcción de lo rural y lo oral en la literatura hispanoamericana." *Revista de Crítica Literaria Latinoamericana* 21, no. 42 (Segundo semestre 1995): 57–71.

———. "Trastierra y oralidad en la ficción de los transculturadores." *Revista de Crítica Literaria Latinoamericana* 29 (1989): 25–38.

Pease G.Y., Franklin. "Las versiones del mito de Inkarrí." *Revista de la Universidad Católica*, 3 December 1977, 25–41.

Rama, Angel. "*Los ríos profundos*, ópera de pobres." *Revista Iberoamericana* 122 (1983): 11–41.

———. "Los ríos profundos del mito y de la historia." *Revista de Crítica Literaria Latinoamericana* 2 (1980): 69–90.

Randall, Margaret. "¿Qué es, y cómo se hace un testimonio?" *Revista de Crítica Literaria Latinoamericana* 36 (1992): 22–45.

Ricoeur, Paul. "The Model of the Text: Meaningful Action Considered as Text." *Social Research* 38 (1971): 529–62.

Rivero, Eliana. "Acerca del género 'testimonio': Textos, narradores y 'artefactos.'" *Hispamérica* 46–47 (1987): 41–56.

Rohter, Larry. "Nobel Winner Finds Her Story Challenged." *New York Times*, 15 December 1998, A8.

Rowe, William. "Arguedas: El narrador y el antropólogo frente al lenguaje." *Revista Iberoamericana* 122 (1993): 97–109.

———. "El grafismo no fonético como modelo de comunicación en *Hijo de hombre* de Augusto Roa Bastos." *Escritura* 30 (1990): 313–19.

Senghor, L. S. "Rapport sur la doctrine et le programme du parti." Paper delivered at the Constitutive Congress of the African Assembly Party, Paris, France, 1959.

Sklodowska, Elzbieta. "La forma testimonial y la novelística de Miguel Barnet." *Revista/Review Interamericana* 12, no. 3 (1982): 375–84.

Sommer, Doris. "Sin secretos." *Revista de Crítica Literaria Latinoamericana* 36 (1992): 135–53.

Spitta, Silvia. "Hacia una nueva lectura del mestizo en la obra de José María Arguedas." *Hispamérica* 24, no. 72 (1995): 15–26.

Strathern, Mary. "Intervening." Review of *Waiting: The Whites of South Africa*, by Vincent Crapanzano. *Cultural Anthropology* 2 (1987): 255–67.

Vera, Bensa. "La *Canción de Rachel*: La literariedad de su testimonio." *Revista/Review Interamericana* 19, no. 1–2 (1989): 65–76.

Vera León, Antonio. "Hacer hablar: La transcripción testimonial." *Revista de Crítica Literaria Latinoamericana* 18, no. 36 (1992): 181–99.

Watanabe, John. "Unimagining the Maya: Anthropologists, Others, and the Inescapable Hubris of Authorship." *Bulletin of Latin American Research* 14, no. 1 (1995): 25–45.

Webster, Steven. "Dialogue and Fiction in Ethnography." *Dialectical Anthropology* 7, no. 2 (1982): 91–114.

Zambrano, María. "Lydia Cabrera, poeta de la metamorfosis." *Orígenes* 25 (1950): 11–15.

Zimmerman, Marc. "*Testimonio* in Guatemala: Payeras, Rigoberta, and Beyond." *Latin American Perspectives* 18, no. 4 (1991): 22–47.

Index

Abakuá, 49, 60, 62, 66

Abrahams, Roger D., 141

Academy of Sciences (Cuba), 123, 125, 128, 136, 147

Acosta Saignes, Miguel, 55

Africanism, 30–32, 186n8, 186–87n13

Afro-Cuban culture, 25, 27–30, 34–39, 41, 42, 46–48, 51, 58, 59, 61–62, 65, 66–69, 122–23, 124, 138, 144, 149, 164

Ak'abal, Humberto, 158

Alberti, Rafael, 44

Alcor, 173

Alianza Popular Revolucionaria Americana, 75

Alonso, Carlos, 21–23, 164, 184n4

Amauta, 77

Amnesty International, 158

Andean tradition, 15, 25, 73–78, 80–84, 86, 88, 94–95, 97, 99, 102, 108, 110–13, 115, 119

animals, 43, 118

anthropology/anthropological discourse, 12–14, 20–21, 24–26, 119–20, 156, 161; and Arguedas, 13, 20, 74, 76, 81, 82, 89, 91, 93, 94, 96, 97, 99, 105, 106, 108, 111, 164–67, 181; and the arts, 111, 165; and Barnet, 12–13, 20, 122–23, 125–31, 139–41, 165–67, 181; and Burgos, 149–50; and Cabrera, 13, 20, 27, 34, 36–39, 44, 49, 51, 53, 56, 60, 64, 70, 163–67, 181; and collecting, 27–28, 39–40, 45, 78, 83, 92, 187n22; and cultural description,

51; ethnography/ethnology, 12, 19–21, 24–34, 36, 40–43, 47, 48, 50–52, 54–58, 60–66, 70, 71, 72, 74, 76, 78–83, 88–94, 96, 101, 104–6, 110, 111, 114, 115, 117–20, 123–28, 132–33, 135–41, 147–50, 161, 163–67, 188n45, 190n 11, 190n19, 191–92n45, 194n8, 195n35, 196n49; and insider/outsider positioning, 13, 60, 81, 120, 122, 129; interpretive, 127, 195n35; and literariness of anthropological writing, 20, 96, 115, 138–39; and mediation, 12–13, 25–26, 91, 106, 108, 165–66; and representation, 26; self-reflexivity of, 12; as socio-historical critique, 125, 131; and Spanish American narrative, 163–67, 183; systematic nature of, 94, 163; and taping, 127, 135, 139, 141, 151–52

Apurímac River, 102

Aragón, Gabriel, 85

Araníbar, Carlos, 117

Archivos del Folklore Cubano, 187n19

Argentina, 181

Arguedas, Arístides, 77

Arguedas, José María, 11, 13–16, 19, 20, 23–26, 72, 73–120, 122, 143, 148, 161, 168, 174, 176, 178–79, 181–83; and anthropology, ethnography, or folklore, 74–86, 88–97, 99, 101, 104–6, 108, 110–18, 125, 131, 139, 164–67, 181, 190n11, 190n19, 191n39, 192n65; autobiographical style of, 79–83, 89–90, 94, 97, 108; bicultural

Yeats, W. B., 172
Yoruban language, 33, 38, 39, 44

Zambrano, María, 50

Zimmerman, Marc, 156, 197n68,
197n71
Zumthor, Paul, 15, 184–85n14